JESUIT EDUCATION

Christian Maturity (P. J. Kenedy, 1955)
Work and Education (Loyola University Press, 1959)

JESUIT EDUCATION

An Essay on the Foundations of Its Idea

JOHN W. DONOHUE, S.J.

NEW YORK
FORDHAM UNIVERSITY PRESS
1963

To the memory of

FATHER LEO M. WEBER, S.J.
(1893–1952)

Master of Novices
Saint Andrew-on Hudson
(1928–1942)

CONTENTS

FOREWORD

The scriptural admonition to "think of the rock you were hewn from, of the hidden depths whence you came" (Isaiah 51,1), can apply, it seems, to institutions as well as to persons. For an institution that is continually evolving an occasional review of its origins is especially salutary. As life finds its expression in growth, both internal and external, so a living institution will grow and expand. But the growth of a living institution must be carefully nurtured if it is to be in accord with the aims and the intentions of its original designers. The words of the Prophet Isaiah, then, advise us to renew our vision at its source.

Jesuit education is a living institution and we can compare it to a living organism capable of growth and development. From the viewpoint of education, this organism requires the lengthy period of training for its teachers and the periodic replacement of teachers who either change to administrative work or who retire from the classroom. Amidst such changes, the continuity of an explicitly known and applied tradition must be insured. This continuity of tradition has been a constant aim in the 400-year experience of Jesuit education.

The aim, nevertheless, must be fulfilled by taking means. In the United States this concern for clarification has been the continual preoccupation of the Jesuit Educational Association from its beginnings to the present day. No sooner had the Association been formally organized in 1934 than plans were immediately under way for a statement of the essential characteristics of Jesuit education.

The present volume, therefore, has something of a history behind it and it will be well to indicate it at least in broad outline. No one who is familiar with the contemporary effort at formularizing the objectives and curriculum of a single institution will be surprised at the time and effort required to describe a *system* of education which attempts to inform a plurality of institutions—high schools, colleges, universities. In 1941, the Executive Committee of the Jesuit Education Association appointed a subcommittee, Father Allan P. Farrell, S.J., and Father Matthew J. Fitzsimons, S.J., to begin work on a statement of Jesuit principles of education. The ensuing report to the Executive Committee, entitled *Objectives and Procedures of Jesuit Education,* was, owing to circumstances, tentative and incomplete. Nevertheless, several printings of the report to meet the demand for copies both in this country and abroad were evidence of interest in the subject and of the need of such a formulation.

In continuance of the work of clarification, an Institute of Jesuit Deans was held in Santa Clara, California, in 1955. The members discussed the objectives and curricula of Jesuit education for ten days and duly reported their conclusions. Two years later, the authors of the first report, Fathers Farrell and Fitzsimons, on a sabbatical leave in 1957–58, were able to amplify their earlier treatment in a larger and valuable study.

The next step was to hold a meeting in Chicago in 1959 of delegates from various regions of the country. This *Workshop*, as it was called, made a remarkable contribution by clarifying the nature of the volume which would be written by Father John W. Donohue, S.J., who was officially appointed to the task. I am happy to state that Father Donohue has faithfully and generously fulfilled the task assigned to him—as the present volume will reveal. The Jesuit Educational Association, therefore, expresses its gratitude and appreciation to the author for this careful and stimulating and contemporary study.

Although in the present century there have been several impressive and scholarly volumes on the sources of Jesuit education published in this country and in Europe, there is always need for stating anew the bases of a far-reaching system of education.

As Father Donohue remarks, "a good-sized shelf of books" would be necessary to treat satisfactorily the long and evolving history of Jesuit education and to discuss the large issues which confront Jesuit high schools, colleges, and universities today. It is our hope that a series of monographs on details of Jesuit education and a series of reports on experiments in the same field will follow. This volume, then, can be considered as the first of a series of publications and can serve as an incentive for further studies and for experiments.

Finally, I may quote two statements from Father Donohue's book that will give an example of the insight and felicitous grasp of essentials that the author displays. The first is from his *Preface:*

> The social continuity of the Society of Jesus throughout four centuries argues to the maintenance of an essential identity amid vicissitudes and change for otherwise the institution would either have perished or been substantially altered. And since any school is influenced by the philosophy of those who conduct it, some distinctive Jesuit outlook has quite likely shaped Jesuit schools from the time of St. Ignatius until the present and given them a family likeness which persists deep down despite the radical differences induced by disparate environments in successive ages.

The second quotation is taken from Chapter VII:

The Jesuit schools are understood as extensions of the inspiration and action of the Society itself since they are concrete embodiments of its apostolic aim.

On the part of the Association, I am happy to express our thanks to The Ford Fund for the Advancement of Education, and especially to its Vice President, Dr. Alvin C. Eurich, for a generous grant which enabled us to inaugurate the efforts which led to the publication of this volume.

EDWARD B. ROONEY, S.J.

President of the Jesuit Educational Association

PREFACE

This is a book about educational theory. An alert reader may be inclined to take warning and echo Hume's cheerful critique of all speculative exercise: "Consign it to the flames." For it must be admitted that discussions of the principles or philosophy of education are proverbially judged to be tedious. If they actually are, it is to some extent unavoidable. Education is a topic of frightening complexity and the single term labels a manifold reality whose extension is nearly as wide as that of life itself. Even practical works on teaching procedures or school management are likely to seem dull enough since the actual business of teaching is hard and slow and piecemeal. Those without firsthand experience may suppose it to be largely a matter of gesturing toward boundless seas from some peak in Darien. They do not realize that, before the vision of Sophocles or Einstein can be pointed out, somebody has to spend hours teaching the elements of language or physics and that books on methods aim to ease these pedestrian tasks. The theoretician, for his part, is even more handicapped than the practitioner because he works at a level of abstraction which scarcely allows escape from truism and cliché. If one discusses being, or atoms, or the twelve-tone scale one has, of course, to abstract the subject treated. But abstract concepts about education, even when they are legitimately derived from reality, seem only mildly nutritious precisely because men's chief concern is with the whole of education as a concrete activity in the real and contingent world and with theory only insofar as it clarifies or expedites this activity. It is certainly hard to conduct the theoretical inquiry without losing awareness of that vital process, with all its limitations and shifting colors, which enfolds the student, the teacher, the matter to be learned, the direction and goal of the learning and the dynamic acts of teaching and learning themselves. Yet if that awareness is lost, one wanders in an airless jungle of platitudes.

On the other hand, a certain minimum of educational theory is essential, if educational practice is to be sound. It is not wise to dismiss it as frivolous on the grounds that theory is usually unable to supply direct solutions for the insistent problems encountered in running a school day by day. For there are certain other intractable questions from which the hard pressed schoolman retreats when he refuses to look up from the time-consuming and rather satisfying detailed work of his daily routine in order to ponder those spacious formulations of objectives and procedures which fill the front pages of school catalogues and yearbooks or ornament commencement speeches and superintendents' annual reports. A man who is tempted to such evasion needs to see, as the (London) *Times Educational Supplement* once put it, whether he "can stand the fierce glare of idealism after a gruelling day's work in a world of hard facts." At least, he must be philosopher enough to keep his aims and policies under critical surveillance for even the best practices tend to petrify. He should know, besides, that all historic forms of schooling have been undergirded by some conceptualization of their academic and moral ideals, although it is true that these theoretical foundations have not generally been laid down by professional philosophers. The goals of character education, for instance, are most often provided by a religion or by a social movement which has assumed something of the aura of a religion. The goals of intellectual education owe less to the recommendations of philosophers than to those heroes, savants and saints who articulate the deep, if unsystematized, perceptions and feelings to which an era vibrates, when it is shaken by developments in thought or in the arts or by technical and scientific transformations, or by the passion for national self-determination, or by new geographical discoveries.

In any case, educational theory exists and is important even when it is not impressive. Moreover, its limitations are at least diminished in those philosophies of education which have been stimulated by actual school experiences. Plato may never have managed a republic but he was a dedicated teacher. Isocrates and Quintilian, St. Thomas and Newman, Dewey and Montessori all fashioned theories partly from the lessons they learned in classrooms. The principles dealt with in these pages pertain to a realistic theory of this latter sort. We are trying to summarize here the foundations of Jesuit educational practice and particularly those bits of educational theory which can be discovered in certain documents stemming from the first six decades of Jesuit history. These are the *Spiritual Exercises* and the *Constitutions* of the Society of Jesus, both written in the sixteenth century by St. Ignatius, the founder of that Society, and the celebrated plan for curricula and methods which appeared in 1599, more than forty years after Ignatius's death, under the title *Ratio atque Institutio Studiorum Societatis Iesu.*

All these documents, however, owed a great deal to their authors' experiences as well as to their philosophical and theological convictions. St. Ignatius had himself lived out those central Christian truths which his little book of exercises inculcates not by homily but by stimulating and guiding the reader's personal effort, under grace, to convert those beliefs into behavior. The *Constitutions* are practical, though not exhaustive, directives for the organization of life and work in a religious order and they were given careful trial before their definitive promulgation. The *Ratio Studiorum,* coming half a century after the first Jesuit schools were established, codified the best of what several generations of teachers and administrators had learned not simply by drawing out the educational implications of their religious and philosophical positions but also by observing the practice of other late Renaissance teachers and by reflection upon their own work in the schools. Any elements of educational theory embedded in these sources will have been derived from or at least thoroughly tested in life and action.

A contemporary student of the *Ratio* is apt to think, in fact, that its theoretical content is hardly visible amidst the serried ranks of precise regulations for principals, teachers and students; for courses of study and teaching methods. The first draft of that *Ratio* remarked succinctly that its concern was precisely with school management—*de administratione scholarum.* But if you want a school which will really promote sound learning, said Suarez, the most distinguished Jesuit theologian of those days when the *Ratio* was new, you need first of all a sufficient number of diligent teachers and then an exact plan and method of teaching, *ordo ac methodus.* This the *Ratio* of 1599 certainly supplied.

A methodology, however, is not a complete philosophy of education nor even one of its proper parts. It is true that the rationale of method may be grounded on philosophical or theological bases which themselves enter into the substance of an educational theory. Yet it is equally true that the same specific pedagogical procedures may be warmly defended by quite different philosophical anthropologies. Both the Thomist and the instrumentalist, for instance, will insist that there is a genuine learning only in terms of the pupils' own desire and activity and both can logically defend a stress on problem-solving experiences in school although they may buttress the case with quite diverse reasonings. The really central theses of the theory underlying Jesuit education are not likely to be derived, therefore, from an analysis of methods, however distinctive, but rather from reflection upon the nature of man and upon the character of the educational process in general and that of Christian education in particular. Consequently, this book will devote some pages to a rapid sketch, admittedly impressionistic and incomplete, of certain fundamental categories suggested by such reflection.

A Jesuit school, however, is also commonly thought to have a characteristic flavor of its own, even as a Benedictine or a Quaker or a Buddhist school has its individual tone. That this in turn indicates the presence of an underlying theory, at least in the sense of a tradition preserving significant traits and convictions, is a reasonable supposition.

The social continuity of the Society of Jesus throughout four centuries argues to the maintenance of an essential identity amid vicissitudes and change for otherwise the institution would either have perished or been substantially altered. And since any school is influenced by the philosophy of those who conduct it, some distinctive Jesuit outlook has quite likely shaped Jesuit schools from the time of St. Ignatius until the present and given them a family likeness which persists deep down despite the radical differences induced by disparate environments in successive ages. For the most part a family spirit of this sort consists of nuances introduced into the charter of aims which may be common to many schools or in a distinctive organization of the school experience itself. It is apt, therefore, to be rather intangible even though real. In the pages that follow, however, it is presupposed that beneath the letter of the *Spiritual Exercises,* the *Constitutions* and the *Ratio* such a vital spirit can be discerned. It will consist of certain fundamental persuasions, attitudes and commitments which are antecedent to the work of Jesuit education yet contribute significantly to its inner life so that the minute and sometimes trivial or archaic prescriptions of the *Ratio* are to be seen as more or less successful attempts to incarnate insights and principles which themselves constitute an authentic fragment of educational theory.

This at least is the conviction of the Jesuits themselves. The *Ratio* of 1599 governed the practice of Jesuit schools from the time it appeared until the Society of Jesus was suppressed in 1773. After the Society was restored in 1814 an attempt was made to revise this *Ratio* but the day was past when any detailed school plan could fit the needs of many disparate national cultures in the old and new worlds. Nevertheless, as we shall remark in Chapter II, Jesuit legislation down to our own day has always supposed that there are "principles of sound pedagogy which have been wisely set forth by our father (St. Ignatius) in the Fourth Part of the *Constitutions* and elaborated by the *Ratio Studiorum,*" as the *Epitome,* or digest of the Society's law, puts it and that the method characteristic of the Society should be "everywhere preserved as far as possible." For as the 27th General of the Society, John Baptist Janssens, remarked in 1947 in a letter on the various ministries of the order: "How valuable for our own times is the traditional pedagogy of the Society, based as it is upon the principles which we ourselves have drawn from the *Exercises* and our rules. . . ."

No doubt these principles must be distinguished from the accidental forms and colorations they have received in their various historical concretizations and need to be adapted to successive eras and milieus. That need was recognized long ago by the French Jesuit Joseph de Jouvancy when he published in 1703 his *Ratio Discendi et Docendi,* an extended essay on the Jesuit pedagogy for secondary schools. It had an official character because it had been commissioned by the 14th General Congregation of the Society in 1687. In his Preface Père Jouvancy adverted to the aphoristic character of many of the *Ratio*'s prescriptions and to the necessity of penetrating to the spirit beneath them. These wise regulations, he said, are like seeds which must be nourished by meditation and experimentation if they are to bring forth fruit.

The present study is an essay in such meditation. It is not strictly textual, however, since it tries to draw out the implications of the educational principles in the *Spiritual Exercises,* in the *Constitutions* and in Jesuit school legislation with special emphasis upon the *Ratio.* It also tries to provide these themes with a larger framework and to indicate their logical plenitude without claiming that the sixteenth-century Jesuits themselves made all this explicit. There are limitations to this genetic approach, of course. Jesuit education is, in the United States particularly, very much a thing of the present and is not adequately understood merely by going back to the point of its origins. For if a living and growing entity evolves toward a complex and more potent maturity which the embryo only foreshadows, then a study of its genesis will not yield full understanding. It is at least equally necessary to look forward to the successive stages and to the goal of the development and to keep in mind that Aristotelian wisdom which maintains that it is not the seed which is first in importance but the guiding ideal of the perfect flower. Propositions of this sort are, to be sure, primarily verified for individual organisms, but if they are analogously applicable to institutions, then it would be wise to examine the unfolding history and the dominant purposes of a school type as well as its relatively rudimentary beginnings. On the other hand, the genetic study, though insufficient of itself, is not without its uses especially in the case of an educational system which has a strong reverence for its tradition. The past is a partial key to the future and one cannot grasp the meaning and design of an evolution without attending to origins.

The focus of this essay, however, is confessedly limited in three respects. For to understand fully the seminal principles of Jesuit education, one would need to trace their reduction to practice and their complexification over the course of four hundred years in most nations of Europe and the Americas and in many parts of Asia, Africa and the Pacific Islands. Account would also have to be taken of the cultural currents within each of these countries for the France of today differs not only from the contemporary United States but from the France of

Louis XIV. A complete investigation of this Jesuit tradition would like-wise require a systematic canvass of those Jesuit commentators who have not merely expounded the teaching techniques recommended by the *Ratio* but have also paid some attention to its philosophical and religious foundations. Finally, a study of Jesuit educational concepts ought logi-cally to consider the large issues which confront Jesuit high schools, colleges and universities today to see whether or not these concepts contribute to the definition and resolution of those problems. But these three tasks would require several lifetimes in which to employ the in-formed skills of historians and experts on every phase of education from the newest methods of teaching Latin grammar or modern mathematics to the best administrative practices in legal and medical training and the product of this industry would necessarily be a good-sized shelf of books. Yet perhaps there would be room on that shelf for a modest and tentative inquiry into the abiding spirit which fashioned the great documents stand-ing at the beginning of the Society of Jesus's history, a spirit which transcends the context of its sixteenth-century origins and may well in-form Jesuit schools anywhere, at any time.

When this book was in manuscript, it was read and painstakingly commented upon by more than a score of American Jesuit teachers and ad-ministrators. In every case, their observations were highly instructive and many of them have been absorbed into the text. Where a suggestion was not acted upon, it was because the writer could not see the question just as his critic did or because the revision called for would have required another, though indeed a much better, book. To read these wise com-mentaries, however, was to recognize just how provisional the present essay is. The reader must be warned, therefore, and by no conventional disclaimer, that these pages represent only one Jesuit's understanding and interpretation of that tradition which they seek to transcribe.

                                                         J. W. D.

The School of Education,
Fordham University
July 31, 1962
Feast of St. Ignatius Loyola

PART ONE
THE CONTEXT OF THE IDEA

Chapter I

ON MOTIVES AND ORIGINS:
ST. IGNATIUS AND EDUCATION

*The teachers should . . . inspire the students to the
love and service of God our Lord, and to a love of
the virtues by which they please Him. They
should urge the students to direct all their studies
to this end.*
Constitutions of the Society of Jesus, IV, xvi, 4[1]

On July 31, 1556 St. Ignatius Loyola died in Rome in his sixty-
fifth year. He had been living there for nearly two decades, absorbed in
the work that was his as the founder and first General of the Society
of Jesus. The Apostolic Letters of Pope Paul III had constituted that
Society a religious order within the Catholic Church in 1540. Subsequent ages would be often bemused by a mythical image of this order,
whose members are popularly known as Jesuits, a myth romantic and in-
exact at best, lurid and unsavory at worst. But the matter-of-fact perspective of Canon Law saw the Society simply as one of those social entities or subgroups within the total Catholic community which
are technically known as Religious Institutes. The members of any
such institute follow a determined rule in pursuit of their common
quest for personal perfection and for the Christian service of others.
They are governed by Superiors whose authority is derived from the
Roman Pontiff and they usually live in houses of the institute and
share common board and lodging. Their manner of communal religious life is not adopted for a time only but permanently and the
members bind themselves to observance of the evangelical counsels by
vows of poverty, chastity and obedience. These are public vows since
they are accepted in the name of the Church by a legitimate ecclesiastical superior. The Society of Jesus is, moreover, an order rather
than a "congregation" because it is an institute in which solemn vows,
rendering the acts contrary to themselves invalid as well as unlawful,

3

are pronounced and it is a clerical institute because most of its members are priests or destined to be.

This order which had begun as a tentative aspiration of Ignatius had, by the time of his death, grown to include over a thousand Jesuits organized into twelve administrative divisions or provinces and maintaining about a hundred different establishments.[2] Thirty-three of these institutions were, though with varying degrees of complexity, secondary or middle schools of the sort that on the Continent are frequently called "colleges"—*collège, collegio, kolleg.* The work of education was then, as it has continued to be, a chief ministry of the Society. Still, it was not the only form of the Jesuit apostolate and to write the full history of the Jesuits during the past four hundred and more years, would be, in fact, to touch upon most of the major themes and movements in the history of the Church during these same four centuries.

It is no part of the purpose here even to summarize that Jesuit history and so it will be enough to make one or two observations about it. The story of the Society, and consequently of its schools, falls into two periods. The first of these extended from the establishment in 1540 to the suppression of the Jesuits by Clement XIV in 1773. The second period began with the restoration of the Society by Pius VII in 1814 and has continued until the present. In 1749, the year of the last complete census before the turmoil which culminated in that suppression, there were 22,589 Jesuits in the houses in Europe, in the Western hemisphere and in the Far East. Half of these were priests and the rest were either Jesuit seminarians, called scholastics, or coadjutor brothers. In the 39 provinces there were then some 845 educational institutions. Some of these were seminaries either for Jesuits only or enrolling students from dioceses and other religious institutes as well. More than six hundred of them were secondary schools or colleges which sometimes had Faculties of Arts (Philosophy and Science) attached. Most of them were in Europe but they were also found in the Latin American colonies and in the Asiatic provinces. The schools were often housed in handsome buildings and were always tuition-free because they enjoyed a certain income from foundations set up for them by benefactors. After the suppression, the governments of the Catholic nations of France, Spain, Portugal, Poland and Austria confiscated these resources and sometimes employed them to start state-controlled schools, for in many regions the Jesuits had had a virtual monopoly on secondary education.[3]

In 1814 the restored Society resumed its school work almost from scratch. By 1960 there were 34,687 Jesuits in some 77 provinces and vice-provinces in Europe, North and South America and the Far East as well as in numerous mission territories in Africa, Asia and Oceania. More than a fifth of these Jesuits were in provinces of the United States where the educational work of the Society has known its greatest modern expansion. In the world as a whole, the Jesuits of 1960 maintained 878 educational complexes which included 4,059 different schools with more than nine hundred thousand students and taught or administered by better than 32,000 non-Jesuit faculty members and some 12,000 Jesuits, or about a third of all the personnel of the Society. These schools included 289 seminaries for Jesuits themselves and more than a hundred seminaries for students preparing for the diocesan priesthood. There were 2,471 elementary schools, usually attached to parishes and often in mission areas. There were 817 secondary schools and 482 institutions of higher learning including the American universities with their numerous colleges and professional schools.[4] Today, however, although the Jesuit engagement in education is greater, absolutely speaking, than it was at any time before the suppression, it bulks far less large relatively. In the years since 1773, all the nations of the West have created extensive systems of public schools and within the Church itself many other religious institutes are now dedicated to the work of education.

These historical pegs and broad statistics will need some particularization later but for the moment they rough in enough background for some reflection upon St. Ignatius's own contribution to this enterprise of Jesuit education. Reflection of this sort is necessary not only because the history of Jesuit education begins with St. Ignatius but also because of the intrinsic importance of his contribution to that history. This importance can be suggested obliquely by recalling that the program spelled out for the sixteenth-century Jesuit schools looked, on paper at least, very like any other Renaissance prospectus. The proximate educational aim of those schools was quite admirable but undeniably limited. Whitehead, who appreciated both the strength and the limitations of the tradition honored in those Jesuit *collegia,* has persuasively summed it up and actually equated it with "liberal education" at its best.

> In its essence a liberal education is an education for thought and for aesthetic appreciation. It proceeds by imparting a knowledge of the masterpieces of thought, of imaginative literature, and of art. The action which it contemplates is command. It is an aristocratic education implying leisure. This platonic ideal has rendered imperishable services to European civilization. It has encouraged art, it has fostered that spirit of disinterested curiosity which

is the origin of science, it has maintained the dignity of mind in the face of material force, a dignity which claims freedom of thought. Plato did not, like St. Benedict, bother himself to be a fellow-worker with his slaves; but he must rank among the emancipators of mankind. His type of culture is the peculiar inspiration of the liberal aristocrat, the class from which Europe derives what ordered liberty it now possesses. For centuries, from Pope Nicholas V to the school of the Jesuits, and from the Jesuits to the modern headmasters of English public schools, this educational ideal has had the strenuous support of the clergy. [5]

Nevertheless, the same ideal had its dangers. For one thing, it needed to be translated into manageable school programs and such programs always tend first to oversimplify and then to harden and grow stale. This happened with the Renaissance humanism of the early Jesuit schools as one can see by reading Père Joseph de Jouvancy's famous commentary on the official Jesuit school plan, the *Ratio* of 1599.[6] This treatise was intended as a handbook for young Jesuit teachers, an *Instructio ac Methodus,* to help them prepare and conduct their secondary school classes. It everywhere manifests the informed skill and ardent dedication of an expert teacher but one who moves, nonetheless, within a rather narrow and formalistic framework—at least by contemporary standards. Latin and Greek dominate the curriculum, as they did then in all secondary schools. Tagged on to the study of these languages is a grab bag of materials designed to nourish stylish ease and erudition in Latin composition: bits of Rhetoric, Poetry, History, Chronology, Geography and Philology or *Polymathia*. By this last were meant snippets from certain specialities, such as the science of ancient coins, which were judged appropriate acquisitions for the liberally educated gentleman. Literature is here made to serve chiefly for the development of a correct Latin style. Plato is absent from the long list of recommended Greek authors but Quintilian's presence is strongly felt for he is the authority cited almost exclusively. This will remind the educational historian that the ideal celebrated by Whitehead really owed more to Isocrates and Quintilian than to Plato.

The details of the school practice in this little book of Jouvancy are sound enough so far as they go but they represent no real advance over the official *Ratio* of a century before. Indeed, the Jesuits who were engaged from 1548 until 1599 in the experimentation and reflection which ultimately fashioned that *Ratio* manifested a freer and more imaginative spirit than Jouvancy displayed for all his skillful detail.

But quite apart from the natural tendency to petrifaction, this Hellenic model of liberal culture is intrinsically circumscribed, as Whitehead also noted, and for this reason it cannot fairly be made the archetype by which all other forms of education are measured. It did neglect science and technology, although each of these has a humanizing potential. Most remarkably, despite its favor with churchmen, it also neglected philosophy and theology. It neglected education for social action and service in favor of a privileged dilettantism. It had its gaze fixed too uncritically on an elite which was often, in fact, simply an aristocracy of wealth and birth rather than one of talent. St. Ignatius, himself of good birth, quite reasonably cultivated the nobility of Spain and Italy as well as highly placed ecclesiastics because these were the only people who could expedite the work of civil and religious reconstruction since they had a monopoly on power and riches. But those tempestuous, inbred and self-centered princes and dukes, infantas, queens and duchesses frequently gave slight evidence of natural gifts and little was heard from them once changes in the economic and political order had curtailed their inherited prerogatives.

The interesting fact, however, is that Jesuit schools did not also disappear when that Quintilian exemplar of the *liberalis homo et eruditus* was eclipsed. If today the Dean of an American Jesuit University graduate school, or the Dean of a Jesuit medical or law school, the administrators and professors in a Jesuit college of liberal arts or one of the faculty in a Jesuit school of education or business or social service or foreign service or the principal and teachers of a Jesuit high school in Cincinnati or Tampa, El Paso or Boston want to search out the spirit and perennial aims of Jesuit education they will do well to ask how it was that the Society's educational work escaped burial with the late-Renaissance recipe for "liberal education." They will discover that those controlling purposes which led the Society into school work in the first place subsequently preserved its capacity for renewal and flexibility. For these aims of the educators themselves were not tied to any one cultural context and so they could join forces with and make use of the specific and intermediate aims intended by schools in a variety of contexts.

But it is precisely to St. Ignatius that the appreciative grasp and formulation of those Jesuit purposes in education is chiefly owed. Despite the common Renaissance cast of their curriculum, the first Jesuit schools very quickly acquired an individual tradition, principally by reason of their carefully detailed organization and the character of the men who staffed them.[7] St. Ignatius himself was largely responsible for both these bench marks. It was he who insisted upon careful school planning and it was he who set their master ideal before the members of the Society. This ideal was, to be sure, simply the full register of the Christian ideal but to a considerable extent each Jesuit was formed to this Christian pattern by making the Ignatian *Spiritual Exercises* and by his daily life in that distinctive social milieu, the Society of Jesus, whose *Constitutions* were also substantially the work of Ignatius. Those *Constitutions* make it very clear that the Society of Jesus is impelled to the work of education from an apostolic motive since it believes that sound schooling can help conduct men to salvation.

The importance of this religious motivation is central. Among the Jesuits personally guided by St. Ignatius was Pedro Ribadeneira who wrote one of the earliest commentaries on the spirit and law of the Society.[8] Over the top of the brief chapter on education in this *De Ratione Instituti Societatis Iesu,* Ribadeneira fixed the inquiring title: "Why Does the Society Teach Boys Grammar?" A question, however, which begins with *why* is usually a question about motives and differs significantly from questions introduced by *what?* These latter are queries into the nature of things: What is a liberal education, what should the secondary school mathematics curriculum include, what is the ideal relationship of faculty to administration? *Why* asks about the *finis operantis,* the purpose of the worker as distinguished from the *finis operis,* the purpose of the work. No doubt a direct opposition between these two purposes must mean the frustration of one or both of them but it is perfectly possible for an agent to intend a personal end which is added or parallel to those ends which the nature of the activity itself dictates. The pilot of a commercial airliner may fly to earn his living or because he finds such work more satisfying than a desk job yet this does not prevent him from devoting his energies to the management of a safe and competent passage while he is in the air. For if he is not seriously concerned about every detail contributing to comfort and security, the goal of the flight will hardly be achieved.

For any thorough discussion of a human phenomenon some attention to the *why,* to the motivation of the participants is necessary and where education is concerned it will often be particularly instructive for a defect in the teacher's purpose may well vitiate his teaching. The sour and brutal schoolmaster in *Tom Sawyer* had been disappointed in his ambition to study medicine and kept school merely to support himself although the work galled him. There is a special interest, moreover, in asking why the Society of Jesus devotes itself so largely to education. It was certainly not compelled by the religious vocation itself or by any ineluctable impulse deriving from its own law or from external pressure to apply more of its members to the works of teaching and scholarship than to missionary expeditions in remote lands or to preaching and the giving of retreats or to various chaplaincies. Finally, and this is our chief point here, it will be seen that the true source of vitality in Jesuit education is indicated by the answer to a *why* rather than a *what*. That is to say, the Society's enduring purposes and motives in conducting schools are the forces that have made it possible to sustain this work across space and time. If an educational theory did no more than answer questions about curriculum and method, the schools built upon it would inevitably become obsolete and perish. For these factors, by their very character, depend considerably upon a determined cultural epoch and do not contain within themselves the sources of that living spirit which enables an institution to survive. The secret of vitality and continuity must be sought at a deeper level.

That level is touched when one turns to the Ignatian documents which are the fountainhead of the Jesuit spirit. It is in these strong and energetic formulas of Ignatius himself that one finds the Jesuit world view and inspiration indicated. These are, of course, nothing more than the Christian view and inspiration but here they have been passed through the alembic of one saint's powerful realization. It will be worthwhile to consider somewhat fully how that religious perception of St. Ignatius, so humanistic in a profoundly Christian sense, so radically pragmatic in its judgment of all reality beyond the reality of the soul related to God, so decided in its preference for active service nurtured by love— how all this gave to Jesuit education a basic orientation which has thus far kept it from a fatal immobilization at any fixed historical point and has made possible the continual vigor of this ministry.

St. Ignatius and Education

Any reflection on St. Ignatius and his work is hedged about with difficulties. To begin with, this is obviously a delicate matter for Jesuits themselves to discuss and yet one must point out, as unaffectedly as possible, that Ignatius of Loyola was one of those men through whom God changed the face of the Church. In this he was like Paul, Augustine and Francis of Assisi. He decisively influenced, for instance, the practices of Christian piety although not everyone has relished that influence. He introduced new concepts of the structure and purposes of a religious institute, and through the Society he founded, he significantly affected the apostolates of the foreign missions and education. A career so remarkable must be treated with reserve by his spiritual descendants, if they are to avoid a chauvinistic air. They cannot, in any case, be tempted by corporate pride, if they recall, to use a favorite Ignatian metaphor, that a saint is only God's tool: *instrumentum conjunctum Deo.*

Quite apart from these special considerations, however, all students of the life of Ignatius must find the subject a formidable one. The figure may seem, at first, to be simple enough, although the life was crowded with momentous events, but the simplicity is an illusion grounded upon caricature. Closer examination suggests that although Ignatius's character may not have been psychologically intricate and enigmatic, it was certainly profound and did manage to synthesize quite contrasting traits. He was born, among the last of a large family, in 1491 in the manor house of the Loyolas, the well-to-do, ruling family of a country district in the Basque province of Guipúzcoa. He was not, therefore, properly a Spaniard at all for the Basques have their own distinctive ethnic, linguistic and cultural tradition. From the handsome volume of photographs and accompanying text which Leonard von Matt and Father Hugo Rahner prepared, one can get some notion of how pleasant that rural world is even now with its villages and farms, its orchards and groves of oak and chestnut all lying within the shadow of the Pyrenees.[9] In early boyhood, Iñigo, as he had been called at Baptism, led the leisurely, comfortable life of the rustic nobility in a remote valley where children were awakened at daybreak by the creaking of the mill, the gossip of the doves on the roof and the yelping of the hunting dogs in their kennels.

When he reached his teens, however, he was accepted as a page in the palace of his father's friend, Juan Velásquez de Cuellar, chief treasurer of the royal court of Castile. There in the town of Arévalo, some four hundred miles from his birthplace, Iñigo got an education of sorts in the tradition of chivalry which owed as much to the medieval ideal of knighthood as it did to the Renaissance concept of the courtier. Instead of poring over Donatus's grammar like an industrious bourgeois in a dusty schoolroom, this son of a proud, provincial aristocracy capered in the flashing regalia of a court gentleman and practiced sword play. He liked to read, to be sure, but vernacular romances, not the forensic outbursts of Cicero. Aristotle's *De anima* meant nothing to an admirer of the amorous quests of Amadis de Gaul. The antiquarian enthusiasms of the Renaissance scholars would have seemed quite mad to this spirited child of an older culture in whose breast a genuine piety and a lusty taste for adventure jostled one another. He could not have understood the enthusiasm of a Poggio finding the complete Quintilian buried amid rubbish in the Abbey of St. Gall nor the raptures of the Florentine academy burning votive lights before the bust of Plato. For his part, he dreamed of rescuing fair ladies from dungeons, not Latin manuscripts and he lit tapers before the shrines of the saints, not the philosophers.

When Iñigo was twenty-five, Ferdinand of Aragon died. In the years immediately following there was a good deal of unrest in the Iberian peninsula while Ferdinand's sixteen-year-old grandson, the future Charles V, was consolidating the first stages of his imperial career. In 1521, one of the brief wars which marked this period found the forces of the French king besieging the Navarrese town of Pamplona which numbered among its most determined defenders, Iñigo de Loyola, who was then in the service of the local Duke of Nájera, the viceroy of Navarre. In the course of the assault on the citadel, a cannon ball shattered one of Iñigo's legs. It was badly set and the victorious French allowed him to be returned by stretcher to Loyola. There the leg was dislocated and reset.

The shock and pain of these fearful experiences threatened to extinguish Iñigo's life but at a critical point he rallied and began an extended, weary convalescence. During those days of boring immobility he asked for books and his devout sister-in-law gave him a life of our Lord by Ludolph of Saxony and a Spanish version of the *Flos Sanctorum*. These were scarcely what he had been looking for but he read them for lack of anything else and they served as conduits of the grace which began to work a momentous conversion in him. He alternated his devout readings with worldly daydreams of glory and mental composition of flowery speeches to the lady in whose service he would like to have enlisted. After a while he noticed that the devotional readings and the thoughts of pilgrimage and penance which they inspired left him peaceful and happy, whereas the worldly fantasies had just the opposite effect.

Finally, in the early spring of 1522 his determination crystallized. With his leg mended, though imperfectly, he left his ancestral home forever. First he embarked upon what he himself called his years as a pilgrim. These included some months rich with graces and decisive spiritual experiences in the town of Manresa, a journey to the Holy Land and a continually expanding and effective concern not merely for prayers and asceticism but for the service of others. It was this apostolic zeal that led him to begin in his thirty-third year the second of his two educations. At Loyola and later on in the palace of Arévalo, he had acquired accomplishments which were real enough but neither scientific nor scholastic. He loved music, novels and courtly manners. He became equally skilled in the Biscayan dances and the tough arts of a soldier. He studied no theology but he was formed in a firm loyalty to the Church. This first education left lasting traces. In the book of the *Spiritual Exercises,* one of the pivotal "exercises" is a meditation upon the Kingdom of Christ which is designed to convert the meditator into a "noble knight" who will serve the Lord promptly and diligently. It aims to secure this conversion by inviting the exercitant to reflect upon the generous manner in which a great human leader will be supported by his ardent followers. But the good king who is envisioned in this parable is certainly no Renaissance prince. It is a Louis IX rather than a Cesare Borgia or Henry Tudor that one must have in mind here.

After Ignatius revised his goals and set his whole course for the service of God he realized that for a useful ministry he required more than these sprightly skills of the gentleman. He needed to work his way through the traditional curriculum of grammar and rhetoric, philosophy and theology which an educated priest would be expected to have followed. In the early sixteenth century the little boys of Barcelona had their first Latin lessons in a public grammar class subsidized by the Town Council and taught by a regent of the local university. In 1524, Ignatius squeezed himself down into the benches beside these shrill scholars to "learn by heart," as he said, the rudiments of grammar. For the next eleven years he applied himself to the standard academic regime. After Barcelona there was a sort of hodgepodge at Alcalá: *Terminos de Soto,* he told a questioner long afterwards, *y phisica de Alberto, y el Maestro de las Sententias.* But Spain was not very kind to him then. He was continually badgered by ecclesiastical inquisitors suspicious of the spiritual guidance he provided for young men and devout women and in any case his studies suffered from the somewhat haphazard methods in vogue. At last, in 1528, he got to Paris and followed there a carefully articulated program that appealed strongly to his own acute feeling for form and order and the proper subordination of the lower to the higher: grammar reviewed at Montaigue; the arts at Sainte-Barbe, amid the humanistic breezes; theology with the Dominicans at the convent of the rue Saint-Jacques.

This project was noteworthy enough in itself and doubly so when we remember that Ignatius in the first flush of his conversion was all for large-scale exploits, all for outreaching even such legendary spiritual athletes as the hermit Onuphrius who lived in a cave of the Egyptian desert for seventy years in solitude. But it must be noted that this whole long program from the tussles with Latin declensions in Barcelona to the taking of the Parisian Master of Arts in 1535 was, for Ignatius, strictly pragmatic in intent. During the last three years of his life, one of the younger Jesuits who worked with him in Rome, Luis González de Cámara, wormed out of Ignatius, bit by bit, an oral account of his early life. Speaking of himself and his studies in the third person, the founder said: "After the pilgrim [i.e. himself] understood that it was not God's will that he remain in Jerusalem, he kept thinking on what he ought to be doing, and finally felt more inclined to study so as to be able to help souls."[10] It was not love of learning for its own sake that inspired him but an implacable and practical devotion to a purpose which learning might serve. This is the characteristic Ignatian viewpoint in which the finality of education is directly governed by a Christian concept of the finality of life itself and schooling is made to minister to the over-arching aim of love of God and love of mankind for the sake of God.

It is this attitude, of course, which sharply distinguished Ignatius from the conventional Renaissance humanists—not only from a Bembo, but also from an Erasmus whose recipe for Christian humanism called for a rather simple amalgam of classical culture with the Christian faith. Father Leturia, the leading twentieth-century authority on Ignatius's early years, reminds us that Erasmus thought love of letters admissible only *si propter Christum,* but one cannot image St. Ignatius talking about love of letters at all.[11] On the other hand, his attitude was also quite unlike that of St. Bernard. In the tenth part of the *Constitutions* he bids the members of the Society to cultivate diligently all those human resources which will make them *useful.* Their learning is to be exact and thorough and they are to acquire some eloquence for effective preaching and teaching. And if this notion of *utilitas* seems to some like a profanation of the academe, still any demand for studies and teaching would have appeared highly questionable to St. Bernard. *Monachi non est docere,* Bernard said more than once, *sed lugere.* Penitential tears are the business of the monk, not teaching. And he exhorted the clerics of his day: "Flee from the midst of Babylon, flee and save your souls."[12] But the sixteenth century was not the twelfth just as it is not the twentieth either. Jesuits were accordingly bidden to study the tactics of the king of Babylon and to join battle with him rather than to retreat. For the end of their Society is not only to look after their own salvation but also to work tirelessly for the salvation of others. Indeed, these two objectives are so closely linked that they are often presented as forming, in a sense, a single aim since the individual goal is achieved through the vocation of service.*

It was during his Paris stay that Ignatius gathered about him the group of six young men who were to form the nucleus of that Society of Jesus. On the Feast of the Assumption, 1534, their common resolve took its first form when together they vowed chastity, poverty and the making of a Palestinian pilgrimage provided that it could be done within the next twelve months. This pilgrimage did not, in fact, prove possible but the autumn of 1540 found Ignatius, who had been ordained in 1537, a resident in Rome. There on September 27, Paul III issued the first pontifical approbation of the new Society and decreed that it should bear the name of Jesus—*quam Iesu nomine insigniri cupimus.* The last sixteen years of his life were spent by Ignatius as the first General of the Society which he had founded and to which he gave an example of practical and indestructible zeal. There is a moving lesson to be drawn from the contemplation of the saint at his desk in Rome, busy with plans and those

---

*In a comment upon these pages while they were still in manuscript, the Reverend Robert F. Harvanek, S.J. remarked on the importance of emphasizing St. Ignatius's fondness for joining two related yet different ideas in a single formula, particularly when it is a question of enunciating broad aims. Ignatius liked to conceive the goal, as Father Harvanek observed, as complex or polar. He sets, therefore, "piety and learning" as the end of education or directs his Society toward the twofold end of personal salvation and perfection along with apostolic work for the perfection and salvation of others. It may be added, however, that this latter formula has been approached by commentators in two rather different ways. Some have been most impressed precisely by the duality of the goals and, indeed, by a certain contrast, if not tension, set up between them. They see the man, whose vocation is to the "active" life, as "polarized" between the call to praise God directly, which attracts him toward contemplation and solitude and the call to the ministry which attracts him toward service and interpersonal affairs. This approach brings out very well the fact that there is question here of two real aims, although one is more important than the other, and not simply a single aim joined to a set of means. Other commentators prefer to stress the essential bond between the aims. They fear that too strong an emphasis upon the duality and polarization might lead to a crippling sense of opposition between the praise of God, on the one hand, and the service of the neighbor, out of love of God, on the other. If this should happen, men may complain that their apostolic work withdraws them from God. This will be forestalled, it is felt, if one insists upon the truth that those committed to this sort of work, love and serve God precisely in and through this service of the fellow man. Those who favor this second approach prefer, therefore, to speak of a single aim which has two aspects. In either of these approaches, a duality is recognized and the heart of the problem is seen to be that of effecting a synthesis of both elements in one human life and work.

letters which now fill twelve thick volumes; testing, weighing, watching
and acting. To think that one brought up amidst the quixotic ambitions
of a fading chivalry should have put aside the pointless reveries and ambitions of a caballero to work for the world from a little desk is to appreciate what grace can effect in a noble nature.

But the figure at the desk is, as suggested, also somewhat mysterious because of the apparent antinomies it enclosed. Ignatius was
endlessly kind and affable but he could be a fearsome corrector even of
the minor faults of his subjects. He was astonishingly courageous but
confessed candidly that the election of Paul IV, a Pope who took a very
dim view of the Jesuits, made every bone in his body tremble. He
learned and practiced the most delicate and pure prudence and yet all his
life he was something of a storm center. He was both a lofty mystic and
a great social activist; an "absolutist" where ends were concerned because his whole life was centered upon God and yet a thoroughgoing
empiricist in the matter of practical policies and means. Perhaps his personal history accounted in part for his unusual blend of a hardheaded
realism with a romantic idealism—if that latter adjective can be used
without overtones of sentimentalism or anti-intellectualism. Ignatius
had been formed in two different cultural traditions without being absorbed by either. He had the accent of fervor and chivalry which we asso-
ciate with the Middle Ages and the accent of prudent reason and practical scientific concern which strikes us as more characteristic of the
modern world. He knew both these spheres and yet managed to tran-
scend each because he was larger than his context, one of those exceptional men who, while necessarily humanized by an actual society, still
surmounts this matrix, as a prophet does. His own life blended all these
themes. There is Ignatius riding in the sunset to keep vigil at Montserrat
and dreaming great dreams as he goes and there is Ignatius dealing
methodically with a thousand details pouring into his Roman office. His
Spiritual Exercises echo the first of those themes when they make their
strong appeals to courageous idealism and the desire for true greatness
—all of it summed up in the phrase that youth finds so winning: *Como
noble caballero de Christo:* like a noble soldier of Christ.[13]

But this theme is insufficient by itself and so it is not the only note
struck by the *Exercises*. It would not have attracted everyone perhaps,
and certainly no one can rise to it at all times. But Ignatius interwove
with the challenge to heroic magnanimity, another and quite different
kind of emphasis—a down-to-earth and level-voiced insistence on programs, details, reflective examinations of progress, careful self-analysis,
discipline and use of the technique of divide and conquer. And all this

because love and idealism are finally proved by deeds, not words. Those who look only at this second side of the coin will find Ignatian spirituality and Ignatian educational theory rather too methodical, self-conscious and even tough. But all these one-sided views are deceitful. The real Ignatian flavor is found in that insistence on keeping simultaneously and steadily in sight the most exalted ends along with the most exact and concrete means for achieving them. Since the ultimate goals of Christian life and education are largely given to us by the Christian faith itself, the major part of our own task, aided by grace, has to do with working up a solid technique for achieving these goals. If to take means seriously is to be a modern man, Ignatius was pre-eminently modern.[14]

Yet he could address himself so decisively to questions of means, of policy and technique, precisely because he had a most tenacious grasp of the end he sought. In fact, the impression he conveys of having transcended his milieu can be explained on the psychological level by the matchless intensity with which he penetrated a few pivotal religious truths and realized them with unremitting devotion in practice. Consequently, to schematize St. Ignatius's "philosophy of education" we need only disengage these fundamental certainties and indicate their relevance for educational theory. Such an approach is not necessarily artificial, for it is not inappropriate to think of Ignatius under the formality of an educational theorist. He has not bequeathed us, of course, anything like a complete theory of education, for most of the speculative questions never occurred to him and besides he was no philosopher. But he was greatly interested in the education of character, in the making of the good man, and in this he shares the fundamental concern of all great philosophers of education.

One might comb the Ignatian documents—the book of the *Exercises,* the *Autobiography,* the *Constitutions* and *Letters*—looking for pedagogical details which could be sifted into our modern categories. To suggest but one example: the fourteenth annotation in the *Exercises* instructs the retreat director to have a care for the particular character and condition of the exercitant and this has been cited as an instance of respect for individual differences. It is, of course, though St. Ignatius might have thought it simply basic common sense. But in any case, more important than these details are the central themes which constitute a rich lode that Jesuit educational tradition has always mined, even if only unconsciously. Many problems will arise in a Jesuit school or university today for which there is no detailed and specific answer in the Society's Institute. Their solution will be authentically Ignatian, however, if it represents the concrete application of that full tradition in which the Jesuit educators themselves have been formed. Guidance in these junctures comes from a man's total Jesuit background and that background includes certain essential features of the Ignatian accent in education which need to be sketched out here.

Before turning to the Ignatian theory, however, we may recall succinctly St. Ignatius's practical contribution to the actual business of education. Under God he founded the Society of Jesus, organized it with a prescient and informed wisdom and provided the first orientation to those works of scholarship and teaching which are the constituents of its educational enterprise and were accounted in 1947 by the twenty-seventh Father General as first among its ministries.[15] In all these projects, what distinguished St. Ignatius, the administrator, was his astonishing synthesis of a venturesome foresight with prudent realism. For instance, he gave his Company an Institute of reasonable flexibility, quite novel for its time, and thereby left it free to follow the developing lines of social and apostolic necessities. "As we see the matter here," he remarked in a letter to a Jesuit in Spain, "what we ought to do in our Lord is to leave the Society free in its movements so as to be able to undertake tasks of more general import, which we cannot do if we are tied down to particular works."[16] The order was, consequently, left open to growth and inspiration in a way that would have been impossible if it had been rigidly focused upon some sharply determined work like ransoming captives or preaching crusades. Here one can see that Ignatian genius for tranquilly maintaining in steady balance an absolute sureness regarding basic aims and a careful but imaginative experimentalism in the evolution of practical policy. The result of his thought and decision was that significant innovation which saw a religious order become so involved in teaching not only theology but also the humanities and natural sciences as to make education its characteristic work, the one which it "has esteemed beyond others and cultivated with the greatest zeal."[17]

The story of Jesuit education, therefore, underscores the unusual insight of St. Ignatius. He could hardly have known, at least naturally speaking, the lineaments of that new world toward which his own transitional age was moving. In the post-Renaissance centuries, two distinctive actualities would appear in the matter of education. In the West, the ideal of some formal schooling for everyone would become an unquestioned principle even as it gradually became an economic and political necessity. At the same time, the control of popular instruction would largely pass from the church to the state in most nations of the Atlantic community. On the North American continent, a new republic would come in time to exemplify strikingly both these actualities. Its Catholic citizens would find themselves living, it is true, in a pluralistic society where the public schools are technically neutral toward religion. But at the same time these Catholics would be sharers in the economic abundance of the United States and would be prepared to support their own schools—if someone were prepared to conduct them.

Thus it has happened that the pre-eminent apostolic activity in a culture such as ours is probably that of education. At other times and in other places a people may have transmitted its way of life through vehicles other than the school. Perhaps the Athenians were as effectively initiated into the Hellenic idea and ethos in the amphitheatre or assembly as in the makeshift classrooms frequented only by a minority. But in twentieth-century America this task is made to devolve very largely upon the school. This is not to say that such a situation is wholly desirable but only that it happens to be the real one. So that if Americans today want to work for the good of their neighbor there is simply no better place, no more sensitive and vital area than the school. This is not to pretend that it is an easy place to work. Teaching is now as ever a business of much sweat and anxieties, having its unique rewards, but fertile also in failures and disappointments. Nor is the school the only place to work; other apostolic activities are also essential. At present, however, the civilization of intelligence and the formation of conscience, the examination of life's central issues and the acquisition of intellectual resources wherewith to meet them are more than ever the charge of the school. But since personal fulfillment and ultimate redemption are profoundly conditioned by, or intertwined with these processes the work of teaching is now of unparalleled religious import. It was the wisdom of St. Ignatius to have realized, even though the future was opaque, that education is a job of considerable significance at any time and to have shrewdly surmised that it would become more so and therefore to have launched the Society of Jesus upon this apostolate in which it works alongside other religious groups and dedicated laymen and laywomen.

This launching, of course, was not accomplished either on the spur of some visionary moment or by a single, fully detailed decision. The Society of Jesus had not, after all, been founded precisely or even chiefly to teach the humanities to little boys and that is why Ribadeneira had felt compelled to ask himself just why it did teach boys grammar. Today as always, in fact, the ministries of Jesuits are wide ranging and various. But long ago, under the guidance of St. Ignatius himself, it did evolve the understanding of its apostolic vocation to include secondary educa-

tion and eventually the conduct of higher education in all its complexity
as a specification of that broad commitment to teaching in the widest
sense which was always implied by its basic dedication to the defense of
the Catholic faith and the advancement of mankind in Christian belief
and behavior. The details of the evolution have been carefully traced in
a number of studies.[18] The newly formed order passed by a series of steps
from the establishment of houses of study exclusively for scholastics, as
the young Jesuits preparing for the priesthood were called, to the admission of "externs," or non-Jesuits, to those classes. From thence it proceeded to the foundation of schools and universities expressly designed
for the general humanistic education of lay students or for their subsequent specialization in professional areas. The whole development was
canonically sanctioned by the papal letter or *bulla* of Julius III, *Ex-
posit Debitum,* of July 21, 1550, which declared that the Society exists to
defend and advance the faith by, among other means, public *lectiones*
—schools which directly ministered to the welfare of the Christian
commonwealth, as Ribadeneira had noted when he answered his own
question.[19]

This specific concept of secondary schools for young boys was
weighed carefully before it was conclusively accepted by St. Ignatius
some time between 1551 and 1556. His hesitation was prompted by
prudence. The idea of priests, brothers and sisters teaching the arts
and sciences as well as philosophy and theology is commonplace today
and the framework of their religious life has been adapted to accommodate a work second to none. But it was a considerable novelty in the
sixteenth century and there was little in the way of precedent to sanction
or tested procedures to support it. We get some appreciation of how matters then stood when we see what care commentators like Suarez and
Ribadeneira exercise in refuting the implication of dangerous innovation
in this whole business. They feel obliged to show that it is not abhorrent
to the desirable decorum of religious life. It has admirable patristic precedent, they point out, in the examples of St. Jerome and the third-century
school of Alexandria where Clement and Origen shone. In any case, as
Suarez argued, if the military orders could defend the Church with
physical weapons, the teaching orders may surely defend it with the
spiritual weapons of instruction and scholarship.[20] Besides, as Ribadeneira observed, the aim of Christian schools is twofold, both moral and
intellectual, and no one will deny that the formation of youthful character is a suitable occupation for persons who by profession are trying to
lead a life of moral excellence. As for teaching letters or secular subjects,
it is enough to note, he continues, that the Church of God has always

claimed this care as its own. He adds pleasantly that his own times are calamitous because the world is everywhere oppressed by the depraved morals of Catholics themselves, by corruption in government and by the "foul swill" of heresies. The educational apostolate is therefore crucial and "I do not know whether any other work better serves the divine majesty than this humanistic instruction of youth."[21]

St. Ignatius had been of the same mind and he had converted his conviction into action. So much for an epitome of his practical education work. The second theme, that of his educational theory, is less easily stated. Did he entertain any substantial notion of Christian humanism, that is to say, of a religious vision of life with distinctive implications for education? If so, what was it? One may reasonably maintain that he did have such a concept of life and education (essentially identical, of course, with the Christian concept of these realities) and that this can be justly described as humanistic. It was not, to be sure, the baptized Ciceronianism favored by devout humanists, although Ignatius was quick enough to employ skills of this sort when they were at hand. He sent Ribadeneira to Belgium in 1555, with the hope that Pedro's eloquent Latin sermons would ingratiate the new Order with the Court and his confidence was justified. But the humanistic dimension of Ignatius's own thought is more radical than any particular curriculum can adequately represent. It is a humanism for three chief reasons among others: because it affirms the exceptional dignity of man in the contingent universe and advocates his full and ideal development; because its precise concern is for mankind, for the entire human race rather than for some select portion of it; and because it takes seriously that historic process in which men live and which forms them even as their own responsible decisions are in turn shaping it.

The theme of man's dignity and pre-eminent role among visible created beings is a leitmotiv of the *Exercises*. It is announced at the very beginning in the consideration which we are invited to make of what Ignatius called The First Principle and Foundation. This principle asserts that man was made to praise, reverence, and serve God and that "the other things on the face of the earth are created for man to help him in attaining the end for which he is created."[22] But these phrases are no more than a spare restatement of the revelation which dominates the first chapter of Genesis. God is shown there making man in the divine image and giving him "dominion over the fishes of the sea, and the fowls of the air, and the beasts, and the whole earth" which he is to fill and subdue. This insight into man's distinctive and unique position, does not, however, imply that the material world is without intrinsic value. On the contrary, Christianity affirms that all of nature reflects the imprint of God Who gave it being and continually sustains it in existence. If the first meditation of the *Exercises* focuses upon the ordination of material creation to man's fulfillment, the final meditation, the Contemplation for Attaining Divine Love, requires us to think of God dwelling in these very creatures, "working and laboring" in all the elements, all the plants and animals upon the face of the earth.[23] The world is good in the first place because God made it; not simply because it satisfies human needs.[24]

Nevertheless, although the universe is honored as the work of God, pervaded by His creative presence, still it is true that when Ignatius's humanistic vision searches out the deepest theological meaning of that world, he finds it precisely in the ultimate instrumental vocation of things. "I hold it as an established truth," he said, in a letter to Gian Pietro Carafa, the future Paul IV, "that God our Lord has created everything in this present life for the service and good of men." And to the Italian duke, Asconius Colonna he put his favorite theme thus: "In this life a thing is good for us only insofar as it is a help toward life eternal and evil insofar as it is an obstacle to it."[25]

This vision of instrumentality must be emphasized as strongly as possible because it was not only central to Ignatius's own thought but lies at the very heart of the Jesuit concept of education and is encountered at many levels from specific questions of curriculum to generalized formulations of broadest goals. It is bound to scandalize both the absolute humanist and the absolute positivist because on the one hand it assigns a subordinate function to art and knowledge and on the other it denies the final self-sufficiency of the visible world. Yet no other concept is at once so thoroughly humanistic and respectful of all nature and at the same time so loyal to man's divine vocation. A twentieth-century Jesuit scientist has summarized this most perceptively. In *The Divine Milieu,* Teilhard de Chardin paraphrases that foundation principle of Ignatian thought. In our universe, he writes, all souls are made for God in Christ though only faith tells us this. In this same universe it is equally true, and a matter of simple observation, that every other reality, even material is made for our souls. All the energies of the tangible world are continually nourishing the human spirit in one way or another and are taken up by it. Thus it happens that all other reality, even material, attains to God through the mediation of our souls.[26] This world from which we draw not only nurture, shelter and medication but from which we fashion our books, pictures, statuary and those musical instruments whose voices liberate the spirit—all this is at the service of man who ought, in turn, to employ it for the service of God. The infrahuman world provides man with the means and the occasion for the flowering of his human potential and if man seeks God, as he ought, this world itself reaches and praises the Lord through the human voice and action.

In the second place, Ignatius's view is authentically humanistic not only because it sees man as the crown of the cosmos but also because it grasps the unity of mankind, the totality of all men in a single human family. Consequently, it is not crippled by any limitation to males only or to Europeans alone or just to the wellborn. It is humanity itself that the *Exercises* have in mind in their great central meditations even though the immediate purpose of these meditations is the conversion of an individual heart. It is *Man* who is created to praise God, not just certain men. The sinner is invited to humble himself by contrasting his life with the immensity of "all men." The Incarnation is understood as decreed by the Trinity "to save the human race" lest everyone go down to hell. And when the Lord does come, He designs to win the whole world, not part of it and so He sends the disciples enrolled under His standard in every age "throughout the world to spread His sacred doctrine among all men, no matter what their state or condition."[27]

This humanity envisioned by St. Ignatius is no Platonic archetype set above the clash and groaning of history. He thinks of the actual unity of all those human beings composing the real human family rather than of the specific unity indicated by the concept of humanity. It is, therefore, men in time that concern Ignatius and a strong sense of history is felt across the *Exercises* despite their laconic and stenographic structure: the history of the fall and redemption; the history of the Kingdom of Christ, the Church in this world continually engaged with activities and things to be done; the history of the individual Christian soul whose choices are so fateful that the aim of the *Exercises* is to help him avoid a fatally wrong decision. Indeed, this appreciation of each person's worth keeps Christian humanism perfectly balanced so that despite its social character the individual is never subordinated to the collectivity as a means to an end.

For, after all, this Ignatian humanism is not merely humanistic. Any Renaissance theorist might have set man upon a pinnacle, concerned himself with mankind's collective fate and appreciated the momentous character of the historic process. Ignatius, as a man of faith, goes beyond this for he entertains a conception of life that is Christian as well as humanistic, and remote, indeed, from the ideologies of secular humanists whatever their century. But the most important truth about man when he is set within this Christian perspective is that of his relationship to God. "Man was created to praise, reverence, and serve God our Lord, and by this means to save his soul."

In our own day a fundamental insight into the importance of relationships, into the relatedness which is at the very core of life, has been widened and deepened by the studies of philosophers, sociologists, physicists and psychologists as well as by theologians. "To be related," no longer seems, as it did to the medieval metaphysician, the faintest of ontological categories. Instead, existence is seen to mean existing in and by relationships, existence at the intersection of myriad relations. Hegel had pointed out that to understand an object requires that it be understood in its relation to other things. A Christian philosopher like Marcel will stress the importance of human interrelatedness; the American social thinkers like James, Dewey and Mead spoke in similar fashion and a psychiatrist like Harry Stack Sullivan built a complete theory of personality in terms of interpersonal dealings. Now we see more clearly that which was always true: how the infant yet unborn lives in relation to its mother from whom the lifeblood flows; how the child, the youth and the man live by relating themselves to the natural world which warms, feeds and comforts them or is assimilated through knowledge, and by their community with other men. Americans, of all people, should have no difficulty in appreciating this notion since they know the reality so well. For as Robert C. Pollock has put it:

> Here in America, the positive significance of society for the development of personal life stares us in the face, for society in our country has assumed an extraordinary public character, being spread out around us in a great web of relationships, within which each one visibly leads his life. Where else is it so obviously true, as in America, that man is indeed, as it has been said, a "knot of relationships!"[28]

We can easily, therefore, appreciate Ignatius's penetration through religious faith to the centrality of that supreme relationship, the one which enfolds and grounds all else and to which all others are finally instrumental—the relationship of man to God. For the Christian, the whole of human life swings in a great arc out from God, the source, and back to God, the goal, "the beginning, middle, and end of all our good," as Ignatius once put it.[29] It is true that man must humanize himself and develop the resources of the universe for only thus can he articulate that basic relation of love. Man is indeed the being capable of self-consciousness and freedom and these powers cannot be put at God's service unless they are developed and they cannot be developed unless, as Gilson remarked, their rights are integrally respected.[30] But as far as Ignatius was concerned, the ultimate purpose of this development of liberty and mind is that we should act and that in acting "Our one desire and choice should be what is more conducive to the end for which we are created." It was his custom for over twenty years, from 1532 until his death, to close his letters with the wish that both he and his correspondent might have the grace to know God's will and to accomplish it completely.[31]

What all this orientation might mean for practical educational issues is suggested, to take a single case, by the twelfth chapter of the Fourth Part of the *Constitutions* which Ignatius wrote for the order he had founded. This chapter deals with the disciplines to be taught in a university, that is to say, in an institution beyond the middle school. It begins with a clear statement of purpose: "The Society's goal" (the word used is *scopus* which may also mean "target"), "and the goal of its studies is to help our fellow men to know and love God." This dual aim then provides a standard for deciding what shall enter the university curriculum. There will obviously be a faculty of theology since that is the most appropriate academic means to the end desired. Latin and Greek will be taught, along with the arts and the natural sciences, either because these are useful for theology or because they appear to cultivate the intelligence and thereby dispose it for ecclesiastical studies. Hebrew, Chaldaic, Arabic and Indian may be taught, "if they should appear to be useful or necessary for the goal laid down." Medicine and law were pursuits rather remote from the charter assigned to the Society by its Institute and so this twelfth chapter concludes that the Jesuit universities will not have these faculties or at least that they will not be staffed by the Jesuits themselves. But that left the door sufficiently ajar and in America today there are five Jesuit medical schools and thirteen law schools besides seven of dentistry, eight of engineering, three of pharmacy, nine of nursing and one each of music, journalism and foreign service, although Chaldaic is nowhere formally professed. The fundamental principle of Ignatian humanism perfectly supports and governs this development which was useful and wise in light of that immutable Christian purpose which constituted the Society's goal.

This view of education as ultimately instrumental may trouble some minds. Is it not true, one might ask, that intellectual and cultural values are inherently precious, are good in themselves and not merely as useful tools for reaching something else? Of course they are, and St. Ignatius knew this and nowhere denies it. He simply does not address himself to that point, for he surveys the terrain from an exceedingly lofty elevation and his dominant concern is with the final and total picture. Had he adverted to this matter, he would surely have agreed that no man can consume his life in a chemistry laboratory or in reading the dull but necessary books that every student must get through unless, besides other motivations, he is also sustained by an insight into the inherent worth of the intellectual endeavor itself. But if such a man is a Christian, he will also know that within the larger perspective this excellence appears as an intermediate good, having about it the quality both of a goal and a factor. For the man is more than a chemist or historian or artist and his life is not comprehended by his professional career. In the final reckoning, the whole realm of scientific and creative work is ordered as a means to a transcendent and absolute value. Saint differs from saint and Ignatius once warned that we should not compare saints. It might be observed, though, that since St. Thomas Aquinas was a great scholar as well as a great saint, he will serve to remind us of the essential goodness in the quest for truth, while St. Ignatius will keep before us an equally pertinent principle by reminding us that the search itself must be, as it can be, a service of the God of truth.

The contribution of revelation to Ignatius's humanism was not limited, however, to this emphasis on man's prime relation to God and the instrumental character of other things in the light of that relationship. Christianity has an historical dimension too; one which points to a record of conflict and tragedy. In the concrete order men have found it desperately hard to choose God rather than the world. Even some Christians who assent fully to Ignatius's firm, brief formulas and acknowledge that they ought to select from the teeming riches of life only what will give God glory, still think this cannot be done save by violent truncation. Yet a Christian humanist of Ignatius's stamp does not wish to see reality impoverished but only rightly ordered. To this end a man must, it is true, cultivate a prior detachment which will keep him from supplanting the supreme good with a subordinate value that has been idolized. But since detachment of this depth is hard to come by, the human drama is often darkened by failure. Because Ignatius knew this, his own outlook was colored by a characteristically Christian blend of optimism and pessimism.

His faith in Providence and in the Redemption sustained a certain ground tone of optimism. Because the Divine Majesty is infinite and unshadowed Love and Goodness and because the Word Incarnate has already insured the ultimate triumph of those who are loyal until death, a sincere Christian has an indestructible hope which has as its psychological and emotional effect a kind of moderate optimism. Moreover, since the Lord calls for our cooperation, human action and enterprise in the divine service are neither meaningless nor optional. But St. Ignatius joined to this sanguine spirit a realistic and even tragic sense of evil. This second theme, which in itself may be accounted pessimistic, he embodied in some striking images which symbolize truths of great consequence. A number of the spiritual exercises, for instance, turn the exercitant's attention to the fact of moral evil or sin. To establish the appropriate mood for these meditations, he is directed to think of his soul as imprisoned in the corruptible body and of that composite which is himself, body and soul, as exiled here on earth among brute beasts. In a subsequent meditation on the Incarnation, there is a panoramic survey of human history as it appears apart from the saving intervention of God. The time dimension is fluid, the scenes melt into one another and yield a desolate impression of chaos in which men are born and die and between these mysterious poles busy themselves swearing, blaspheming, wounding and killing one another in a vast confusion that brings nations blindly down to hell. The great meditation on the Two Standards opens with a smoky tableau of Satan enthroned in Babylon and dispatching his janissaries over the globe to ensnare men in a destructive pride through the lures of money, power and prestige.

Although this sobering vision of evil very much tempers Christian optimism, it does not stifle it. It serves, instead, to define the exact nature of the true humanistic task which is to re-establish that order and harmony in human life which evil has blasted. The *Exercises* have, as their preliminary note itself announces, for "their purpose the conquest of self and the regulation of one's life in such a way that no decision is made under the influence of any inordinate attachment."[32] To put it another way, they aim to reinstate or to preserve men in their essential vocation. That vocation is ultimately a vocation to happiness in the affective vision of God but in this life it is a vocation chiefly realized through a service which actively incarnates and validates love. Ignatius, observes an experienced commentator, chose the word *service* as being "more precise and less subject to illusion" than *love*.[33] This service is not necessarily a matter of dramatic exploits. It must always involve abstention from the sin which ruptures the relationship with God but thereafter it will most often mean a large-hearted fidelity to the modest tasks of a modest role in the Christian ranks.

By reason of its optimistic strand, therefore, the Ignatian humanism is fundamentally hopeful and energetic and by reason of its realistic awareness of sin and the corruption of freedom it avoids both a rationalistic over-confidence and naive meliorism. "Even at Rome," said Ignatius in a letter of November, 1538, "there are not wanting those who have no love for the light of truth and life which the Church teaches."[34] His humanism is also particularly inclined to underscore the need for action and responsible decision. It respects intelligence but awards primacy to the moral virtues. St. Ignatius does not deny the classic thesis which locates man's happiness in the pure contemplation of noblest truth. But this happiness can be achieved only in the immediate vision of God which constitutes heaven. Consequently, the Ignatian humanism, which is a theory for the right conduct of this temporal life, concerns itself less for happiness than for service; less for fruition than for action. Christian service is actually nothing but effective love. On this earth, indeed, St. Thomas observes, we are more intimately united to God by charity than by knowledge for we can love God directly while we cannot yet "see" him directly. The love-service of the Christian normally focuses upon the person of Christ the Lord who has an imprescriptible right to our devotion because He is God and, at the same time, irresistibly inspires it because as the Incarnate Redeemer He is both a Man who can be visualized and the author of our salvation who has loved us first. The main thrust of the *Exercises,* in fact, is to bring before the exercitant this incomparable figure of our Lord for the Ignatian humanism is thoroughly Pauline, thoroughly Christo-centric. The knowledge and love of Jesus is its dynamo and its goal is that joyful and practical homage which these forces empower. "Let him go forward" said Ignatius of the ideal member of his Company, "in the spirit of love . . . swiftly, joyfully, perseveringly . . . *cum animi hilaritate.*"[35] And once he gathered many of these threads into a letter he sent to the young Jesuit scholastics at Coimbra in Portugal, writing in part:

> . . . You live in an age when you must show your desires by your works. Look around you: where is the divine Majesty honored, where is His tremendous greatness venerated, where is His most holy will obeyed?
>
> . . . See the misery into which souls are plunged . . .
>
> . . . What need there is to prepare yourselves for all manner of work and struggle to make of yourselves efficient instruments of divine grace for such a work! Especially when there are so few loyal workers "who do not seek their own advantage, but that of Jesus Christ." (Phil. 2, 21)[36]

These foundations of St. Ignatius's humanistic theory are the premises from which certain practical conclusions for the ordering of school programs and for their administration were drawn by the saint himself in the Fourth Part of the *Constitutions*. Several decades later the editors of the *Ratio Studiorum* continued the task of translating Christianity's broad imperatives for education into precise details of classroom procedures. By its very nature a task of this sort is never finished and must be shouldered by each generation. For Jesuit schoolmen, however, the experience and the accumulated wisdom of their predecessors is wonderfully instructive for their own work. In the next chapter we shall sketch the evolution of that wisdom by describing the documents which chiefly preserve its written form and by summarizing the story of their composition.

NOTES: CHAPTER I

1. In Chapter II the origins and content of the Jesuit *Constitutions* are briefly summarized. Most of the material on education is found in the fourth of the ten parts of this book of the *Constitutions*. The quotations from the Fourth Part in these pages are taken from the translation by George E. Ganss, S.J., which is included in his study, *Saint Ignatius' Idea of a Jesuit University* (Milwaukee: Marquette University Press, 1954). The passage quoted as an epigraph here for Chapter I is taken from p. 330 of that translation which will henceforth be cited as *Ganss*.

2. A handy compendium in which one can find some of the meager statistics available for sixteenth-century Jesuit history is that of J. B. Goetstouwers, S.J., *Synopsis Historiae Societatis Iesu* (Louvain, 1950). One of those provinces existing in 1556 was actually a mission to Ethiopia and it ceased after some years.

3. An interesting account of the manner in which confiscated Jesuit properties were employed to finance state schools is provided by N. Hans, "The Dissolution of the Society of Jesus in the Eighteenth Century and its Financial Consequences," in *Education and Economics: The Year Book of Education 1956* (Yonkers-on-Hudson: World Book Company, 1956), pp. 137–146.

4. These statistics are taken from William J. Mehok, S.J., "Jesuit Schools of the World: 1961," *Jesuit Educational Quarterly,* 25 (June, 1962), pp. 42–56. Father Mehok's study indicates some of the difficulties of gathering accurate statistics when the educational enterprise is so vast and when account must be taken of national differences in defining schools and reporting figures.

5. Alfred North Whitehead, *The Aims of Education: And Other Essays* (New York: Macmillan, 1929), pp. 70–71.

6. Joseph de Jouvancy, S.J. (Josephus Juvencii), *Ratio Discendi et Docendi*. The edition cited here is a relatively late one (Paris: Augustus Delalain, 1809), p. 214. The first edition was in 1703.

7. On this point see the two best general studies of the historical origins

of Jesuit education: J. B. Herman, S.J., *La pédagogie des Jésuites au XVIe siècle* (Louvain: Recueil de Travaux, 1914), pp. 52, 55, 161 and François de Dainville, S.J., *La naissance de l'humanisme moderne* (Paris: Beauchesne, 1940), p. 250.

8. Petrus Ribadeneira, S.J., *De Ratione Instituti Societatis Iesu*, trans. from Spanish into Latin by Laurentius Carli, S.J. (Rome: Civiltà Cattolica Press, 1864). The original Spanish text was first published in 1605.

9. Hugo Rahner and Leonard von Matt, *St. Ignatius of Loyola: A Pictorial Biography*, trans. John Murray (Chicago: Henry Regnery and Company, 1956). For a complete biography of St. Ignatius see Paul Dudon, S.J., *St. Ignatius of Loyola*, trans. William J. Young, S.J. (Milwaukee: Bruce, 1949) and for studies limited to the saint's earlier years, James Brodrick, S.J., *Saint Ignatius Loyola: The Pilgrim Years 1491–1538* (New York: Farrar, Straus and Cudahy, 1956) and Pedro Leturia, S.J., *Iñigo de Loyola*, trans. Aloysius J. Owen, S.J. (Syracuse: Le Moyne College Press, 1949).

10. The original text of the autobiographical reminiscences gathered by González is printed in the multi-volume source series, *Monumenta Historica Societatis Jesu*, whose individual tomes have been appearing from Madrid and Rome ever since the first in 1894. The autobiographical fragment is found in the section of the series called *Monumenta Ignatiana*: Fourth Series, I (Madrid, 1904). The lines quoted are on p. 66. Their English version here is from *St. Ignatius' Own Story: As told to Luis González de Cámara*, trans. William J. Young, S.J. (Chicago: Henry Regnery Company, 1956), p. 36. St. Ignatius' description of his studies at Alcalá, quoted in our text, is found on p. 70 of the *Monumenta* edition.

11. Pedro Leturia, S.J., "Why the Society of Jesus Became a Teaching Order," trans. V. J. Yanitelli, S. J., *Jesuit Educational Quarterly*, 4 (1941), 41, note. This study originally appeared as "Perchè la Compagnia di Gesu divenne un Ordine insegnante," *Gregorianum*, 21 (1940), 350–382. The journal in which the translation appeared is one of private circulation but this is not the case with *Gregorianum*.

12. Quoted by Philippe Delhaye, "L'organisation scolaire au XIIe siècle," *Traditio* 5 (1947), 227, text and note 14.

13. See Hugo Rahner, S.J., *The Spirituality of St. Ignatius Loyola*, trans. Francis John Smith, S.J. (Westminster: Newman Press, 1953), p. 112.

14. "The world has not suffered from absence of ideals and spiritual aims anywhere nearly as much as it has suffered from absence of means for realizing the ends which it has prized in a literary and sentimental way." John Dewey, *Individualism—Old and New* (New York: Minton, Balch and Company, 1930), pp. 29–30.

15. John Baptist Janssens, S.J., "Epistola ad Societatem 'De Ministeriis Nostris,'" *Acta Romana Societatis Iesu*, 11 (1947), 315. This journal is one of private circulation.

16. See *Letters of St. Ignatius of Loyola*, selected and translated by William J. Young, S.J. (Chicago: Loyola University Press, 1959), letter to Michael de Torres, September 10, 1546, p. 102. In a letter to Mat-

thew Sebastian de Morrano, February 22, 1549, Ignatius remarks that
the Society cannot undertake a work like the direction of convents because, according to its Institute, it "must, so to say, have one foot on
the road, ready to hasten from one place to another." *Ibid.*, p. 187.

17. Janssens, S.J., *op. cit.*, p. 319.
18. These studies include, in addition to the previously cited books of Ganss
    and Herman and the essay by Leturia, Allan P. Farrell, S.J., *The
    Jesuit Code of Liberal Education* (Milwaukee: Bruce, 1938). Father
    Farrell's book contains the fullest account of the evolution of the
    Ratio Studiorum, an account based upon manuscript sources.
19. "Among the enterprises which the Society has undertaken for the good
    of the commonwealth, not the least, surely, is the burden it has as-
    sumed of teaching boys the rudiments of grammar by making schools
    available to the public." Ribadeneira, *op. cit.*, p. 510. The essential
    material from the bull of Julius III may be found in *Societatis Iesu
    Constitutiones et Epitome Instituti* (Rome: Apud Curiam Praepositi
    Generalis, 1949), pp. 8–20.
20. See Franciscus Suarez, S.J., *Tractatus de Religione Societatis Iesu*
    (Brussels: Greuse, 1857), V, 4, 288–89. Suarez was born in 1548 and
    died in 1617.
21. Ribadeneira, *op. cit.*, p. 517. Suarez observes that study of the liberal
    arts contributes to the welfare of both Church and State: "Generalius
    autem loquendo, studia et universitates honestarum artium, non solum
    propter ecclesiasticam, sed etiam propter civilem communitatem et
    utilitatem, necessaria sunt, et ita in omnibus regnis et provinciis recte
    institutis, hujusmodi generalia studia floruerunt." *Op. cit.*, p. 285.
22. St. Ignatius of Loyola, *The Spiritual Exercises,* trans. Louis J. Puhl,
    S.J. (Westminster, Md.: Newman Press, 1951), p. 12, n. 23. This
    translation makes use of the division of the text into numbered sections
    which was first devised for an edition of the original Spanish text and
    its official Latin translation published by Marietti, Turin, 1928. In a
    meditation on sin which is subsequent to the consideration of the
    First Principle and Foundation, the exercitant is directed to consider
    how badly he has used the terrestrial wealth at his disposal, saying to
    himself: "And the heavens, sun, moon, stars, and the elements; fruits,
    birds, fishes, and other animals—why have they all been at my service!"
    Ibid., p. 30, n. 60.
23. *Ibid.*, pp. 101–103, nn. 230–237.
24. Pierre Charles, S.J., *Createur des choses visibles* (Brussels: Edition de
    Renouveau, 1946), p. 47.
25. The letter to Cardinal Carafa (or Caraffa) was written in 1536 and that
    to Colonna in 1543. The passages quoted here are from *Letters of St.
    Ignatius of Loyola, op. cit.*, pp. 30, 69.
26. Pierre Teilhard de Chardin, *The Divine Milieu* (New York: Harper
    and Brothers, 1960), 27–30.
27. St. Ignatius of Loyola, *The Spiritual Exercises, op. cit.*, pp. 12, 29, 44,
    49, 61; nn. 23, 58, 95, 102, 145. These are the meditations on the
    Principle and Foundation, one's sins, the Incarnation, the Kingdom of
    Christ and the Standard of Christ.

28. Robert C. Pollock, "The Person in American Society," in *Catholicism in American Culture:* Semicentenary Lecture Series 1953–54 (New Rochelle: College of New Rochelle, 1955), p. 45.

29. From a letter to St. Francis Borgia in 1545. See *Letters of St. Ignatius of Loyola, op. cit.,* p. 83.

30. Etienne Gilson, *Christianity and Philosophy,* trans. Ralph MacDonald, C.S.B. (New York: Sheed and Ward, 1939), pp. 116–117.

31. The sentence beginning, "Our one desire" is the final sentence in the First Principle and Foundation, *The Spiritual Exercises, op. cit.,* p. 12, n. 23. For St. Ignatius's formula for closing letters see Paul Doncoeur, S.J., *The Heart of Ignatius: The Ignatian Concepts of the Honor and Service of God,* trans. Henry St. C. Lavin, S.J. (Baltimore: Helicon Press, 1959), p. 57.

32. *Spiritual Exercises, op. cit.,* p. 11, n. 21. Our comment on the exact nature of the task of Christian humanism echoes Erasmus's well-known formulation of education's aim: *Instauratio bene conditae naturae.*

33. Pinard de la Boullaye, "Ignatian Spirituality," in Jean Gautier (ed.), *Some Schools of Catholic Spirituality,* trans. Kathryn Sullivan, R.S.C.J. (New York: Desclee, 1959), p. 214. Writers on the thought of St. Ignatius all sound alike since they are saying much the same thing. This is inevitable because Ignatius was a man of few ideas. These few, however, he propounded and lived with an unmistakable clarity. The concept of service of God in the Church is one such idea and all who study Ignatius are bound to underscore it. The term "service," as Father Rahner observes, is not without its ambiguities and so he is at some pains to distinguish the Ignatian concept from the servility inculcated by totalitarians. *The Spirituality of St. Ignatius Loyola, op. cit.,* p. v. In the United States, if one is not mistaken, the word has never been seriously discolored and still evokes an admirable image of responsibility and even generosity. In any case, it meant for Ignatius the best of which men are capable.

34. *Letters of St. Ignatius Loyola, op. cit.,* p. 36.

35. *Constitutions,* VI, 1, 1. The full text of the *Constitutions,* both the original Spanish and the official Latin version, can be found in the *Monumenta Historica Societatis Jesu, Monumenta Ignatiana,* Third Series, Volumes II (1936) and III (1938).

36. The letter was written from Rome in May, 1547. There is a complete English translation by Father Young in *Letters of St. Ignatius of Loyola, op. cit.,* pp. 120–130. The translation of the excerpts quoted here in the text is taken from Doncoeur, *op. cit.,* p. 47.

CHAPTER II

ON SOME DOCUMENTARY SOURCES

Those sound pedagogical principles which were wisely set forth by our Father in the Constitutions *and developed by the* Ratio Studiorum . . .
Epitome of the Institute of the
Society of Jesus[1]

In 1581 a Neapolitan, Claudio Aquaviva, was elected the fifth General of the Society of Jesus. He was then thirty-eight years old and he was to hold office until his death almost exactly thirty-four years later. His generalate was the longest, the most distinguished and, if we exclude that of Father Ricci who was General when the Society was suppressed, the stormiest of any of the successors of St. Ignatius. Under Aquaviva's direction the works and membership of the order advanced impressively to the sporadic accompaniment of violent commotions raised around him by men both outside the Society and within it. The record of this accomplishment and turbulence is detailed in any standard history of the Jesuits. Not the least of Aquaviva's achievements was his success in fulfilling St. Ignatius's plan for a handbook of administration and method designed to unify and organize school procedures for all the Jesuit institutions. Shortly after his election, he had appointed a twelve-man committee to take up the still unsettled matter of constructing this *Ratio Studiorum* but that group does not seem to have effected anything. The work really got under way on the Feast of the Immaculate Conception, 1584, when Aquaviva led a little delegation of six Fathers to kiss the slipper of Gregory XIII and ask a pontifical blessing on the task they were about to begin—most laborious, *tam operosum,* as they subsequently reported it to have been.[2] For the next six months these deputies worked in the Penitentiary of St. Peter's and in the summer they moved to Sant' Andrea on the Quirinal hill. They had come together from various countries—Spain, Portugal, Austria, Germany, Italy and France (although the representative of the French province was actually Scottish by birth)—and they provided a good cross section of opinion. Each day they met for three hours in committee and the rest of the time they sifted through all the earlier Jesuit school plans as well as through contemporary educational treatises and also canvassed their fellow Jesuits for recommendations. The result of their studies was a book made up of connected essays on two chief topics: the determination of the opinions that were to be defended in Jesuit seminaries, so far as disputed theological questions were concerned, and the organization of the courses in grammar and humanities which would be followed by all students, those going on to theology and those bent on careers in law or trade. This document, known today as the *Ratio* of 1586, was originally issued in a limited edition since it was professedly tentative and experimental and designed for consultation, not permanence. In 1882 the German Jesuit, G. M. Pachtler re-edited it for the series, *Monumenta Germaniae Pedagogica,* in which it occupies some two hundred pages.

After this 1586 *Ratio* had been reviewed by Aquaviva and his advisors, as well as by small committees in each of the twenty-two provinces then in existence, it was put to a revision and another version, differently organized but substantially and often verbally the same, appeared in 1591.[3] Once again judgments were freely proffered, collected and collated from the Jesuit schools throughout Europe and in 1599 the final draft of a *Ratio atque Institutio Studiorum* was formally approved and promulgated by Aquaviva with the hope that it would be put into practice smoothly and cheerfully—*facile suaviterque.* It remained mandatory for all Jesuit institutions until the suppression in 1773.

The *Ratio* of 1599 is commonly supposed to be a classic expression of the Jesuit accent in education and the honorific references to it in the Society's law would appear to support this view. Still it is certain that neither the distinctive Jesuit nuances in education nor the *Ratio* itself can be understood without looking back from 1599 to the documents that preceded and shaped that definitive school plan and forward from 1599 to the legislation which followed and modified it. Moreover, as we shall indicate in Chapter IV, the total Jesuit philosophy of education necessarily includes all the themes of any adequate Catholic philosophy of education, even though these may not be mentioned by the *Ratio.*

The *Ratio* of 1599 is likely to puzzle, if it does not repel even a well-disposed reader who happens upon it for the first time. Its letter seems to overlay and obscure its spirit as often as it succeeds in expressing it. Nevertheless this spirit can be discerned, after some reflection, just as a noble melody can be discerned beneath a less perfect orchestration. But for this discernment one needs to read the *Constitutions* of the Society and certain earlier educational documents along with the first two drafts of the *Ratio*. It is from all these writings that the authentic properties of Jesuit education are to be distilled and in the second part of this book we shall try to group these distillates into a tentative synthesis. At this point, though, a few observations on those basic documents and on their history will be useful. It is not necessary to draw up an exhaustive topical analysis either of the Fourth Part of the Constitutions or of the various drafts of the *Ratio* since this work has been admirably done for contemporary English readers by Father Ganss and Father Farrell.[4] The documents themselves, however, and the process by which they were evolved suggest or embody certain characteristics of the Jesuit approach to education and it is simply these that we wish to underscore here. We shall begin by looking at certain questions that a twentieth-century student might raise if he opened the *Ratio* of 1599. Thereafter we shall make some comments, first on the origins and over-all characteristics of the section on schools in the Jesuit *Constitutions,* then on the collection of documents which antedated the first draft of the *Ratio* as well as the three versions of that *Ratio* itself and finally on certain significant stages in latter-day Jesuit legislation.

The *Ratio* of 1599 is actually a collection of thirty sets of rules prefaced by a letter of transmission from Aquaviva. In an English translation it occupies about 140 pages.[5] Some of these sets are lengthy. There are 50 rules for the Prefect of Lower Studies who today would be called a secondary school principal. Other sets are short. There are only three rules for the professor of mathematics. As one reads these various directives one can perceive the general outlines of the institution for which they were designed and this image of a sixteenth-century school might be further clarified by asking three questions. What are the analogies in our own American educational system to the various levels of the institution envisioned in the *Ratio?* From what sources were the characteristics of that institution chiefly drawn? How ought one go about properly evaluating the school whose portrait emerges from the *Ratio?*

To the first question there is really no adequate answer since it is not possible to find an exact contemporary parallel to those late Renaissance schools. The *Ratio* describes a complex institution having three chief divisions. At the top, both logically and from the point of view of prestige, was the theological course or Faculty of Theology—the term "Faculty" signifying in this context a broad area of instruction. Theology was normally studied only by seminarians, either Jesuits themselves, those of other orders or those preparing for the diocesan priesthood. Below it was the *Facultas Artium* which might anachronistically be labeled the collegiate liberal arts course. It included the study of philosophy which also had some scientific work subsumed under it. The main focus of interest, however, the level of instruction to which the *Ratio* devoted most attention and the one found in all the Jesuit *collegia,* either with or without a Faculty of Arts added to it, was a school called the Faculty of Letters (Language Studies) or the *Gymnasium*.[6] It was divided into a program with five main sections: three classes of grammar studies whose readings and exercises are carefully spelled out in the *Ratio,* a class of Humanities which stressed Poetry and a class of Rhetoric. These "classes" were not necessarily a year each in length. A boy might spend less than a year in the first grammar class but two years in Rhetoric. He could start clambering up this ladder as soon as he had acquired the elements of literacy in an elementary school. This meant that he would scarcely have been admitted to the Jesuits' Latin classes before he was seven. Children less than that age, said the six Fathers who worked up the 1586 draft of the *Ratio,* are merely troublesome anyhow and need nurses not schoolmasters—*molestissimi et nutricibus potius indigent quam ludimagistris.*[7] After completing the studies of the Lower School, students might follow the program of the Faculty of Arts and still complete the whole course by fifteen or sixteen. Not a few, however, went no further than the first five-step cycle.

Now one may ask whether this curriculum of the *Gymnasium* constituted it a secondary school somewhat analogous to the twentieth-century high school. The terms themselves are certainly fluid enough and if a secondary school be defined tautologically as the middle school between the abecedarian exercises of the elementary classes and the professional specialization of the university, the Jesuit *collegium* was a secondary school. But any attempts to match it in terms of its curricula with some phase of modern systems is apt to mislead as much as to enlighten. In America today the secondary school is perhaps better understood as the school of adolescence whose pupils fall within the age limits of 12–14 to 17–19. But such a definition would not fit neatly the sixteenth-century Latin grammar schools either of the Jesuits or the Protestants not only because there were young children on the first rungs of these institutions but also because their programs manifested less concern for special educational needs created by the developmental problems of adolescence.

It will be best therefore to define these first Jesuit schools in their own terms—Latin Grammar schools with a lineage running back through the Middle Ages to Quintilian's Rome and Isocrates' Athens. They were not unlike similar places conducted by Lutherans in Strassburg or Anglicans at Eton. A boy paced through pretty much the same sort of program in any of these institutions. There was drill in morphology and syntax and some consideration of style and literature in the higher classes. The school was a Grammar school—a place which Dr. Johnson defined with blunt lucidity as one "in which the learned languages are taught grammatically."[8] What is to be noticed here is that the Jesuit's first concern was for secondary education and it was there that they achieved their most spectacular success. Their educational ideals were, so to speak, most fully realized in the work of the middle schools. Even today, apart from the theological seminaries, Jesuit education throughout the world is largely at the middle level between the elementary grades and university specialization, except in the United States where a number of complex collegiate and university centers have grown up, particularly since the end of the First World War. It is true, of course, that the Jesuit "colleges" in many countries outside the United States include work considerably beyond the ordinary American high school and represent something like a combination of our secondary school with the junior college.[9] In fact, the American Jesuit universities had as their nineteenth-century progenitors just such middle schools or "colleges," in the older sense: Faculties of Letters to which a year or two of philosophical studies were added.

The present school legislation in the Society's *Epitome* manifests this same primary concern for secondary education. Under the general heading, "The Instruction of Youth," the first specific directive points out the desirability of establishing schools open to the public and adds, "at least secondary schools (*scholae mediae*)."[10] This does not imply a speculative judgment about the superior importance of secondary over elementary or higher education, although a case could be made for such a conviction especially in our own culture, where the high school seems to be the focal point of more crises and problems than are the schools above and below it. When the Society of Jesus embarked upon education, however, it was precisely this Latin Grammar or middle school which appeared to be the most promising area for development. To teach little children the alphabet was judged an uneconomical employment of the Order's resources. The existing universities were firmly controlled by their own staffs and it would have been expensive to start new ones. In any case the rising middle classes wanted neither the arts nor theology but the socially approved badge of Latinity for embryonic lawyers and merchants.[11] Most of the Jesuit effort went, therefore, into providing the schools that were in demand for the sake of reaching the people who demanded them. But it is also true that the Jesuit theory of curriculum put these literary studies in lowest place and viewed them as the logical conduit to the philosophy and science of the "Arts" faculty which was designed to be climaxed in turn by the full theology course or by some other professional specialization in the university.

In the next chapter we shall sketch the daily routine of one of these seventeenth-century Jesuit "colleges" by deducing it from the *Ratio*. Let us note now, though, that the procedures to be described were very like the procedures praised by all Renaissance schoolmen and that Quintilian was the father of most of those methods. It is sometimes said, for instance, that the distinctive hallmark of Jesuit pedagogy is the "prelection." This is a technique originally evolved for the teaching of classical literature. It is a type of textual explanation and commentary in which the teacher prepares his class for the next set of lines or the next assignment by discussing with them its problems, values and special points of interest. But as Père Herman shows, the prelection recommended by Erasmus hardly differs from that of the *Ratio Studiorum* and both are closely linked to the method of Quintilian—*noster Quintilianus* as Ribadeneira once called him.[12] The sixteenth-century pedagogues, indeed, were persuaded that Quintilian's *Education of an Orator* (*Institutio Oratoria*) had determined forever the ideal of instruction. And not only the sixteenth century. When Jouvancy published his commentary on the *Ratio* in 1703 he cited no other authority for his recommendations on classroom method than the great first-century Spaniard who was once Rome's most celebrated teacher of rhetoric.

It is a commonplace of educational history, however, that Quintilian himself codified the inspirations and elaborated the techniques of his Athenian predecessor, Isocrates. When Isocrates was a boy, Socrates had foreseen two possible careers for him. He might become an orator or, should "a more divine impulse" lead him to metaphysics, he might become a philosopher. In the actual event, Isocrates became neither an orator nor a philosopher. Timidity prevented him from ever speaking in public during all his ninety-seven years but he did become the wealthiest and most successful Greek rhetorician and the basic architect of an ideal of literary culture. This ideal dominated secondary education in the Western world until that education ceased, less than a century ago, to be the prerogative of the wealthy or the gifted and became a stage of common schooling. It was Isocrates who canonized eloquence as the supreme cultural expression; who reduced science and mathematics to the function of "gymnastics of the mind," preparing the intelligence for rhetorical composition; who stressed the importance of pupil activity and unceasing practice; who made the love of honor and achievement the pivotal device of motivation.[13]

Because the heritage of Isocrates and Quintilian was common to all Renaissance schoolmasters, Johann Sturm, who began his long rectorship of the Lutheran gymnasium in Strassburg at about the same time St. Ignatius was settling in Rome, was convinced that the first Jesuit schools stole their plan of organization and their materials from himself. The likenesses were actually owed to the fact that Sturm and the Jesuits were not only handling similar problems in a similar cultural context but were drawing upon certain common sources and subscribing to the same general ideal of intellectual culture—the Renaissance ideal of perfect Latin eloquence.[14] "Exercise all diligence and effort," said Rhetius, a distinguished Jesuit teacher in 1557, "to bring your students as swiftly as possible to the mastery of a pure and incorrupt Latin style." This was echoed in a phrase from the first rule for the Professor of Rhetoric who is bidden by the *Ratio* of 1599 to make Cicero the sole model of style, *ex uno fere Cicerone.*[15] In addition to this aim, both Sturm and the Jesuits taught the learned languages by methods built upon the Quintilian inspiration and honored in practice at the University of Paris in the first decades of the sixteenth century after having been successfully employed, even earlier, in the Low Country Schools conducted by Erasmus's first teachers, the Brethren of the Common Life. Outside the classroom, in that turbulent age, new inventions were being devised, new philosophies were being created and new continents were being explored. It is true that reports of these novelties were sometimes done in Latin but it could scarcely be said that classical culture had in the sixteenth-century work-a-day world anything like the dominance it enjoyed in the sixteenth-century classrooms of Winchester, and Eton, or Strassburg and Geneva or in the Jesuit *collegia* in Spain, Portugal, France, Germany and Italy. All these schools inhabited a rather windless world where the impact of change was muffled enough to make possible the use, well into the latter part of the century, as standard textbooks of Latin grammar the *Ars Minor* and *Ars Major* of Aelius Donatus, the fourth-century instructor of St. Jerome.[16]

The chief business of the middle schools, the first five classes in a Jesuit *collegium,* was a close study of Latin with some attention to Greek. The pupils took the language apart almost word by word, examining the nuances of each term and the proper use of each Latin particle and busily compiled for their own use a list of choice phrases culled from the Latin authors. The sixteenth century's own apt image for this curious process was that of anatomization.[17] It occupied all a student's time in his first two classes, those of lowest and middle grammar; most of his time in the highest grammar class and a good deal of his attention in the class of humanities or poetry and in the class of rhetoric.

Since the originality of the *Ratio* does not lie, then, either in the curricular materials it prescribes nor yet in the pedagogical devices it carefully traces for bringing about mastery of these materials, one may easily fail to appreciate the distinctive characteristics of those schools whose experiences the *Ratio* first formulated and thereafter regulated. The very fact of their existence was, of course, novelty and contribution enough. Erasmus may have recommended the same sort of methodology as the Jesuits but Erasmus founded no network of schools. It is fair to say that the Jesuits practically created secondary education in many seventeenth-century European countries so that, if you wanted this sort of schooling, it was to one of the Jesuit colleges that you went. It is hard to appraise these institutions justly at our present distance. They may be credited with rather too much or with too little. Depending upon where the critic stands, he may judge them either progressive or reactionary. Père de Dainville draws an attractive picture in which the Jesuits and other sixteenth-century humanists appear, by contrast with their monastic predecessors, as forerunners of the child-centered school since they stood for greater pupil freedom, for lessons filled with delight and interest, for a new accent on creativity, for a reasonable ideal of character education and for pleasant class surroundings and a judicious seasoning of the school term with holidays, games and contests.

In any case, those early Jesuit schools were usually characterized by three notes which together constituted an authentic innovation: a certain originality in the school program itself, a firm belief in the value of order, graduated curricula and tested methods and, finally, a staff of teachers devoted to their work and professionally well prepared. It is true, so far as the first of these notes is concerned, that the *Ratio's* program and methods were not strictly original but it is not unreasonable to maintain that its arrangement of its borrowed materials into a firmly organized system of progressive steps was new. In any case, the care for exact order and method which this organization incarnated was not only a characteristic of Jesuit educational theory but also a novel element in its era.

It is hard for us to appreciate this now since today the organization of education and the luxuriant elaboration of its administrative apparatus have become professional specialties in themselves. But when the Society of Jesus took up the work of education as a prime part of its apostolate it needed first of all to put that work on as sound a base as possible within the confines of the academic ideals then regnant. This had to be done, moreover, at a time when school procedures were, by twentieth-century standards, crude and chaotic. Indeed, the *Ratio's* elements of novelty will scarcely be discerned unless the context in which it was drawn up be kept in mind. When the Jesuits opened their first school at Messina, in Sicily in 1548, and insisted upon their students following a graduated progression of studies, they found themselves opposing a tradition of genial electivism more disorderly than Eliot's system at its height. For in the schools of Italy, as Ignatius's secretary, Father Juan de Polanco noted, it was not unknown that urbane young men attended lectures in philosophy before they had learned how to write.[18] What was needed first of all was an organization of the administrative and teaching offices which would be clear, exact and thorough but would not eliminate all room for spontaneity and initiative on the teacher's part and would not encase the student in a passive routine of monotonous regularity. Père Herman, indeed, once remarked that the only general principle of a strictly theoretical sort in the *Ratio* is that which holds: Variety is good because satiety is bad.[19] In any case, the efforts made by Jesuit schoolmen for half a century, efforts culminating in the *Ratio* of 1599, were aimed at securing order and unity without eliminating freedom and diversity.

These schoolmen themselves probably constituted the Society's most distinctive contribution to educational practice just as a prime concern for effective teaching dominates its pedagogical documents. That concern is for the selection and formation of dedicated, competent men whose classroom work will join the purest idealism to a technical proficiency based upon mastery both of subject matter and teaching skills. In the final chapter we shall return to this point, for it is central. More than one thoughtful observer has actually concluded that the wisest characterization of Jesuit education is that which simply holds it to be a Christian education given by Jesuits.

The Constitutions

If we wish to examine, in the order of their occurrence, the chief documentary sources of this Jesuit dedication to education and its concrete expression in a care for well-organized school procedures and well-trained teachers, we must begin with the book of the *Constitutions* of the Society of Jesus which stands in first place logically as well as chronologically.[20] At the outset a certain caution is in order. For Jesuits themselves, these *Constitutions* are uniquely venerable since together with the *Spiritual Exercises* they are the chief vessels conserving the distinctive Ignatian heritage. In the case of the *Constitutions,* however, that heritage can seem somewhat intangible since it is not fully spelled out but only suggested. This is even more true, of course, of the *Ratio* which not only lacks the authority and prestige of the *Constitutions* but on the surface appears to deal merely with concrete school details not all of which remain pertinent. The *Constitutions* are certainly always relevant but not infrequently fragmentary. For as a distinguished twentieth-century German Jesuit has observed, they:

> . . . provide no unbroken and consistent picture of the Society. They consist of isolated, almost aphoristic statements. Certain important points are emphasized, often subordinate and incidental directions are also added. They are not, therefore, scientifically constructed theses which, taken in their entirety, present a complete plan of the Society; they are a collection of rules, that have sprung from a distinctive interior atmosphere and attitude, have been observed and carefully tested in experience and eventually committed to writing as a kind of practical directive which neither represents nor reproduces the original spirit but serves only to mark its practical application.[21]

What is said here of the *Constitutions* taken as a whole applies very well to their Fourth Part in which educational matters are treated. But it may be noted that the *Spiritual Exercises,* which do not discuss such determined affairs as the organization of a religious order or a school, but focus upon the eternal and inner significance of all human life are not tied to the context of any single historical moment as the *Ratio* and the factual prescriptions of the *Constitutions* are. The burden of their message easily transcends the matrix of the sixteenth-century world and is as relevant today as ever.

But to some extent, what one finds in the *Exercises* one finds also, implicit and latent perhaps, in the *Constitutions* and to a very much lesser degree in the *Ratio.* This is a certain vision of life, and consequently of education, which is not so much a tradition as the ideal which tradition should serve. This deposit has been brought more fully into consciousness and has been rounded out through four centuries but Jesuit teachers and their colleagues can still profit from the insight afforded by their foundation documents. To do so means, of course, that they must neither diminish their heritage nor confuse it with incidental procedures which really constitute only one historically valid way of reducing to

practice certain gnomic principles which can have many other concretizations.

It is in the Fourth of the ten parts or "books" into which the *Constitutions* are divided, that St. Ignatius treats of education. The somewhat
episodic character of the treatment is indicated when one sees that he
does not devote any real discussion to the general aims of education although nowadays this topic is exhaustively, if inconclusively, examined
by conferences and committees, panelists and symposia and the authors
of a swarm of books and papers. Perhaps Ignatius and his immediate
successors, including the authors of the *Ratio,* saw no special problem
here just because they had so vivid a sense both of human destiny and of
their own apostolic purpose, that *unicus scopus*—service for the greater
glory of God, the sanctification and salvation of themselves and all other
people, the more universal good. Certainly the intensity of Ignatius's
convictions preserved him from any fear of losing sight of this basic
aim or drowning in a sea of minute policy decisions. At any rate, he was
quite content to formulate the goals of the school broadly, firmly and
rapidly—the teaching of letters and the good moral habits required of
a Christian—and then to get on at once to questions of means and techniques.

If he had been asked to define the role of educational theorizing he
would very likely have said, in light of his own practice, that its concern
should be with order and method, with the tools of the educational enterprise, with *how* rather than *what* or *why.* His own customary procedure also suggests certain attitudes that might be brought to bear upon
just such a work. In the tasks of administration and organization, St. Ignatius was realistic, accepting the limitations of the contingent framework within which he had to operate. If the way to get a school founded
was to cultivate the local duke, the duke would be cultivated.[22] Ignatius
was also extremely careful to insure orderly system in all arrangements
and highly confident of its value. He was endlessly painstaking and always moderate, or to use his own words, discreet in his regulations.[23] In
short, he tackled the actual business of setting up school strictly in
empirical fashion. He asked himself, quite like a good pragmatist, what
means promised to be most effective for that end which he had always
in sight. When his selection had been made after prolonged and prayerful
consideration it was then tested in action before the policy was definitely
adopted.

The construction of the *Constitutions* was, therefore, a lengthy
process which occupied St. Ignatius, to some extent or other, from 1543
until his death in 1556. It was also something of a group process because

he often sought the advice and opinion of his fellow Jesuits and, although the content of the *Constitutions* is entirely his, he left a good deal of the actual drafting to that chief secretary, Father Juan de Polanco. When the first version was finished it was reviewed in Rome by a gathering of representative members of the Society who met from November, 1550 until the following February. A year later, the document was promulgated experimentally and Ignatius's trusted emissary, Father Jerónimo Nadal travelled about Europe to explain it in each Jesuit house. The Latin translation of Ignatius's Spanish text was finally published two years after his death.

The ten parts of the *Constitutions* are of unequal length and have chiefly to do with the selection and admission of suitable candidates for the Society, their subsequent spiritual and intellectual formation, their assignment thereafter to the Order's various ministries and certain of the ideal characteristics desired both in the individual Jesuit and in the collective life of the whole Company. One finds everywhere that firm instrumental orientation which views all things save God in practical terms of their utility for the divine service which leads to divine union. Moral virtue, as we should expect, is more esteemed than learning but the latter is by no means despised since it is a most excellent apostolic tool. "Great learning and great virtue are to be sought after," Ignatius once wrote the young Jesuits studying at Coimbra in Portugal, "and perfection to be looked for in both, yet to virtue must always be given the preference."[24] Since the love of the Lord has primacy, there is constant emphasis on abjuration of the struggle for status and upon mortification so that this love may not be stifled or inhibited. In the preamble to the Fourth Part of the *Constitutions* which treats explicitly of educational matters, abnegation is called the necessary foundation for the intellectual work of a religious man. A great deal is also made of that purity of intention which finds God in all things and in them serves Him alone. This incarnates a truly mystical impulse. The structure of due subordination of subjects to superiors is also outlined and all are exhorted to cultivate cheerfulness since St. Ignatius knew very well that the melancholy man is practically immobilized.

The Fourth Part itself has seventeen chapters which discuss both the Jesuit scholastics' own education and the work of the schools conducted by the Society. These chapters are for the most part rather brief and contain, as all the sections of the *Constitutions* do, both the original regulations and the subsequent "clarifications" which Ignatius added whenever experience showed that some point was obscure.

Eight of the chapters, the seventh and the eleventh to the seven-

teenth inclusive, take up matters of organization and program affecting
both the Jesuit scholastics and the lay students in schools open to the
general public. The remaining chapters have to do only with the first of
these two groups or with aspects of the foundation and government of
educational institutions.[25] The discussion includes, as it usually does for
any topic treated in the *Constitutions,* formulations of certain broad,
perennial aims or attitudes along with some highly precise regulations;
in this case regulations for the curriculum, the time-order, the teaching
methods and administrative procedures. One section will enunciate with
an austere eloquence the abiding motives of love and service which
alone are to prompt the Society in its educational labors, while another directs that once a year those institutions which owe their existence
to some rich man's benefactions shall present this founder or his rela-
tives with a wax candle bearing his coat of arms or some pious insignia.[26]
The reader of these pages is left with at least three impressions. He will
discover, in the first place, several themes which add up to general orientations in education. These are culture-free and therefore applicable
anywhere although they are naturally not very helpful for solving the
procedural questions which constitute the majority of school problems at
any given moment.

Secondly, it will be evident that there are also sizeable lacunae
here, for many aspects not merely of a complete educational theory but
even of a complete guide to school management are not included. To
some extent this omission was deliberate. Speaking of the education of
character, for example, the seventh chapter of the Fourth Part makes
the basic point that students should "absorb (*hauriant*) along with their
letters the morals worthy of a Christian." It adds immediately: "Since in
matters of detail there will be considerable variety consequent upon the
differences of localities and persons we shall not descend to particulars
here." But Ignatius's fondness for order and method prompted him to
follow this, in turn, with yet another directive recommending that each
individual school work out the details for itself, using the practices of
the Roman College as a model. The existence, however, of these gaps
cautions us against reading into those brief chapters any integral educational scheme either in fact or in the intention of the author. The *Constitutions,* as was suggested before, are a partial collection of representative
rules, not a complete plan of life or of education. For a full understanding of Jesuit education, therefore, it would be necessary to see how historical practice has filled in the picture for which the *Constitutions* provide only a partial sketch.

Finally, one may well feel that some of the recommendations both of the *Constitutions* and of the *Ratio* are very rudimentary and others rather mistaken. But when we read that the rector is to give the library key only to those scholastics whom he judges need it, we must remember that this document is four centuries old and in certain respects inevitably reflects its age. Libraries, after all, were kept locked in most American colleges well into the nineteenth century not simply because there was little enthusiasm for student browsing but also because books were still sufficiently rare. The directives about the library key, moreover, must be set within the context of what precedes and follows it:

> If possible, there should be a general library in the colleges. Those whom the rector judges to need a key to it should have one. Furthermore, each one should have the books which are necessary for him.[27]

There is no doubt, of course, that the spirit of *Lehrfreiheit und Lernfreiheit* which the nineteenth-century German universities popularized is not found in this Fourth Part of the Jesuit *Constitutions*. But no one with a sense of history could reasonably have expected it to be. There *is* found here, however, a hierarchy of educational values in which the more universal values at the summit, the ones which take precedence, are of such a nature as to open the whole system to enrichment by subsequent developments. The strong esteem for learning and the pervasive pragmatic approach to the techniques which promise to assist this learning make it easy to assimilate the ideals of scholarly excellence and research which were matured long after St. Ignatius wrote. In like fashion, the interest in character development makes it equally logical to assimilate tested developments in guidance procedure.

In the second half of this book, St. Ignatius's ideas about education will be set out in some detail. The point to note here is that he was perfectly aware of the partial character of those educational recommendations and so he himself built into them these corridors to further advance. His own specific directives did not add up to a systematic organization of every aspect of a Renaissance school program but they did provide for such an organization. In the thirteenth chapter of the Fourth Part of the *Constitutions,* Ignatius called for the eventual construction of a "separate treatise" which should arrange in detail such particulars as time-order, schedule, curricula and pupil exercises. It was this directive which Aquaviva fulfilled forty-three years after St. Ignatius's death when he issued the *Ratio Studiorum* of 1599. In time, many of the specific solutions of that *Ratio* would become obsolete, though the spirit of the document would remain an inspiration for Jesuit schools. But at least four of the *Constitutions'* basic convictions about education will outlast any *Ratio* since they are perennial so far as Jesuit schools are concerned. The first of these is the Ignatian belief in the primacy of the moral over the intellectual virtues. This means that holiness is judged to be more valuable than erudition but it does not mean that intellectual values are underrated. On the contrary, there is also, as a second characteristic, a high esteem for intellectual development coupled with that distinctive instrumental estimate of its worth. There is, in the third place, a strong appreciation of careful educational planning and patient attention to the discovery of the best means and policies for achieving the school's goals. Finally, there is the acceptance of St. Ignatius's principle of adaptation which he applied everywhere, not merely to school questions. Although Ignatius left to that future tract, the *Ratio Studiorum,* the spelling out of most practical matters, he himself laid down this great principle which by its very nature, as well as by its explicit inclusion in the *Constitutions,* occupies higher ground than the rules of the *Ratio.* He directed the attention of Jesuit schools to the provisions of that anticipated school plan, but with this warning: that it was to be adapted to places, times and persons—*id dumtaxat monendo, illa locis, temporibus et personis accommodari oportere.*[28] This is, to be sure, a principle dictated by the very essence of all education and it was clearly repeated for our own times by Pius XII when he observed: "The work of education, since it must be carried on in a specific environment and for a specific background (*milieu*), must constantly adapt itself to the circumstances of this background and of this environment. . . ."[29] In the historic event, this principle of adaptation appears as a prime characteristic of Jesuit educational activity when that activity is viewed in its entirety over four centuries.

Forerunners of the *Ratio*

Adaptation, however, means that there are factors which have an abiding value and are not to be jettisoned but preserved precisely through adaptation. Much of this present book will be taken up with a consideration of these latter elements. Some of them are to be found, as we have seen, in that Fourth Part of the *Constitutions* and others can be disengaged from the *Ratio Studiorum* which the *Constitutions* called into being. The seed sown by Ignatius culminated in the *Ratio* of 1599 only after decades of preliminary spadings. A good deal of time was required to shape a school plan to its final form and in the process sixteenth-century Jesuits showed themselves enthusiastic practitioners of group dynamics and of an empirical approach to practical problems. To appreciate the extent of those endeavors and the numerous introductory sketches which preceded even the first version of the *Ratio,* one need only page through the collection of 132 documents gathered up in the *Monumenta Paedagogica.* This is a bulky volume of over nine hundred pages which was published in Madrid in 1901 as part of that great, continuing series called the *Monumenta Historica Societatis Iesu.* Its materials were edited from manuscripts preserved in some eighteen codices. They are not all impressive and the collection itself is cheerfully described by the editors as a "farrago." It includes certain very early formulations of the purposes of the Jesuit *collegium* and the procedures to be followed in founding it. Then there are complete school plans like the *De Studiis Societatis* of Father Jerónimo Nadal, the Majorcan who was one of St. Ignatius's most trusted collaborators. Nadal was the rector of the first truly "public" Jesuit school opened at Messina in Sicily in 1548 and he may well have begun his plan at that time although he did not finish it until some years later, perhaps about 1565.

An informed twentieth-century writer, rather unsympathetic toward Nadal, has remarked that the *Constitutions* and the three versions of the *Ratio* in 1586, 1591 and 1599 introduced modifications in Nadal's scheme without, however, substantially altering the general approach.[30] So far as the main lines go this is not an unreasonable judgment. One does find in Nadal, for instance, that clear statement of the primacy of the moral aim which characterizes the later documents and quite disaffects the secular classical humanist. Let everything be so arranged, writes Nadal, that piety holds first place in the studies of both the Jesuit scholastics and the lay students: *ut in studiis primum locum pietas obtineat.*[31] Nevertheless, he recognizes that proper allowances must be made for the difference in status and vocation between these two groups. In academic matters, Nadal's plan prescribed Donatus for the grammar classes, Aristotle for the students of philosophy and St. Thomas as the author to be followed in the theology courses. At the same time it made room for some study of science, musical theory and mathematics— Euclid, Ptolemy, the "triangles" of John of Monteregio and the use of astrolabes. There are rules for all officials, particularly for rectors, and an explicit ordering of the classes from the little abecedarians through the three grammar sections, to poetry and rhetoric. Nadal descends even to such particulars as the readings, the written work and the disputations which are to occupy the students of letters as well as those in philosophy and theology. All this is very like the *Ratio* published nineteen years after his death and certainly influenced by his work.

The *Monumenta Paedagogica* arranges most of its material according to the countries from which it came: Italy, Portugal, France, Germany, Austria and Belgium. The Italian section is by far the lengthiest because it includes a large number of memoranda from the Roman College which was the most prestigious of the Jesuit schools and also a center for pedagogical research of this sort. In the nature of things, a definitive *Ratio* could hardly have been produced by one man. Yet one man did make an impressive and influential attempt at it. Among the documents emanating from the Roman College is a rather long-winded program, the *De Ratione et Ordine Studiorum Collegii Romani* of Father Diego Ledesma which takes up more than a hundred pages of the *Monumenta*.[32] Ledesma was a Spaniard, born in 1519, who entered the Society as a priest in his late thirties. He died after eighteen industrious years, most of them spent at the Roman College teaching and working over the thorny questions involved in organizing a sound administrative and curricular structure. More than a third of the items in this collection were either written by him or received his editorial attention. A contemporary biographical sketch suggests that Ledesma, though a man of admirable zeal, was also a somewhat anxious spirit and in his school plan one detects a certain rigorousness. In his blueprint for the Roman College, written about 1575, he lays down the law very strictly and spells everything out in detail—classes, repetitions, exercises. There is not much room for the creative teacher but perhaps this is just as well. If the teachers followed the pattern Ledesma favored they might not have had time or energy for creativity. For in an earlier memorandum Ledesma had advocated ever greater mortification upon the part of teachers. He recommended that they be granted no exemptions and that in addition to their classes they exercise themselves daily in domestic duties about the house, even those of the lowliest sort: *etiam sordidis et infimis*.[33] The *Ratio* of 1599 would reject this explicitly. One can say of Ledesma's plan what Père Herman said about part of it: a bit too long, too minute and too constrictive of the teacher. Nevertheless, it also contributed significantly to the ultimate formation of the *Ratio Studiorum* of 1599.

The *Ratio*

The process of that formation began, as we noted, in 1586 and of the three drafts of the *Ratio* the first is by far the most interesting. The reason for this is indicated by Aquaviva in a letter transmitting this trial version to various provinces for consideration. In order that their brethren might be better informed and judge more wisely, the six deputed Fathers incorporated in their statement, explanations and defenses of their proposals.[34] The Ratio of 1599 would eliminate all these reasonings so as to make a briefer handbook for busy schoolmen but all elements of theory were thereby likewise eliminated since theory is to be found in the arguments supporting the rule or detail.

In the *Ratio* of 1586 a reader not only encounters reasons, theories, digressions and occasional witticisms but also gets a vivid picture of the actual world in which the authors lived and wrote. It is apparent, for one thing, that all is not perfect in the Jesuit schools of the day. There are some difficulties with the students, difficulties with the curriculum and difficulties with the teaching. The difficulties with the students are the least serious simply because they are as perennial as youthful human nature and one cannot do much about them. The architects of this *Ratio* have begun, in any case, with the supposition that the Society is conducting schools and that this is a good work. They do not think themselves obliged to defend the very notion of teaching little boys grammar as Ribadeneira had felt constrained to do in the commentary mentioned earlier.

Once he decided to grapple with that point, Ribadeneira had to handle the contention that teaching is a more difficult task than religious life can accommodate. According to this objection, he reports, it is too hard to manage a mob of boys who are by nature so frivolous, restless, garrulous and indolent that their own parents can't control them. Thus it happens that the young Jesuits who are put to the business lead an excessively strenuous life, are quite worn down and even lose their health. Many of these men, moreover, are persons of talent who might be doing worthwhile scholarly work were they not impeded by all this puerile nonsense.[35]

But the venerable Ribadeneira demolishes this disaffection briskly. He has already pointed out that civil and ecclesiastical leaders alike agree that the foundation of any well-ordered state, the fountain from which all its blessings flow, is the proper education of its youth in letters and morals. He has marshalled an impressive crowd of saintly forerunners since he is more anxious to cloak the Jesuits with the protective mantle of tradition than to secure their reputation for innovation. He lines up, among others, the Alexandrians, Clement and Origen; the holy anchorite extolled by Chrysostom for having left his dear solitude to labor in the education of youth; Jerome who taught literature to the sons of the wellborn in order to lure them to a following of Christ and the somewhat ambiguous case of Cassianus, a Christian teacher who was enthusiastically hacked to pieces by his pagan scholars when his

faith was discovered. Surely, then, a work carried on by so many holy
and distinguished men (including the Dominicans and Augustinians
whose schools in Spanish towns have been seen by Ribadeneira himself),
cannot be inconsistent with the authentic spirit of religious life. It is
hard work, he grants, but it is abundantly compensated by the glory it
gives to God. What if the teachers are fatigued *capite atque animo?* Do
the other works of the Society provide only mental and spiritual recreation? If men of the world don't mind ruining their health to make a little
money, surely a religious man can endure some physical discomfort for
the purchase of heaven. And if there is anyone who looks down on the
work of teaching in a secondary school because it keeps him from those
loftier studies which would bring fame to him and to the Society, let him
consider over and over, *etiam atque etiam,* that God rewards, not those
activities which men esteem, but those which offer the greater homage
of humility and love. Let him remember, too, that the more imposing and
prestigious pursuits are not always the best or most useful.

This bracing position will simply be assumed rather than argued by
anyone whose business it is to map out curricula and class schedules,
just as the physicist assumes that the study of physics is worthwhile.
The various practical difficulties are not, however, dissolved without a
good deal more work and it was to those that the committee of six
turned. The first Jesuit schools were often established under conditions
far from ideal. In his *Chronicon,* a chronological history of the Society
from the birth of Ignatius up to 1556, Polanco spoke frankly of the
damages sometimes incurred when schools were accepted before there
was an adequate supply of trained men to staff them. The young Jesuits
who were not yet ordained were intended then, even as they are now, to
teach for a few years at a point in their course of studies which found
them equipped to do so with profit both to themselves and to their students. But occasionally the pressures of those disturbed times led to the
premature employment in small schools, *collegiolis,* of scholastics who
were both ill prepared and sadly overworked. The results could not help
but be, as Polanco noted, injurious to the young Jesuits themselves, some
of whom lost their vocation, and to the Society as a whole.[36]

But even under ideal conditions there would still have been the
necessity of devising the best arrangements of the curriculum and the
shrewdest methodology for achieving the desired aims, in this case principally the aims implied in the notion of Latin eloquence. Unless this
were done the teachers and administrators would be constantly tinkering
with these elements and an exuberant spirit of improvisation, for which
St. Ignatius had no enthusiasm, might well take over. Besides, given the

cultural unity which still prevailed in Western Europe, a school plan like the proposed *Ratio* would make possible a good deal of similarity among Jesuit institutions so that the culture acquired by boys in Cologne might have a fraternal resemblance to that acquired by boys educated in Paris, Palermo, Lisbon, Ingolstadt or Prague.

This notion of unity or conformity in the content and details of a school program does not recommend itself unreservedly to contemporary educators although everyone would agree that the fundamental principles of thermodynamics or the inflection of French irregular verbs ought to be the same wherever taught. In any event, by 1832 when the Society of Jesus, having been suppressed in 1773 and restored in 1814, came to revise the celebrated *Ratio* of 1599 that ideal of unity was no longer possible of achievement to anything like its former extent. The development of national traditions required a reasonable acknowledgement from the schools in the various countries and one could not now devise a detailed program applicable everywhere. On the other hand, there is something to be said and Robert M. Hutchins, for one, has often said it, in defense of the notion that it would be a good thing if all the people of the world, to say nothing of all the people of the Atlantic Community, did possess a certain common core of culture as the base of international cooperation. Perhaps the West with its common technology, common political ideals and common roots in the historic traditions born in Athens, Rome and Palestine does actually possess some such core. At any rate, if the sixteenth-century Jesuit ideal of conformity and unity is interpreted as an aspiration after this sort of community it still has much to recommend it even though the days when the nine-year-old in Vienna followed the same schedule as the nine-year-old at La Flèche and used the same textbooks are gone forever.

In the second part of this book we shall be drawing upon the thought of that 1586 *Ratio,* as well as upon other central Jesuit documents, for some notion of the permanent elements in the traditional Jesuit approach to the triple task of intellectual, moral and social education. Here we want only to call attention to some instructive characteristics of the methods employed by that committee of six, who were the principal authors of the *Ratio,* since the two subsequent versions are considered modifications of their work. In the first place, they did not act as though all constructive criticism and wisdom began with themselves. When they handled a question they took advantage of the accumulated observations of their predecessors, particularly Nadal and Ledesma, and they were also ready to absorb sound practices derived from any source. In fact, they defined their task at one point as precisely this selection of the best that was available: *In optimo seligendo laborandum est imprimis.*[37] The second and longest section of their report finds them moving leisurely about from topic to topic in some twenty-seven essays which inquire into the conduct of classes, repetitions and disputations, the formation of teachers, the arrangement of curricula, vacations, time-orders, prizes and degrees.

All these discussions manifest a willingness to confront genuine problems. There were serious difficulties, for instance, about the preservation of the morale of teachers in the Lower School since they were looked down upon by the higher faculties and they themselves feelingly compared their work to laboring all day in an oven.[38] Moreover, many of them were young teachers who remained in the classroom only a few years before going on to further studies. There was, therefore, the problem of diminishing the bad effects of this frequent turnover of personnel which produced, said the six Fathers, "tragedies."[39] Then there were problems with teachers of literature who grew bored and repeated the same material with minor variations and gave up demanding themes and exercises from their students. A deadly chill came over their classes: *frigent plane omnia.*[40] Nor was all well with the teaching of theology in the seminaries. The students sometimes complained that their professors' commentaries were a waste of time. There were further defects in the classroom procedures: too much passivity, too little pupil activity. The committee writes a long argument against the practice of dictating notes during a lecture. While the teacher dictates, they say, the students think only about getting it down. If he follows up with an explanation they pay no attention because they are tired out or imagine they already have it or busily proofread their notes to make sure they omitted nothing.[41] The authors of the *Ratio* of 1586 wanted more attention given to Greek in the secondary school but they also wanted it taught more efficiently. As it is now, they complain, boys grow old learning to conjugate a single model verb. They insist that the library have an annual budget allotment, for teachers without books are unarmed soldiers.[42]

Besides taking these and other real problems under study the Fathers handled them all in an open-minded fashion and frequently gave both sides of a puzzling question. These discursive and theoretical elements make their document more interesting than its modified successors but they also made it less suitable as a statute. The *Ratio* of 1591 consequently cast the material in the form of rules and omitted the discussions. The final version of 1599 streamlined the structure even more and left out all reasonings so that only spare statements of procedures remained. The reasonings had already been amply reviewed; the choices that appeared wisest had been made. The task was finished. As the seventeenth century opened the Jesuit school had a firm charter spelling out its practical operations.

Later Documents

There were those who thought that this charter had, in fact, been established forever and that the *Ratio* of 1599 was, as Father Sacchini, the Society's second official historian put it, eternal: *in omnem parabatur aeternitatem.* The world of 1600 was certainly changing fast enough to make such a prediction rash even though the acceleration of technological and cultural change was relatively slower than it is today. After the restoration of the suppressed Society, the *Ratio,* as was noted previously, was re-examined and a trial revision was issued in 1832. This was not a very extensive revision but neither does it appear ever to have become obligatory for the whole Society. It was not officially promulgated as a law either by one of the Society's legislative assemblies, a General Congregation, nor by one of the Fathers General, as the *Ratio* of 1599 had been promulgated by Aquaviva. When Father Roothaan, the General in 1832, sent the revision to the provinces he explained his intention. The document was offered for "use and practice," so that after having been tested, then again corrected, if necessary, or enlarged, it might be given "the force and sanction of a universal law." In the event, however, this process of emendation and definitive issuance never took place and the revised *Ratio* has come to be regarded, in fact, as directive rather than obligatory.

That process of final emendation would, in any case, have been enormously difficult and it would certainly not have been possible to descend to detail in the fashion of the *Ratio* of 1599. Some significant additions were made, however, by those who drew up that trial revision of 1832. In 1599 the great vernacular literatures had, for the most part, yet to be written and the *Ratio* not only says nothing about studying such literature but only reluctantly permits the use of the vernacular in actual teaching and then chiefly in the lower classes. The *Ratio* of 1832, however, made room for Shakespeare and Racine. It also wrote ten additional rules for the Professor of Physics. One of these directs the teacher to consider it his professional obligation to keep abreast of his field since there are new advances in science every day. The principles of adaptation to the needs of the time and of receptivity toward new values are implied in these changes even though a melancholy nostalgia for other days can sometimes be detected in the comments of Father Roothaan's letter accompanying the revision of 1832.[43]

In 1923 the domestic law of the Society of Jesus was reorganized in light of the new Code of Canon, or ecclesiastical, Law which had been promulgated by Benedict XV some four years earlier. The precepts which govern the order and schematize its ideals and way of life include, in first place, the prescriptions of Pontifical law which are common to all religious orders and then those which are proper to the Society. Next in importance are the formulations of the *Constitutions* of St. Ignatius which are themselves approved by the Apostolic See, and all those decrees of the Society's legislative assemblies, the General Congregations, insofar as these had been ratified by that twenty-seventh Congregation convened in 1923. Finally this *Epitome,* as the reorganized summary is called, assimilated all the decrees of the Society's successive generals, of whom there had been 26 by 1923, provided these decrees were originally issued for the entire order and were judged to be still in force.

The Fourth Part of the *Epitome,* like the Fourth Part of the *Constitutions,* deals with the Society's educational work and does so in general terms rather than in the concrete detail that characterized the *Ratio.* It has two main foci: the intellectual and spiritual formation of Jesuits themselves and the conduct of their schools throughout the world. Under the second heading, Jesuit teachers are simply directed to conserve, so far as possible the distinctive methodology recommended by the *Ratio* and to make themselves familiar with the principles of pedagogy set forth in the *Constitutions,* elaborated by the *Ratio* and commented upon by Jesuit writers on school questions. But the *Epitome* does not itself specify the character of that methodology nor the precise principles it has in mind. Since 1954 there has been a new *Ratio Studiorum Superiorum* governing the studies in Jesuit seminaries in accord with the directives of Pius XI's Apostolic Constitution of 1931 on the organization of ecclesiastical faculties. There is no such code for Jesuit secondary schools, however, or for institutions of higher education. The *Epitome* did direct that each province draw up a set of plans for its own needs. In this work, moreover, the teachers and the directors of studies were to be consulted. These plans were then to be submitted to the General for his approval and after suitable trial would be made official for the regions concerned.

In the United States a tentative effort at this sort of codification had begun even before the twenty-seventh General Congregation met in 1923. For in 1921 an Inter-Province Committee on Studies had been formed with representatives from each of the four provinces then existing in this country. That committee met annually for a decade. It was succeeded by a special Commission on Higher Studies appointed by Father General Ledochowski in December, 1930. The new Commission was directed to appraise the state of Jesuit higher education in the United States and report its findings directly to the General. It was composed of six members who among them represented all the provinces which by now numbered seven: California and Oregon which were jointly represented by one delegate, Chicago, Maryland-New York, Missouri, New England and New Orleans. The chairman of the Commission was one of the most distinguished Jesuit scholars of his day, Father James B. Macelwane, a geophysicist who was at this time the dean of the graduate school at St. Louis University.

In the letter establishing this Commission, Father Ledochowski had directed its attention to four problem areas. There was first the matter of securing "united purpose and concerted action" in the work of the American Jesuit institutions of higher education. Secondly, the Commission was asked to evaluate the actual standing of these colleges and universities when compared with their best secular counterparts. The Commission was also to study the relationship of the Jesuit schools to the various accrediting agencies on the American scene. Finally, it was to make recommendations for the sound professional preparation of teachers and their securing of appropriate academic degrees.[44]

The Commission held seven meetings in various cities during 1931–1932 and produced a 234-page mimeographed report. This report was remarkably honest, not to say blunt. It was also concrete and forward looking so that thirty years later its comments still seem timely enough. The report was forwarded to the Father General together with observations on it drawn from the provinces. August 15, 1934 was the four-hundredth anniversary of the day when St. Ignatius and six companions met at Mass in a chapel on Montmartre and made the private vows which, though they did not realize it then, marked the first step leading to the foundation of the Society of Jesus. Father Ledochowski chose this anniversary to issue an *Instruction* for the guidance of the Jesuit schools, colleges and universities in the United States. No doubt the report two years earlier of the special Commission had contributed to the formation of this document. The Commission had, to take a single instance, recommended that a national association of Jesuit schools be established and the *Instruction* adopted this suggestion. The *Instruction* itself was to be observed for a time on a trial basis. Father Ledochowski described its fundamental purpose in this way in a letter of transmittal: "It aims moreover at reorganizing our educational institutions, leaving untouched the inviolable principles of our Institute and its *Ratio Studiorum* but combining them with approved modern methods, so that our standard may be equal to the best in the country."[45] In 1948, after some years of practical test, Father Ledochowski's successor, Father Janssens, gave definitive approval to the *Instruction* which had been submitted to slight emendations.

The *Instruction* is brief. It consists of thirty-five articles gathered under three headings or "titles." A good deal that is said beneath them was not treated explicitly in the *Ratio* of 1599. The first title has to do with the promotion of cooperation between the various schools, colleges and universities conducted by the Jesuits in all the major regions of the United States. The second consists of rather general principles on the instructional function itself and emphasizes, far more strongly than any of the seventeenth-century documents did, the importance of academic excellence and of faculty research and publication. The third title treats in similar general but sound fashion of the preparation of Jesuits for informed and skillful teaching. The spirit of the entire document is suggested by its eighth article. This points to an essential task by observing that what is now required is an adaptation of the principles of the *Ratio* to contemporary necessities. In the next chapter we shall suggest certain of the factors which compel this adaptation and in the remaining chapters we shall turn to some reflection upon those principles which are to be adapted.

NOTES: CHAPTER II

1. The *Epitome* or summary of the Institute (collection of laws and legal principles) of the Society of Jesus is described in the concluding pages of this chapter. A recent edition of it was published for limited circulation from the Roman Curia of the General of the Society of Jesus in 1949 and it is this which is cited here by paragraph number. The passage quoted is from n. 397.

2. Up to the present, the standard scholarly editions of the first version of the *Ratio,* that of 1586, and of the definitive *Ratio* of 1599 have been those published in the series *Monumenta Germaniae Paedagogica* as part of a four volume critical edition of early Jesuit educational documents by G. M. Pachtler, S.J., *Ratio Studiorum et Institutiones Scholasticae Societatis Iesu per Germaniam olim vigentes collectae, concinnatae, dilucidatae* (Berlin: A. Hoffman, 1887–94). References to this collection will be cited as *Pachtler* with volume and page numbers. The incident and phrase referred to in the text here are found in Pachtler, II, 28. For a summary account of Aquaviva's generalate see Martin P. Harney, S.J., *The Jesuits in History* (New York: America Press, 1941), pp. 157–73.

3. The second of the three versions of the *Ratio,* that of 1591, is very rare and there does not appear to be any copy of it in the United

States. However, T. Corcoran, S.J. published a hundred pages of selections from it in his *Renatae Litterae Saeculo a Chr. XVI in Scholis Societatis Iesu Stabilitae* (Dublin: The National University, 1927) and references here to that 1591 *Ratio* will be drawn from this volume and cited as *Corcoran*.

4. See Chapter I, under notes 1 and 18. A specialized study bearing on some of these same questions is that of Ladislaus Lukács, S.J., *De Origine Collegiorum Externorum deque Controversiis circa Eorum Paupertatem Obortis 1539–1608* (Rome: Institutum Historicum S.I., 1961). This monograph first appeared in the periodical, *Archivum Historicum Societatis Iesu*, 29 (1960) and 30 (1961).

5. One such translation of the *Ratio* of 1599 is found in Edward A. Fitzpatrick (editor), *St. Ignatius and the Ratio Studiorum* (New York: McGraw-Hill, 1933), pp. 119–254. This translation was made by A. R. Ball.

6. In a valuable study published at the close of the nineteenth century, Bernhard Duhr, S.J. points out that the three-fold curricular division into Faculties of Letters, Arts and Theology was derived from the University of Paris: *Die Studienordnung der Gesellschaft Jesu* (Freiburg im Breisgau: Herder, 1896). In the *Constitutions*, IV, 17, nn. 4 and 5, St. Ignatius adopted this as the basic division of a full fledged university. Another classification which appears in sixteenth-century Jesuit documents is perhaps more functional than theoretical. It divides *collegia* into small or *particularia* if they teach only Letters; medium, *media*, if besides Greek and Latin they also offer *artes liberales seu philosophia;* large or *universalia* when, like the Roman College, they include all three faculties. This description is taken from the *De Ratione et Ordine Studiorum Collegii Romani* of Father Diego Ledesma, the document described in Chapter II and included in the collection, *Monumenta Paedagogica*, a volume which appeared in Madrid in 1901 as part of the collection *Monumenta Historica Societatis Jesu*, pp. 346–47. It might be noted that in these early Jesuit school plans, the conventional academic terms are often employed in several senses. Thus "faculty" sometimes signifies the teachers as a collectivity and sometimes a broad area of instruction. In the *Ratio* of 1599, *Gymnasium* seems sometimes to mean a classroom but it was also taken in the sixteenth century for the total institution as when Father Julius Negrone, in a public address at Brescia in 1579, described the course of liberal arts in the Jesuit *collegium* by remarking: *In hoc gymnasio Philosophia et Eloquentia conspirent amicissime.* Quoted by Farrell, *op. cit.*, p. 108, note 43. A *collegium* is sometimes a place where classes are taught, sometimes simply a residence hall for students. *Schola* in some contexts suggests what we would call a classroom (see the 43rd Rule for the Prefect of Lower Classes and the 43rd of the Rules Common to Teachers of the Lower Classes in the *Ratio* of 1599, Pachtler, *op. cit.*, II, 368, 396) but elsewhere both it and *classis* are closer to the contemporary notion of a "grade." *Gradus* itself frequently points to the level or content of mastery aimed at in a given division of the *collegium*. Thus the Rules for Professors of Rhetoric in the *Ratio* of 1599 begin by enunciating the

gradus of that class. It aims to form the students *ad perfectam eloquen-tiam.* Pachtler, *op. cit.,* II, 398.

7. Pachtler, *op. cit.,* II, 184.
8. Quoted in Vivian Ogilvie, *The English Public School* (London: B. T. Batsford, 1957), p. 115. This whole book is a most interesting account of the fortunes in one country of that academic tradition to which the Jesuit schools also belonged.
9. Of course, such institutions as St. Joseph University, Beirut, conducted by the French Jesuits, or the Ateneo de Manila conducted by the Jesuits of the Philippine province, properly pertain to the category of higher education as this is generally understood in the United States.
10. *Epitome, op. cit.,* n. 377, #1.
11. de Dainville, *op. cit.,* pp. 11, 32.
12. Herman, *op. cit.,* pp. 109, 267–8, 271 and particularly p. 154. On the resemblances found among all Renaissance school programs see *ibid.,* pp. 52, 55, 161 and also de Dainville, *op. cit.,* p. 250, who notes the near identity between the formulas of the Jesuit pedagogical docu-ments and those in the writings of other sixteenth-century humanists. For Ribadeneira's eulogy of Quintilian, *Quintilianus noster exercitatis-simus et peritissimus pueros erudiendi magister,* see Herman, *op. cit.,* p. 138. For a summary, with examples, of the pervasive influence of Quintilian see Herman, *op. cit.,* pp. 131–158.
13. It is in the *Phaedrus* that Socrates's comment on Isocrates is found. See the introduction by George Norlin to the Loeb Classical Library edition of Isocrates's works (London: William Heinemann, 1928–45), I, xvi. In the *Antidosis,* written when he was eighty-two and the fullest ex-pression of his educational theory, Isocrates called such things as as-tronomy and geometry, "a gymnastic of the mind" useful as a prepara-tion for the study of rhetoric, a study which he preferred to dignify by the title of a "philosophy." *Ibid.,* II, 333. On the significance of Isocra-tes's concept of humanism, see H. I. Marrou, *A History of Education in Antiquity,* trans. George Lamb (New York: Sheed and Ward, 1956), pp. 79–91.
14. On the question of the sources of sixteenth-century Jesuit school proce-dures, see the studies already cited by Duhr and Herman. In his intro-duction to a German version of the *Ratio,* Duhr suggested that one rea-son why Sturm thought that such pedagogical techniques as a plentiful use of practice and of written exercises were borrowed from him by the Jesuits was that both he and the Jesuits derived these procedures from the schools conducted in the Lowlands during the last of the medieval years by the Brethren of the Common Life. Herman, how-ever, thought that these characteristic methods were actually inspired by those in use at the University of Paris during the early sixteenth century and certainly the first Jesuit schoolmen always ascribed their inspiration to Paris. Herman granted, nevertheless, that a secondary current of influence, especially on Jesuit schools in such cities as Cologne and Louvain, was that of the Brethren.
15. For Rhetius's comment see the extract from his writings printed as an Appendix by Herman, *op. cit.,* p. 320. For the directive to the Professor

of Rhetoric to draw his style from Cicero alone, see Pachtler, *op. cit.*, II, 398.

16. For examples in early Jesuit school plans, drawn up before 1586, of the recommendation of Donatus's text, see in the *Monumenta Paedagogica, op. cit.*, pp. 87, 89, 108, 619. In this last instance, we find the youngest students described as those *qui Donatum discunt*. By the time the *Ratio* of 1591 was being drafted, the official grammar in the Jesuit schools was the much more recent one of Emmanuel Alvarez (1526–82), a distinguished Jesuit humanist born in Madeira. The *Ratio* of 1591 prescribed his book and its three divisions usually formed the material to be studied in the three classes of grammar. See Corcoran, *op. cit.*, p. 192.

17. See Herman, *op. cit.*, p. 308.

18. Juan de Polanco made this observation in his *Vita Ignatii Loiolae et Rerum Societatis Jesu Historia*, which is usually referred to by the shorter title of *Chronicon*. This history of the early years of the Society constitutes six of the volumes in the *Monumenta Historica Societatis Jesu* and was published at Madrid, 1894–98. The comment cited is from IV, 101. See Farrell, *op. cit.*, p. 93.

19. The principle itself is found in the 24th of the Rules for Teachers of the Lower Classes, Pachtler, *op. cit.*, II, 388: "Exercitationes varias . . . imperet. Nulla enim re magis adolescentium industria quam satietate languescit." The teacher should diversify the exercises, for nothing withers youthful energy more than satiety.

20. There are various editions of the *Constitutions,* both in their original Spanish text and in the official Latin version. One of these takes up tomes II and III in the subdivision of the *Monumenta Historica Societatis Jesu* issued from Rome in 1936–38, as *Monumenta Ignatiana,* Third Series. See Chapter I, n. 35.

21. Peter Lippert, S.J., *The Jesuits: A Self-Portrait,* trans. John Murray (New York: Herder and Herder, 1958), p. 21.

22. One of the early Jesuits, Father John Alvarez, once complained about the need for being gracious to powerful persons and objected that this constituted a bending of the knee to Baal. Ignatius had his secretary, Father Polanco, write a stiff letter contradicting this view. "You do not seem to us to have reasoned well," observes Polanco warmly, "taking as you did so spiritual a view of the matter as to lose all touch with reality in the case." Then he comes to the main point. "You seem to hold that the use of natural helps or resources, and taking advantage of the favor of man, for ends that are good and acceptable to our Lord, is to bend the knee to Baal. Rather, it would seem that the man who thinks that it is not good to make use of such helps or to employ this talent along with others which God has given him, under the impression that mingling such helps with the higher ones of grace produces a ferment or evil concoction has not learned well to order all things to God's glory and to find a profit in and with all these things for the ultimate end, which is God's honor and glory." The letter was dated from Rome, July 18, 1549. *Letters of St. Ignatius Loyola, op. cit.*, pp. 191–92.

23. No doubt Ignatius's own uncomfortable experiences with the Spanish academic arrangements which were far from methodical partly explains his subsequent enthusiasm for exact order and method. Father Rahner believes that an even deeper reason may have been Ignatius's inborn and aristocratic sense of family: "This family-sense is, as it were, the prototype of his matured feeling for form, subordination, and obedience." Rahner, *The Spirituality of St. Ignatius Loyola*, p. 3.

24. The letter was written from Rome in May, 1547. The translation here is taken from Doncoeur, *op. cit.*, p. 91.

25. The Preamble to this Fourth Part of the *Constitutions* summarizes the contents of this whole section: "We shall treat first of what pertains to the colleges, and then of what concerns the universities. With regard to the colleges, we shall discuss first what has relation to the founders; secondly, the colleges founded, in regard to their material or temporal aspects; thirdly, what pertains to the students who will study in them, that is, their admission, well-being, progress in learning and in other means of helping their fellow men, and their removal from studies; fourthly, what pertains to the government of the colleges." Translated in Ganss, *op. cit.*, p. 283. Some of these institutions, as subsequent developments would show, were designed solely for the education of Jesuit scholastics while others were open to the general public.

26. *Constitutions*, IV, 1, n. 3.

27. *Constitutions*, IV, 6, n. 7. The translation is from Ganss, *op. cit.*, p. 302. On the locked library in such nineteenth-century American colleges as Princeton, see John S. Brubacher and Willis Rudy, *Higher Education in Transition: An American History: 1636–1956* (New York: Harper and Brothers, 1958), p. 95.

28. *Constitutions*, IV, 13, n. 2. After the *Constitutions* were written, St. Ignatius added "clarifications" at selected points. The directive which gave rise to the *Ratio* and is cited here is found in one such clarification subjoined to the second paragraph or section of this thirteenth chapter of the Fourth Part.

29. Pius XII, "Education and the Modern Environment." A radio address to the Inter-American Congress on Catholic Education held at La Paz, Bolivia, October 6, 1948, *The Catholic Mind*, 47 (February, 1949), 119. The original texts of the major papal documents and pronouncements are published in the official periodical, *Acta Apostolicae Sedis.* The Spanish text of the speech quoted here, for instance, was printed in the *Acta*, 40 (October, 1948), 465–68, but in these pages we shall quote or cite papal writings in their rather easily available translations in *The Catholic Mind*.

30. R. R. Bolgar, *The Classical Heritage and Its Beneficiaries* (Cambridge: At the University Press, 1954), p. 358. For a full account of Nadal's treatise see Farrell, *op. cit.*, pp. 54–62.

31. Jerónimo Nadal, "De Studiis Societatis," *Monumenta Paedagogica, op. cit.*, p. 89. Henceforth this volume will be cited as *Mon. Paed.*

32. Diego Ledesma, "De Ratione et Ordine Studiorum Collegii Romani," *Mon. Paed., op. cit.*, pp. 338–453.

33. *Mon. Paed., op. cit.*, p. 142. This is from a document by Ledesma

entitled, "Quaedam Circa Studia et Mores Collegii Romani." It is Rule 32 of the Rules for the Provincial in the *Ratio* of 1599 which rejects Ledesma's suggestion. Pachtler, *op. cit.*, II, 262. Herman's comment on Ledesma will be found on p. 33 of his book cited here so frequently.

34. Pachtler, *op. cit.*, II, 11.
35. *Ribadeneira, op. cit.*, p. 510.
36. Polanco, *Chronicon, op. cit.*, III, 152: "Unus vel alter in Societatem admissus fuerat, qui tamen non perseveravit, quod in collegiolis, ubi praesertim tam multae occupationes erant, minime mirandum est." The year under discussion is 1553. Herman, *op. cit.*, pp. 126–9, summarizes these comments from Polanco on the difficulties of the early schools and provides further references to the *Chronicon*. He notes that some of the overburdened recruits not only deserted the religious life but even lost their faith. *Ibid.*, p. 127. Despite the pressures, however, those first schools were successful. In the *Chronicon, op. cit.*, II, 437, Polanco reports that some parents said their sons made more progress in these schools in a few months than they had previously made in one or two years elsewhere.
37. Pachtler, *op. cit.*, II, 155. The precise point under discussion at this stage of the *Ratio* of 1586 is the teaching of Grammar.
38. *Ibid.*, p. 145. The authors of the *Ratio* of 1586 are reporting that the teachers, between duties in the classroom and domestic chores, are quite overworked. "Vix enim aliquando inter scholasticos et domesticos labores respirandi locus est, ut dicant nonnulli, se in pistrino versari toto tempore, quo Grammaticam docent."
39. *Ibid.*, p. 154: "Magistrorum mutatio, quae tot saepe tragoedias excitavit. . . ." To diminish this difficulty the editors of the *Ratio* of 1586 suggest that a young teacher advance with the same class for several years. Thus he will come to know them well and they will not have to get acquainted with a new teacher every year.
40. *Ibid.*, p. 152.
41. For the comment on their professors by the students of Theology, see *ibid.*, p. 73, n. 7, and for the attack on the practice of dictating, pp. 82 ff.
42. For the comment about Greek studies, see *ibid.*, p. 162, and for the remark about the importance of books, p. 178.
43. The *Ratio* of 1832 may be found in Pachtler's second volume. Where it differs from the *Ratio* of 1599 Pachtler printed the two versions in parallel columns. The *Ratio* of 1832 was rather an adaptation of that of 1599 than a new document. The letter of Father John Roothaan transmitting the *Ratio* of 1832 is printed in this volume, pp. 228–233. The phrases quoted in our text are found on p. 228.
44. An interesting account of the *Instruction* and the events which preceded it is that of Matthew J. Fitzsimons, S.J., "The *Instructio* 1934–1949," *Jesuit Educational Quarterly*, 12 (1950), 69–78. The youngest of the seven provinces mentioned in the text was that of Oregon. When the work of the special Commission began this province had not yet been established as a fully independent unit but it was so before the Commission finished its task, for it was erected on December 8, 1931.
45. The comment of Father Ledochowski, from his letter transmitting the

Instruction, is found in a booklet issued for private circulation by the Jesuit Educational Association from its New York Office, September, 1948, under the title: *Instructio Pro Assistentia Americae de Ordinandis Universitatibus, Collegiis, ac Scholis Altis et de Praeparandis Eorundem Magistris* and *Constitution of the Jesuit Educational Association,* p. 8. Both the letter and the *Instructio* were first published in a periodical of limited circulation which prints official documents of concern to the Society of Jesus, *viz., Acta Romana Societatis Iesu,* 7, fascicle 3 (1934), 920–923 for the letter and 927–935 for the *Instructio* which is dated from Rome, August 15, 1934.

CHAPTER III

ON A NOTABLE DIVERSITY OF PLACES, TIMES AND PERSONS: JESUIT SCHOOLS PAST AND PRESENT

*The hours of the classes, their order and methods
. . . will be treated in detail in a special treatise . . .
which should be adapted to places, times and persons.*

Constitutions *of the Society of Jesus, IV, 13*

As the seventeenth century opened, there were in continental Europe perhaps one hundred million people. The Society of Jesus had in 1600 over 8,500 members organized into 23 provinces and, among their other works, staffing some 245 educational institutions. Most of these were *collegia* in which the Faculty of Letters, or secondary education, was the chief concern. The majority of them were in Western Europe although there were others overseas in the Americas and the Far East. It may be possible to outline tentatively a composite profile of these schools for which the *Ratio* had been devised so long as it is remembered that abstractions of this sort are incomplete at best and miss the individual character and actual flavor of any single member of the whole group.

The *Ratio* had, it is true, rules for professors of ecclesiastical studies—theology, Scripture, Hebrew—and for professors of philosophy. To that extent it describes not merely secondary education but certain aspects of higher education. Nevertheless, it devotes much more space to lengthy and explicit regulations for the classes of grammar, humanities and rhetoric. It is no wonder, then, that studies of Jesuit education as it existed from the time of St. Ignatius down to 1773, usually devote most of their attention to the *collège* or academy. That was the classic Jesuit school type which friends admired and enemies deplored. It was this that Francis Bacon had in mind when, in a famous left-handed tribute, he wished that the Jesuits had been free of their superstitions and enrolled on his side. For their schools had, he said, in some sort revived the excellent ancient discipline and he added that the Jesuits "partly in themselves, and partly by the emulation and provocation of their example, have much quickened and strengthened the state of learning."[1]

It was also this sort of Jesuit school that La Chalotais, Attorney General of the Parliament of Rennes, had in mind when he complained in 1763 that after a full course in both humanities and philosophy hardly ten out of a thousand Jesuit alumni could write a good letter. "The work given them to do is so monotonous that it almost inevitably leads to idleness and boredom. Always Latin and composition!"[2] La Chalotais was writing, of course, a century and a half after Bacon when the vitality of the *Ratio* may have declined because its program had lost much of its relevance. Besides, he was bitterly tendentious because he was prosecuting the Society and hoped to see it expelled from France and its schools supplanted by a nationalized system built on the pleasing premise that education "depends only on the State, because it belongs essentially to the State."[3] In any case, these schools had a great noontide and our purpose now is to evoke some memory of their normal routine.

It is not possible, of course, to summarize even in very general terms, the political, intellectual, social, economic and religious forces which were shaking and shaping the consciousness of men in 1600 as Jesuit teachers took their brand-new *Ratio* in hand. But it may be observed that students of the seventeenth-century culture encounter a record of phenomena which, predictably enough, are sometimes comfortably familiar and sometimes not. French Jesuit school masters, for instance, complained that the sons of the well-to-do bourgeoisie wouldn't study because their secure realization of their families' comfortable position gave them a sense of confidence which dispensed them from effort.[4] This rings sympathetically in any century. But the contemporary reader is startled by a page in the *Ratio* of 1586 which recommends that young students be not allowed to attend the public torture and execution of criminals, unless perhaps these be heretics.[5]

It is also evident that if certain tasks of education are perennial, still they acquire a distinctive coloration from epoch to epoch. Every teacher of boys is prepared to struggle with that joyous disregard for etiquette which naturally converts any all-male world into a barracks. Contemporary teachers might be surprised, though, to read the hundred-odd rules which Father Oliver Manare left behind when he inspected the Jesuit schools in Germany in the 1580's. These rules appear to have been designed especially for regulation of the conduct of little lay scholars. They are advised to keep their faces and clothes clean: *mundus non sordidus*. When they go for a walk they should not stamp along indecorously like countryfolk. They should not spit right in front of bystanders but turn their heads courteously to one side. If they have to spit in church, they should rub it out with their foot. In the refectory they should not gobble, nor splash the gravy about nor blow their noses in their napkins. In class they should not chatter among themselves nor laugh at what is said. And so on, in remarkable detail.[6] As de Dainville observed when commenting on similar handbooks of manners which the French Jesuits got up for their students in the next century, these precise directions only serve to indicate the habitual grossness of the age.

In the early documents one also meets with homely advice for the young Jesuit teachers themselves. A set of regulations drawn up for German schools in 1560–61 warns the masters not to shout out the window at pupils. It also contains a noble passage advising them to take as their model Christ, the sole perfect teacher, and to imitate in their dealings with students that patience and benignity which He showed toward simple folk and fishermen and those who were slow to learn.[7] A certain Father Odo Pigenat was provincial in France in the second half of the sixteenth century and he once left a thoughtful memorial after a visit to a boarding school. He directed that the Jesuit prefects who dined with the students should be provided with their own little bottles of wine since the big common jug was out of reach down the table and in any case the wine furnished the boys was excessively watered.[8]

If we were to visit one of those seventeenth-century Jesuit schools we should note in the first place that it was a school for boys and young men only. The *Ratio* of 1591 directed that none be admitted who were so young that they would fuss about trifles as though still at home nor so old as to upset class discipline. Furthermore, all who entered must have learned to read and to write correctly, for otherwise their compositions would be repulsively illegible.[9] By main intent these institutions were day schools and if they enrolled resident students, as they often did, this was by way of an exception which circumstances seemed to require. The boarders paid for their keep but there were no tuition fees for anyone since the Jesuit *Constitutions* required that all teaching be furnished without recompense. It was expected that endowments provided by wealthy civil and ecclesiastical leaders would support the Jesuit faculty and supply for both capital outlay and running expenses.

The schools were often large with well over a thousand students and the size of their individual classes was also daunting. A class of two hundred was not uncommon and one of 450 is reported.[10] Such classes, or audiences, were managed by a procedure originally devised simply to cope with this imbalance between available teachers and enrollments though long afterwards it was praised by certain commentators as if desirable under any conditions. The group was divided up into sections of ten called *decuriae*. One of the ten was captain of the group and he was known as the *decurio*. He at least probably benefited from the arrangements because he had monitorial duties that included hearing the recitations of the others and even, as the second rule for the Professor of Humanities in the *Ratio* of 1599 indicates, the first correction of his fellow students' written work. Experiences of this sort are instructive as a news item in the summer of 1961 suggested. According to this story, the graduate faculty of physics at Harvard had been puzzled by the number of outstanding students it received from an otherwise undistinguished small college. Inquiry showed that this college had a physics professor who let his seniors conduct the freshman classes. They learned a good deal of science in the process.[11] In the Jesuit schools, however, necessity was the first inspiration for this monitorial practice.

The youthful scholars of the *collège* were doubtless robustious enough. An early document preserved in the *Monumenta* directs them to bring to class only books, paper, ink and pen. Knives, shears and all other metal instruments are strictly interdicted.[12] After all, as the German regulations of 1560–61 cited above remarked, the students were presumed to be following not military affairs but the camp of the Muses.[13] The single prescription of the *Ratio* of 1599 which is most widely relished is that which similarly commands the pupil to lay aside his weapons before entering class. No fanciful directive either. The annual letters to Rome, of the rectors in the French *collèges* at this time, regularly reported duels involving students, young enough to be called children, in which one participant was killed.[14] It is true that these bloody incidents were exceptional and were noted for that very reason. Besides, acceptable outlets for youthful energies were always provided. Games in the school yard were a regular part of the program although that German code did declare that students would be punished if they fought, quarreled, dawdled along the road or sneaked off for skating in winter and swimming in the summer.[15]

It will be recalled that a complete Jesuit course included the five stages of the secondary school (three Grammar classes, the first of which might be divided into two steps; Humanities and Rhetoric);

three years in the faculty of philosophy and science and four in theology. At every point on this ladder the main purpose of the teaching was to promote genuine learning by keeping the students actively engaged in tasks that were supposed to insure mastery. *Ut . . . ingenia magis exerceantur* as the lapidary phrase canonizing this activity principle in the *Constitutions* has it: that the powers of the intelligence may be exercised ever more fully.[16] The Jesuit schools believed in creativity and self-expression, to be sure. But they also believed that this was not to be had apart from the discipline of hard work and the apprenticeship of constant practice.

The main classroom procedures for achieving active learning were the teacher's presentation (lecture and explanation); the recitation and other varieties of repetition daily, weekly and yearly; the discussion, which could take all sorts of forms; and the written task or exercise. The main problem was inevitably that of motivation. In the five classes of the Lower School the teachers may well have spent a good deal of time stirring up interest simply because Latin and Greek were not very fascinating in themselves. But the masters would doubtless have said that they were trying to get the boys interested in things that should interest them and which they needed to learn. In any case, the *Ratio* speaks at times of the need for injecting some *fervor* into the philosophical disputations or of methods for enlivening the discussions, *quo magis concertatio fervescat.*[17]

In the theology and philosophy courses the chief business was the lecture. The students were supposed to involve themselves by taking notes and asking questions. This was recommended by St. Ignatius himself in a passage which also provided some advice for private study. In such study, said the saint, a man ought first to puzzle over his problems and then, if he can't solve them, carry them to a conference with his professor.[18] The *Ratio* of 1586 advised the theology lecturer not to hold up the class until the weakest student got the point but to take care of the slower people privately. It also recommended that professors remain for fifteen minutes after the lecture to handle further questions and the *Ratio* of 1599 retained this suggestion. In addition, the Dean (Prefect of Studies) is to keep his eye on the professors and make sure they actually cover the matter assigned for their course.[19]

In the Lower School, particularly in the grammar classes, activity must have flourished to the point of tumult. The chief, though not exclusive aim of the first five-step program in Letters was the acquisition of an intellectual culture equated in practice with the acquisition of a pure Latin style. It was fundamentally a book-centered education whose chief pedagogical devices had been sketched by Quintilian and codified by the practice at Paris which Ignatius much admired. There was first the study, under the teacher's guidance, of great Ciceronian models with the emphasis more heavily on form than content. Thereafter there was a good deal of pupil participation and activity expended on imitation of these exemplars. In the literature course, therefore, the substantial aim was to talk and write like Cicero just as in the arts course the goal was to rethink the thoughts of Aristotle. Perpinian, a distinguished Jesuit educational theorist, neatly linked these two purposes with his somewhat singular view that the chief function of philosophical studies was to furnish ideas with which one's rhetorical productions might be nicely embellished.[20]

A good number of concrete variations specified and diversified these generic techniques. The teacher's "prelection," for instance, began with reading the passage aloud to show the boys how the Latin or Greek words were to be pronounced. This fulfilled the basic meaning of a *praelectio*. But there was also included a full explanation, itself often in Latin, of the texts. Into this analysis bits of geography, scientific erudition, social, economic, political and cultural history were introduced. The *Ratio* of 1591 called that whole process *ratio Latine praelegendi explicandique Auctores* and provided a lengthy model to show how it was to be done. It advised the master to avoid garrulity. If Cicero's words are clear, then adding an explanation is like bringing a candle to the light of noonday. If the passage is obscure, make the explanation brief for wordiness blocks understanding. Don't overwhelm the students with erudition; refer them to books from which they can get more information if they want it.[21]

There was no reason why student recitations should have been stereotyped either. In his plan for the Roman College, Ledesma announced that there were four different ways of conducting a recitation and then proceeded to list nine. Perhaps the best known of the procedures for enlivening these recitations were the *concertationes,* contests which pitted individuals against individuals and groups against groups. The spelling bee is a simple example of this device. On a typical day the boys in the lowest grammar section, to take one instance, spent two and a half hours in class during the morning and the same length of time in the afternoon. Now the teacher would correct written work while the decurions heard recitations of Cicero or grammar rules. Now the teacher himself conducted a class-wide recitation on the lesson of the previous day and then worked over the next passage in a prelection. The last half hour might be given to repetition of the rudiments and rules of grammar or to a *concertatio*. On Saturday there was a review of the whole week's work and an hour of catechism which was the only formal religious instruction provided.

The contemporary teacher may remark that all this has a certain antiquarian interest but is not very pertinent to his own situation. For even if we grant that the classical curriculum in the sixteenth and seventeenth centuries was never so narrow as the vulgarized summaries of textbooks suggest, still it is true that the Jesuit secondary schools of that day, like their Protestant parallels, were fundamentally Latin schools and that the higher faculties had not the breadth nor the vocational utility which we now expect from higher education. A strong concentration on Cicero or Aristotle is no longer desirable nor possible. Still we ought not, for this reason, unthinkingly mock these older schools. After all, any educational institution is necessarily the mirror and vehicle of its age to a great extent. The world in which the editors of the *Ratio* lived was one which made Ciceronian eloquence a prime aim of what we would call general education. The *Ratio* was written for that age and it is not remarkable that it should have reflected this purpose. It would be remarkable, however, were the *Ratio* and the Fourth Part of the Jesuit *Constitutions* also to contain, if only embryonically, certain themes applicable to schools of other times and places—certain abiding principles, to borrow Herman's phrase, beneath that Renaissance rind.

It may, at first, seem unlikely that this should be the case. The *Ratio* is an exact prescription for curriculum and methods accommodated to an age which took the orator as its ideal of the cultured man and Cicero as its ideal of an orator, much as the American frontier honored the lawyer as the true man of parts. But curriculum and methodology are both means to an end. The curriculum is the instrument for fashioning the cultural ideal and good methods, in turn, are adapted to the service of the curriculum in light of what is known about the nature of the learning process. If the goal of the *Ratio* was that of the late Renaissance, then the prescriptions which form its substance are presumably adapted to that aim and are hardly timeless principles forever true. Yet it may be possible to disengage from the documentary sources of the Jesuit educational tradition certain key-categories or master themes, rudimentary perhaps or barely implicit, which constitute a portion of Christian educational theory and retain significance for places, persons and times very different from those of 1599. If, to cite a single instance, that rhetorical ideal is thoroughly probed it will appear to be the concretization of a purpose more universal and more valid than the mere achievement of Ciceronian verbal grace. This wider aim rests on the conviction that the truly human man must possess both wisdom and eloquence; must know something and be able to say what he knows; must be able to think and to communicate.[22] It is an aim which derives support from what we now know about the role of language, communication and reflective thought in the development of a mature personality and a sound concept of self. And when this aim has been achieved it needs no advertisement. It is its own best recommendation for it has been said: "to be able to speak gracefully out of a well-stocked mind is a dazzling talent."[23] It might also be noted that the esteem for human personality and liberty, which we believe distinguishes the Western democracies from totalitarian states, has its roots in the religion that came out of Palestine and the political philosophy that came out of Greece. This suggests another of the values in an education which provides some introduction to classical thought and Christian theology for these studies can wonderfully nourish an informed appreciation of the democratic ideals.

It is true that general aims of this sort are not much help when it comes to working out the specific details of a contemporary American high school or college program but they are useful both as broad goals and as negative criteria. That is to say, whatever else our own schools may be required to do, we can be quite sure that they have significantly failed unless their graduates can speak and write with accuracy, if not with style, and can approach moderate problems without being hopelessly inhibited by passion, prejudice, ignorance or error.

The contemporary student of Jesuit education, then, hopes to discern those elements in its tradition which are still valuable and viable. But such discernment requires an initial recognition of the extraordinary diversity of "places, times and persons" existing between the world in which St. Ignatius died and the American landscape four hundred years afterward. For by recognizing such diversity one is in a better position to distinguish the abiding aspects of Jesuit educational practice from the accidentals which clothe them when they are actualized, more or less perfectly, in diverse historical contexts.

American Jesuit Education: 1956

A summary picture of Jesuit education in the United States in 1956, the year of the four-hundredth anniversary of St. Ignatius's death, will be useful here. These sketchy statistics will underline that fact of diversity by a single illustration. It is a fact which might be just as easily established by reflecting on the exact context in which Jesuit schools find themselves today in Manila or Beirut, in Great Britain or France. But a brief book must have its limitations and throughout these pages the field of contemporary reference will be that of the United States because it is here that they are written. The year 1956 is deliberately selected as a point within that field since it is far enough past to be reasonably fixed yet recent enough to be relevant.

When Ignatius died, the land mass that is now the continental United States was still, so far as Europeans were concerned, unknown and practically impenetrable. It would be another half century before the first permanent settlement was made by the English whose influence on the nation's early history was as dominant as that of Spain below the Rio Grande or France in Canada. In 1956, the nation built up during the three and half centuries following the settlement of Jamestown in 1607 numbered nearly 170 million people. They counted among their characteristics as a group, two faiths, each of which often seemed rather ambiguous: a religious faith, or at least a faith in religion as a good thing and a faith in education. Better than sixty percent of the Americans claimed church membership and some thirty-two or three million of these were Roman Catholics. The common faith in education maintained two distinct yet complementary school systems, the public and the non-public and a quarter of the nation was distributed somewhere along these two ladders running from the kindergarten to the professional school. In higher education the majority of institutions were nonpublic although the public colleges and universities by reason of their size enrolled better than half the students. At the elementary school level some twelve percent of the pupils were in nonpublic institutions nearly all of which were Catholic parochial schools. About ten percent of the young people in secondary schools were also in non-public institutions and close to eighty percent of these were in high schools under Catholic auspices.

The educational work of American Jesuits is almost entirely centered on secondary schools and higher education. In 1956 there were 7496 American Jesuits, nearly a quarter of the world total which was then about 32,000. They were divided into eight American provinces and their numbers included 3971 priests, 2903 scholastics or seminarians and 622 coadjutor brothers. This group of American Jesuits was engaged in a variety of works both at home and abroad. But their principal activity, even in many mission fields, was that of education. In the United States the Jesuits were in 1956 conducting 43 high schools in 23 states from Portland, Maine to Portland, Oregon; from Missoula, Montana to Tampa, Florida. Most of these were day schools but Cranwell in Lenox, Massachusetts, Georgetown in Garrett Park, Maryland and Campion in Prairie du Chien, Wisconsin were chiefly for resident students. The smallest of these schools enrolled 130 students; the eight largest had more than a thousand each and the majority had an enrollment of 500 or better for a grand total of 27,778.

At the same time, American Jesuits maintained, apart from 24 houses of study or spiritual formation designed for their own members, 28 colleges and universities with some 108,841 students, full or part-time, in undergraduate programs of liberal arts, commerce, education and engineering; in graduate studies and in professional schools of divinity, law, music, dentistry, medicine, pharmacy, nursing and social work.[24] The ranks of the teachers and administrators in these schools include not only Jesuits but a large number of laymen and women as well as a few diocesan priests and members of other religious communities. In the colleges and universities, in fact, the non-Jesuit faculty is generally far larger than the Jesuit.

Although the high schools are not co-educational, many of the colleges and the various schools of the universities are. Regis High School in New York City, to which admission is by scholarship grant only, charges no tuition but all the other American Jesuit institutions have to rely upon student fees for at least part of their support since there are now no Renaissance noblemen or prince bishops to found and maintain schools. If there were, they would find the task proportionately more vast than it was in the sixteenth century when expenditures for buildings and instructional materials were relatively modest since these things were themselves comparatively simple and became obsolescent less quickly than they do today. It should, of course, be emphasized that the contemporary American Jesuit institutions could not meet the needs for capital outlay, for new sites, new buildings and equipment and for improvements, were it not for the generosity of the American community in general and the Catholic segment of it in particular. Only the benefactions of individuals, corporations and foundations make possible at present the launching of any new nonpublic schools or the proper expansion of well-established ones.

All these Jesuit institutions are indissolubly both American and Catholic. This is not surprising for church-affiliated schools everywhere are shaped by the needs both of the political and the religious society since they serve both by educating persons who are simultaneously citizens and believers. Stonyhurst, to take a single instance, is not only a Jesuit school but so thoroughly English as to be included in any well-bred list of the eighty or so authentic "public schools." The American Jesuit institutions have, moreover, definite regional characteristics as one can see merely by paging through their catalogues or yearbooks and matching the photographs of pines, snowy slopes, skiers and ice hockey teams at Cranwell in the Berkshires with the palms and lawns and open-air swimming pool at Brophy College Preparatory in Phoenix, Arizona. The handbook of regulations for students at Jesuit High School in Dallas has explicit directions about parking and campus speed limits for "all who drive automobiles to school," while the prospectus of Brooklyn Preparatory in New York contains detailed advice on the various railroads, subways, shuttles and municipal bus lines which may be employed by students of a school situated in a metropolitan area of fifteen million. Superficial phenomena of this sort effectively symbolize, for the informed observer of American customs, those more significant variations in social, economic and cultural patterns which diversify the wide national scene.

There is surely no way to appreciate in depth the range and complexity and individual differences of these American Jesuit schools save by studying their personal histories and examining them on their locations which vary from the seven hundred acres, complete with a lake, of the handsome campus of Spring Hill College outside Mobile to the network of St. Louis University's buildings, crisscrossed by the streets and alleys of a busy urban district. These schools, colleges and universities enjoy a considerable degree of autonomy because the Jesuit *Constitutions* entrust a good deal of responsibility to the local superiors of individual houses. These are, however, duly subordinated to the provincials who govern the administrative divisions called provinces and are themselves, in turn, responsible to the General. The General holds the only elective office in the Society and holds it for life. His power is admittedly great for as Gregory XIV said in his Apostolic Letter, *Ecclesiae Catholicae,* approving the *Constitutions* anew in 1591, the government of the Society is monarchical. The General must, however, govern within the framework of Jesuit law for the service and at the good pleasure of the Church shepherded by the Roman Pontiff.

In recent decades the Jesuit institutions in the United States have also banded together to form that characteristically American thing, the professional organization. This Jesuit Educational Association, as it is called, has a central office in New York City. It was officially created in 1934 by the twenty-sixth Father General, Wlodomir Ledochowski, following the recommendation of a commission of American Jesuits appointed in 1930 for a study of educational affairs. Another fruit of that same study was the *Instruction* discussed in the preceding chapter. The Association has a journal of its own and sponsors an annual meeting which brings together delegates from all the member schools. It also arranges smaller gatherings or institutes for such specialized groups as college deans, high school principals, guidance counselors and teachers of particular disciplines.[25]

The development of modern means of transportation and communication has contributed to this increased awareness and cooperation with one another of institutions which were relatively isolated in the nineteenth century. When that century opened, Jesuit education was represented in the United States by Georgetown, founded in 1789 on the banks of the Potomac and nourished by the traditions of colonial Marylanders who had entered the Society of Jesus before its suppression and survived to see its restoration. In the decades which followed, Jesuits out of Belgium by way of Maryland took over in 1828, ten years after its founding, the direction of the school which would become St. Louis University. French Jesuits came to New York in 1846 from St. Mary's College in Marion County, Kentucky, to staff the little college opened five years earlier by Archbishop Hughes at Fordham. Jesuits from Lyons began school work in Alabama in 1847 and two years later in New Orleans. Jesuits from Turin and Naples opened schools in Santa Clara, San Francisco, Spokane and Seattle on one side of the great Pacific coastal ranges and in Colorado on the other while German Jesuits founded schools across the north central line from Buffalo, through Toledo and Cleveland to Prairie du Chien in Wisconsin. As the United States grew, so did most of these institutions which owed their origin and early survival to the dedication of European Jesuits. These pioneers were soon succeeded by generations of native Americans who entered the novitiates opened by their predecessors and came, in time, to man the older schools and establish a good many new ones.[26]

Even this sketchy survey should point up the vast difference between the education problems faced by Jesuits in sixteenth-century Europe and those which confront American Jesuit schools today. By the measure of twentieth-century quantitative and qualitative complexity, those first Jesuit *collegia* and their *Ratio* must appear comparatively primitive. It is no longer a matter of directing a relatively limited curriculum in secondary schools quite uniformly organized. There are more Jesuit high schools in the United States now than were maintained by the entire Society when Ignatius died in 1556 and their academic and guidance functions are not only intricate but subject to re-examination and continual development. In addition, there are those sizeable institutions of higher education with their undergraduate colleges, their graduate departments and research projects and their professional schools. These are the elements of a system, which, by the standards of an earlier age is one of sophisticated maturity. It finds itself, moreover, situated within an enormously prosperous and dynamic industrial democracy which is beset by grave internal ambiguities and by massive perils from without. In such a climate the attempt to enunciate theory or administer schools successfully or teach in them effectively is formidable.

It may be objected that these pursuits are never easy and that only those innocent of historical perspective or naively self-centered can imagine that current problems are unique. No doubt schoolmen in every age do wrestle with certain issues which continually recur. It is also true that ours is not the only stormy epoch. The sixteenth century was lurid enough; shot through by political agitation and pitiless cruelty within the so-called Christian states; threatened with war and destruction from the East and shaken by very considerable changes not only in manners but in conceptions of value. That too was a century bent on spelling a good many things out afresh although the Renaissance, despite its youthful enthusiasm for reconstruction, does not seem to have innovated so very startlingly if we measure it by the work of profound revision which men today are reluctantly obliged to undertake. But in any event, it is clear that the task of Jesuit education is more involved now than it was in 1599 and no one today would attempt a *Ratio* designed to do for the schools even of a single country what that of 1599 did quite successfully for a good part of the Western world.

We shall not try to detail here all the actual problems which specify this task of American Jesuit education.[27] It will be useful, though, to indicate some of the large problem-areas to which contemporary educational theory must be applied by those who have to devise the middle-range principles and practical policies which will effectively incarnate that theory in a set of realistic means capable of realizing, to some degree at least, the ideal goals.

The most oppressive if not the most proximate category of problems is that which is created by the cosmic uncertainties of the hour. The significance of national power blocks armed with thermonuclear weapons and standing one another off in hostile truce may be ignored by individual men and women immersed in the perennial tasks of making a living, building a home and raising children. It cannot be as easily dismissed by educators since they have a professional obligation to think of the common good and its future. They may find, consequently, that this polarization of the world about two conflicting ideologies, each armed with the capacity for apocalyptic destruction has reverberations for the least classroom. A single instance may serve to suggest how this can be so.

Both Christianity and those democratic nations of the West which have been influenced by this historic Christian faith cherish a conviction that all men possess an intrinsic worth and the moral dignity proper to creatures capable of thought, freedom and love. This conviction does not harmonize well with that thesis of Plato's *Republic* which argues that certain golden men are born to rule and they alone deserve that ideal education which develops the specifically human virtuality and brings the intellectual and moral powers to fullest flower. On the contrary, if it can be shown that there is a basic educational experience which does indeed cultivate the universally human and is, consequently, the best foundation for the vocations of housewife, scientist, corporation manager, mechanic, artist or monk then the idealism of Christian and Democratic education alike directs that all should have some access to this general or liberal education. No doubt variation in individual endowments will require that the gifted, the average and the slow move at a different speed and depth. But the humanizing contact with languages and literature, mathematics and science, history and theology ought not, on this reckoning be barred to the artisans, the men of bronze, or doled out to them in token portions.[28]

Yet the exigencies of global tension may force a different approach in the interests of national survival. James B. Conant has argued that in the secondary school the academically talented youth of both sexes should be recruited for the professions while the remainder are mobilized for highly skilled work in modern industry through a strong vocational program. It must be added that Conant supposes that the youth in vocational training will also spend half their time on English, social studies, science and mathematics. He might also have noted that a vocational education can itself be genuinely humanizing and serve to mature imagination, intelligence and character. But the point of chief interest is that Conant defends his suggestions in terms of the national needs in an hour of desperate technological competition with the Communist empire.[29] It would be rash to resist this scheme as unchristian or undemocratic if, in fact, the very existence of a free nation requires it. It will perhaps be said that such prescriptions fit the designs of a totalitarian state which has no esteem or place for the humanities and only wants to train a small army of scientists and

master technologists supported by a large army of skilled industrial la-
borers, but that for a democracy to adopt this approach means, to
paraphrase De Gaulle, giving up all the reasons for living in order to
preserve life. The defenders of the proposal would insist that the future artisans do have some academic preparation and that the context of
a life in a society with cultural resources as abundant as ours is itself
liberalizing and that, in any event, one can hardly make existence
more humane and free if there is neither hope of life nor soil for freedom.

This dispute, like the debates about the quality of Soviet Education or the alleged softness and loss of purpose in American life may
be insoluble chiefly because exact information is not at hand. It indicates, nevertheless, how solutions to such specific questions as the nature of the high school curriculum or the selection of college students may
depend, to a great extent, upon the facts of terror and perplexity symbolized by the mushroom cloud flowering over the desert.

A second category of problems is shared by the Jesuit high
school, college or university with many other church-related institutions.
It is the abiding problem of fashioning a viable religious humanism. This
is a delicate, never-finished task of synthesis and of harmonious development of man's religious aspirations for eternity with his temporal
aspirations for an authentically human life. It requires the nurture in
unison of the ethical and the technical vocations of man in such wise
that they support rather than impede each other. The Christian ideal of
the educated person is neither the pious boor nor the cultured unbe-
liever but rather one who strives to become both truly human and truly
Christian knowing that unless he is both he cannot successfully be either.
It is the sort of thing T. S. Eliot had in mind when he said on the
eve of his seventieth birthday: "One has to be otherworldly and yet
deeply responsible for the affairs of the world." It is the sort of thing
Pius XII had in mind when he wrote in his first encyclical: "There is no
opposition between the laws that govern the life of faithful Christians
and the postulate of a genuine humane humanitarianism but rather
unity and mutual support."[30] It is the ideal of a rich and integrated human life in which every truly valuable human expression finds a place
and all these values contribute to the supreme value, to release from
egoism into love of God and of one's fellow men for the love of God.

It is, moreover, an ideal given substance and fully realized in the
person of our Lord who expressed in Himself and in His life every genuine human value, each harmonized with all the others in a balanced
and dynamic synthesis. But in practice this achievement of a full hu-

manity ordered to divine service is as rare as great saints are rare. The Christian educator knows that he has failed if he graduates students who are devout but unacquainted with at least the rudiments of intellectual and artistic excellence and unprepared for some useful work. He knows that he has also failed, if the schooling he provides helped to create intellectual and technical virtuosos but in no way helped to make them virtuous. Yet how difficult it is to translate this into schedules and programs and to steer serenely between the shoals of secularism and pietism and to find and support teachers with enough skill, imagination and energy to implement this ideal for those students who can and will respond to it.

Were the Christian educators of the sixteenth century more successful than those of the twentieth in meeting this challenge? To judge by their programs on paper, the *Ratio* included, they hardly adverted to it once they got past the sturdy declaration of their twofold intention of cultivating wisdom and piety, letters and morals. Their work had, to be sure, its notable successes in an age which was difficult enough. But in the sixteenth century, the problem of a Christian humanism was not complicated, as it is now, by two other factors: the unparalleled expansion of knowledge and the effective separation of the zone in which most of this knowledge develops from the zone of religion. The overwhelming accumulation of information in the physical sciences, to take the most obvious example, has often been underlined and we are told that the rate of advance is so great here that the sum of what is known doubles every ten years.[31] In such other areas as criticism, philosophy and theology there is not the same rate of complex amplification. Yet, the erudition, at least, in these fields has progressed astonishingly and, besides, the philosopher and theologian have to take account of the implications of scientific discoveries even though they may not agree that these have altered the intellectual and ethical horizons so drastically as some physicists think.

In a situation of this sort it is obvious that the job of planning the curriculum for a secondary school or for a liberal arts college or even for a professional school is forbidding. By contrast, the authors of the *Ratio* had a simple task. *Noster Quintilianus* had pretty much determined what the *collegium* should teach and even how. The University of Paris had worked out the details of a graduated curriculum and Jesuit schools from the outset followed this pattern. In theology, St. Ignatius had himself decided that St. Thomas should be preferred to Peter Lombard as the basis of lectures. Nowadays the ideal of a certain fundamental intellectual breadth requires careful selection from among manifold disciplines and if superficiality is to be balanced by depth at chosen points, one must be content to be ignorant of a great deal else. It is desirable, certainly, that we know something of that Greek and Roman civilization in which are so many of our cultural roots but this knowledge cannot be acquired at the expense of knowledge of American history or contemporary science or recent theological developments.

None of these intellectual advances logically required a secularized world for their growth yet most of them have, in fact, developed apart from any vital contact with the vision of religious faith. There is no real exigency for hostility between the scientific and the theological outlook; yet they have often seemed opposed in history. Their disparate methods, objects and results have rarely been fully integrated in the living synthesis of an individual person who is at home in both disciplines. Christian educators, consequently, cannot simply move the body of secular knowledge straight into the school and conclude that because it is present and learned it is also assimilated into a unified Christian wisdom. The devout humanists had their problems with classical literature but it was a more rudimentary difficulty and they solved it roughly by simply expurgating the classics. Teilhard de Chardin's brilliant and lifelong struggle to integrate the evolutionary insight with the older elements of a Christian Humanism poignantly suggests how difficult this sort of enterprise is now. Yet the importance of the work is incontestable and is the strongest of arguments for the existence of Christian higher education.

Like any church-affiliated school in the Western world, a Jesuit institution has the obligation of serving two societies—the Church and a civil society which has aims of its own quite apart from those of the religious society though not necessarily antithetical. In some countries this situation is one of considerable tension, for the state is actively hostile toward nonpublic education and its legislation is correspondingly unaccommodating. In the United States the religious school has never felt any sense of inevitable division or irreconcilable conflict of loyalties. Neither the school legislation of the state nor the norms imposed by the powerful, and generally salutary, influence of accrediting agencies has meant that the religious school must adopt an alien set of aims or structures or that its preferences in materials and methods have been unduly inhibited. Nor can the impact of these factors on the curriculum be called oppressive. It is true, of course, that the whole nature of American culture does require a Jesuit high school in Wichita to have characteristics rather different from those of a seventeenth-century academy dealing heavily in classical humanism. But this follows from the nature of education, as we shall see in the next chapter, and is quite another matter.

The Jesuit school or university in the United States does, however, face the financial problems common to all nonpublic institutions in a wealthy country which maintains, and is continually enlarging, the scope of its own fully articulated school systems at local and state levels. In such an environment, the Jesuit institutions have been forced to suspend one of their cherished ideals, that of gratuity of instruction. Yet this reluctant suspension is not illogical, because an even more fundamental Christian principle calls for the employment of whatever morally valid instruments are needed to carry on the work of the religious apostolate and schools with fees are preferable to no schools at all.

Nevertheless, the question of finances is a source of constant pressure. The status of Jesuit institutions as church-affiliated schools is, in fact, often misunderstood. These schools, like most of those conducted by religious orders and congregations, are indeed vitally related to the Church. They are directed by Catholics who are also members of a social group having a special corporate and juridicial existence within the Church. This existence derives ultimately from the approval of the Roman See which, as was noted in the first chapter, is the true source of the authority exercised within the order or congregation by the religious superiors. Since the obligation to provide for Christian education falls chiefly upon the local bishop, it is he who first invites priests, brothers or sisters to conduct a school or college within his diocese. No doubt, the bishop's primary concern is for the specifically religious formation of those committed to his care but he will have recognized that every form of instruction, as Pius XI put it, has a necessary connection with man's final destiny and is, consequently, an object of the Church's solicitude.

Very often bishops will generously assist new foundations or interest themselves in the continued welfare of an established institution. But the typical secondary school or college under the direction of a Religious Institute is not a parochial or diocesan enterprise and does not receive from parish or diocese any regular financial aid. Bishops and pastors have their own churches, hospitals and elementary parochial or diocesan high schools to support and so the responsibility for providing new sites or buildings, finding funds for endowment, scholarships and faculty salaries devolves directly upon the Institute which is the corporate proprietor of these other educational centers. Their financial problem is much like that of any independent school and they, too, must look to the generosity of benefactors for the funds to bridge the gap between their needs and the revenue actually derived from tuition fees. More than one administrator of a church-affiliated school has felt with Henry Adams that money solves all educational problems. Since this commodity is always in short supply and the need for it continually swells, it can seem to some idealistic spirits that school managers are overly preoccupied with material affairs.

As long ago as the sixteenth century, Father Ribadeneira was complaining about Jesuit rectors who were, in his opinion, excessively concerned with putting up new buildings.[32] Nowadays sophisticated critics chide the Christian educator for talking too much about financial needs. Such critics miss two points. In the first place, the basic necessity often *is* precisely financial. Many Catholic institutions are barred from fulfilling impeccable academic ideals not by lack of intelligence or good will but by a simple lack of funds. Moreover, it would, in any case, be snobbish if not Manichean to ignore monetary tools as though they were deplorable and vulgar necessities to be employed but scarcely to be mentioned. For in our civilization, as Teilhard de Chardin reflected when he saw the great cyclotron at Berkeley, dollars are a source of energy, and money "is still, and indeed every day becomes more and more the life-blood of humanity."[33]

Finally, though it hardly needs to be said, American Jesuit schools and colleges have to face permanent educational questions which are at least as insistent and certainly more complex now than ever—questions about the teachers, the procedures and the students.

Questions about teachers—about the recruitment, preparation and adequate recompense of good ones. Any conscientious administrator wants to secure competent teachers and then help them preserve their enthusiasm and enlarge their effectiveness. For the religious order or congregation in school work there are two further and distinctive tasks: that of securing proper vocations to their own ranks and that of providing for their lay faculty members a dignified academic role with its due share of responsibility and professional rewards. The morale of high school teachers must be guarded against corrosion by boredom or a vague sense of inferiority. The college teacher has to be kept from growing indifferent to class work in an exclusive enthusiasm for research or from such a neglect of research as will sterilize his teaching.

Questions about students—about their goals, their problems and their achievements. All these specific issues, of course, presuppose some fundamental concept of Man since it is the educator's philosophy of human nature which ultimately controls, or should control, his practical policies. For the independent school there are also questions about the norms governing selection of students when one cannot accept all applicants.

Questions about procedures. There are new means of communication in educational television, programmed instruction on teaching machines, language laboratories. New organizational patterns, which sometimes sound like echoes from the past, are proposed and the talk is all of team-teaching, teachers' aids and flexible scheduling of students into large groups for instruction and small ones for discussion or for sending them to school eleven months of the year. Questions about administration. Shall it be democratic? How democratic?

Today, more than four centuries after its founder's death, the Society of Jesus thinks of the work of scholarship and education as of prime importance among its numerous and diversified ministries.[34] It understands very well how multi-zoned and intricate this work is, since, after all, it is actively engaged in it. When it approaches educational issues, whether they be issues common to all schools, or to all church-related schools or proper to Jesuit schools, it would wish to treat them within the context of a complete and reasonable philosophy of education. Such a philosophy seeks to relate a generalized discussion of the aims, the curriculum and the methods and agencies of formal schooling to a complete worldview, to a theory of life and value built up both by philosophical reflection upon experience and by theological elaboration of the content of Faith.

The full philosophy of education subscribed to by a Jesuit School is not to be found wholly or even chiefly in any Jesuit documents. For such a school must, in the first place, be a real school and a Christian school and its full educational theory includes all that those essential characteristics require. Here, however, we are principally concerned with determining what the Jesuit family tradition contributes to this total philosophy of the Jesuit school although it is granted that this contribution forms only a fraction of that whole. There are certain enormous differences between a contemporary American Jesuit high school and La Flèche in the time of Descartes; between the Gregorian University in which Bellarmine taught and a twentieth-century university. Much that is commonplace in education today was not dreamt of by the authors of the *Ratio* and so there are no Jesuit principles touching such matters directly even though their theoretical dimension may be susceptible of philosophical or theological development. The president of a modern Jesuit university with its thousands of students, both men and women, its large faculties of Jesuits and non-Jesuits and all the financial, educational and human complexities that flow from this reality cannot find in the *Ratio* or in the *Constitutions* any full specific charter for his institution or any explicit solution for his chief tactical problems. He may, however, find an orientation and some basic directives which do provide for a slender but real unity and continuity between his many-levelled institution and the modest *collegio* which opened its doors in Messina in 1548.

This unity and continuity will not be detected on the plane of curricula and concrete procedures, for civilizations change and so do their demands on the school. Methods also change, often for the better. They are developed not only for greater efficiency but also in the direction of greater humaneness and subtlety. Yet cultures are not wholly discontinuous and men and society have not been substantially altered by four centuries. Man is still the person who is free because he is self-conscious and society is still the indispensable milieu within which, in a very true sense, he becomes human. The Church too has a transcendent continuity and within it since 1540 a particular religious order has perdured despite some astonishing historical fluctuations including an almost total suppression for several decades. It is at least possible, therefore, that there should be an essential core at the center of every Jesuit school, even the least perfect, and that certain abiding categories should specify this institution not merely as a school and a Christian school but as a characteristically Jesuit school. The specifications in this last cluster need not be either perfectly original nor entirely beyond criticism but they do serve to relate the Jesuit schools of the past to those of the present and to link to one another the Jesuit schools dispersed over the earth today. They are the deep causal forces which impose a basic pattern upon that shifting mass of diverse and detailed effects which at first is all that meets the eye. The pages that follow try to call the names of some of these essential categories.

NOTES: CHAPTER III

1. Bacon expressed these sentiments in Book I of *The Advancement of Learning* which is quoted here from the first volume of the old American edition of the complete works of Bacon as edited by Basil Montagu (Philadelphia: Carey and Hart, 1846). In the first comment on the Jesuit schools, Bacon observes: "Which excellent part of ancient discipline hath been in some sort revived of late times by the colleges of the Jesuits; of whom, although in regard of their superstition I may say, 'quo meliores, eo deteriores'; yet in regard of this, and some other points concerning human learning and moral matters, I may say, as

Agesilaus said to his enemy Pharnabaus, 'Talis quum sis, utinam noster esses.' " *Ibid.,* p. 167. Somewhat later he remarks: "We see the Jesuits, (who partly in themselves, and partly by the emulation and provocation of their example, have much quickened and strengthened the state of learning,) we see, I say, what notable service and reparation they have done to the Roman see." *Ibid.,* p. 176.

2. Louis Réné de la Chalotais, *Essay on National Education or Plan of Studies for the Young,* trans. H. R. Clark (London: Edward Arnold and Company, 1934), pp. 43, 49.

3. *Ibid.,* p. 47.

4. de Dainville, *op. cit.,* p. 259.

5. Pachtler, *op. cit.,* II, 181: "Adolescentes nec dimittendi videntur ad spectanda supplicia reorum, nisi forsan haereticorum, vel ad singulare et inusitatum aliquid, exceptis parvulis." A twentieth-century curiosity is the item carried in the June 2, 1961 issue of the (London) *Times Educational Supplement* under the caption, "No Comment." It reported that a few days earlier a woman remarked outside Wandsworth Prison: "I always bring the children to a hanging. They ask questions and they learn not to do wrong and the penalty if they do. I wanted to bring Leslie's brother Francis—he's six—but he was asleep."

6. Pachtler, *op. cit.,* I, 424–31.

7. *Ibid.,* pp. 159, 160.

8. *Mon. Paed., op. cit.,* p. 722. The year was 1585.

9. These points are set out in the Rules for the Prefect of Lower Classes, or as we should call him today, the principal of the high school, in the *Ratio* of 1591, Corcoran, *op. cit.,* p. 208: "In ultimam classem Praefectus nec admittat iuvenes iam aetate provectos, qui nec disciplinam ferunt ipsi, et ferme alios turbant: neque pueros nimium teneros, etiamsi probae tantum educationis gratia mitterentur in scholam, nam dum nugas quas domi facerent, faciunt in schola, mirum in modum onerosi sunt Magistris . . . In Gymnasium quoque nostrum cooptandi non sunt, qui licet rudimentorum Grammaticae satis periti sint, nesciunt tamen recte legere et scribere, quantum satis est. Qui namque horum vitiorum altero laborant, nequeunt eorum compositiones sine stomacho aspici a magistris, ne dum corrigi: et si ante ista non didicerint, vix postea futurum est, ut discant."

10. de Dainville, *op. cit.,* p. 143. For a summary of some enrollment figures in the period 1540–1773, see Robert Schwickerath, S.J., *Jesuit Education: Its History and Principles Viewed in the Light of Modern Educational Problems* (St. Louis, B. Herder, 1904), pp. 144 ff. and Thomas Hughes, S.J., *Loyola and the Educational System of the Jesuits* (New York: Charles Scribner's Sons, 1892), pp. 71–74.

11. *The New York Times,* July 9, 1961, p. 8, E.

12. *Mon. Paed., op. cit.,* p. 244.

13. Pachtler, *op. cit.,* I, 171: "Nulli studiosi . . . arma bellica . . . secum in scholam adferent, cum iam non militaria bellorum, sed literaria musarum castra sequantur."

14. de Dainville, *op. cit.,* p. 264. For the rule forbidding the carrying of weapons to class, which is the fifth of the seven rules drawn up par-

ticularly for "extern" or lay students, in the *Ratio* of 1599, see Pachtler, *op. cit.*, II, 458.

15. Pachtler, *op. cit.*, I, 161.
16. *Constitutions*, IV, 6, n. 11.
17. The *Ratio* of 1599 in Pachtler, *op. cit.*, II, 292, 342.
18. *Constitutions*, IV, 6, n. 8 H.
19. For the recommendations of the *Ratio* of 1586 see Pachtler, *op. cit.*, II, 84 and 98 and for the rules laid down in the *Ratio* of 1599, *ibid.*, pp. 276, 290.
20. Herman, *op. cit.*, p. 222. Cicero was not the only author read. Ovid, Catullus, Virgil and the historians were also prescribed but Cicero's position as the supreme model for imitation was undisputed.
21. Corcoran, *op. cit.*, 257–61.
22. This ideal is implied by a phrase in the Jesuit *Constitutions*, X, 3. Herman, *op. cit.*, pp. 135, 205, pointed to the similarity between it and the ideal of the Renaissance: the man of wisdom and eloquence.
23. This phrase is drawn from an unsigned editorial comment in the (London) *Times Educational Supplement* for June 2, 1961, p. 1125.
24. For a more recent statistical picture see the Appendix.
25. The scope of this American Jesuit Educational Association is stated in its "Constitution," Article III—Objectives: "1. In general, the objectives of the Association are to promote and make more efficient all educational activities of American Jesuits. 2. Specifically, the objectives are the following: a) cooperation of member institutions in furthering the aims of Catholic education; b) promotion of scholarship and research in Jesuit institutions, and publication of the results of such scholarship and research; c) conservation of the permanent essential features of the Jesuit educational tradition, and the necessary adaptation of its accidental features to national and local needs of the time; d) increased academic efficiency of all Jesuit institutions; e) effective presentation of the Catholic philosophy of life; f) corporate cooperation with other educational associations, Catholic and secular; g) collaboration with Jesuit educators and Jesuit educational institutions in other countries on the common problems of Jesuit education; h) experimental study of educational problems in America; i) provision for wider knowledge in the United States of the Jesuit educational system, its theory and its practice." This is taken from a privately printed booklet issued in September, 1948 by the Jesuit Educational Association from its New York Office.
26. A brief account of the nineteenth- and early twentieth-century American Jesuit educational foundations will be found in William J. McGucken, S.J., *The Jesuits and Education: The Society's Teaching Principles and Practice, Especially in Secondary Education in the United States* (Milwaukee: Bruce, 1932). A most interesting study of curricular development in the Jesuit institutions on the Eastern seaboard, is that of Miguel A. Bernad, S.J., "The Faculty of Arts in the Jesuit Colleges in the Eastern Part of the United States: Theory and Practice: (1782–1923)" (Unpublished Ph.D. dissertation, Dept. of Education, Yale University, 1951). Father Bernad has detailed the steps by which the

Jesuit colleges gradually adapted themselves to many of the patterns of organization, curricula and nomenclature common in the American academic world.

27. The Jesuit Educational Association publishes for its membership a periodical, *Jesuit Educational Quarterly,* in which many of these specific administrative and curricular problems are examined.

28. This theme has been persuasively argued by Lorenzo K. Reed, S.J., "Excellence For Whom?" *National Catholic Educational Association Bulletin,* 57 (August, 1960), 267–72. "I intend," said Father Reed, "to propose a new kind of comprehensive high school for Catholic students . . . Its purpose will be to give every student an *academic* education up to the very limit of his capacities." *Ibid.,* p. 267.

29. James B. Conant, "Vocational Education and the National Need," *American Vocational Journal,* 35 (January, 1960), 19. That Soviet education is, in fact, inspired by the desire for industrial supremacy is pointed out by Nicholas De Witt, "Soviet Science Education and the School Reform," *School and Society,* 88 (Summer, 1960), 297: "The Russians orient their educational efforts so as to maximize the returns from it for the advancement of their political, military, and economic objectives. The communists do not believe in education for education's sake. They do not believe in education for the individual's sake. The Russians want no part of liberal or general humanistic education. They want no generalists—only specialists. Their main objective is to offer *functional education* so as to train, to mold, to develop the skills, the professions, and the specialists required by their long-run development programs—specialists who are capable of performing the tasks of running the industrial and bureaucratic machinery of the communist state. And in order to accomplish this, the Russians *were, are,* and *will be* training an army of scientists and technologists."

30. Henry Hewes, "Eliot on Eliot: I Feel Younger Than I Did at 60," *The Saturday Review,* 41 (September 13, 1958), p. 32. The words of Pius XII are drawn from the encyclical, "The Unity of Human Society" (*Summi Pontificatus*), *The Catholic Mind,* 37 (November 1939), 912. They are found also, along with many other instructive passages from the writings of the same Pope, in the valuable volume edited by Robert C. Pollock, *The Mind of Pius XII* (New York: Crown Publishers, 1953), p. 24. This first encyclical was issued October 20, 1939.

31. Robert Oppenheimer, "Tradition and Discovery," *ACLS News Letter,* 10 (October 1959), 10. This is the text of the American Council of Learned Societies Annual Lecture, delivered at the University of Rochester, Rochester, New York, on January 22, 1959. The point cited is one that Oppenheimer has often underscored.

32. *de Dainville, op. cit.,* p. 327, n. 5.

33. Quoted in Nicolas Corte, *Pierre Teilhard de Chardin: His Life and Spirit,* trans., Martin Jarrett-Kerr (New York: Macmillan, 1960), p. 111.

34. See chapter I, n. 15, citing the remark of the twenty-seventh General of the Society of Jesus on the prime importance of educational works.

CHAPTER IV

ON CERTAIN PRESUPPOSITIONS

By the perfect Christian We mean the Christian of
today, child of his own era . . . a citizen and not
something apart from the life led in his own coun-
try . . .

Pius XII[1]

Christian education, said Pius XI in his encyclical letter on that subject, "aims at securing the Supreme Good, that is, God, for the souls of
those who are being educated, and the maximum of well-being possible
here below for human society."[2] This succinct charter directs attention
to the two primary obligations of any Jesuit school. It must, in the first
place, be a *school,* that is to say, an institution which promotes individual self-realization and conserves and renews social life by transmitting its substance to the youth of the given society. It must also be
a *Christian* school, that is to say, an institution which serves the purposes of the religious community, the Church, as well as those of civil
society. These two finalities have much more significance for the integral
theory of Jesuit education than have any of the nuances given either of
them by the Jesuit family tradition. To set forth all they imply for education would be to write a thick book indeed. But it is possible to suggest
a few of the imperatives dictated by the nature of education in general
and of Christian education in particular as a rough framework for subsequent discussions of the distinctive Jesuit accent.

Characteristics Flowing from the Nature of
Education Itself

Education is usually thought of either as a process or as a product. Some notion of the reality itself can be had, therefore, by examining its features from these two angles. In modern industrial democracies, formal education in the schools is so vast and intricate, not to say
chaotic, that it may be hard to seize from it the generic note of educa-

tion considered precisely as a process. This note is no more essential in the rudimentary schooling provided by primitive peoples but it is more visible. The anthropologist sees at once that education, taken widely, is the congeries of activities whereby the older people of any society, in or out of school, pass on to the rising generation that burden of knowledge and skills, beliefs and morals, of traditions and way of life which is the substance of their culture.[3] This communication not only provides the occasion and the means of any individual's personal development but also makes it possible for a society of mortal men to regenerate itself continually. From this point of view, education is usually successful even though it may be far from perfect. The community ordinarily succeeds quite well in transmitting to its children the material it actually does esteem. When the schools are denounced for entertaining small-minded aims or for failing to achieve the goals supposedly approved this really means that society is itself confused or has inadequate aims or is divided in heart between the values honored in word and those pursued in practice.

This also reminds us that academic ideals can only be achieved if education's radical function as an instrument of social continuity is realistically acknowledged. Malice in the social order may on occasion pervert practice and produce, let us say, a biracial public school system or classrooms devoted to propaganda. A sound philosophy of education will not, of course, support nor perpetuate aberrations of this sort. Yet neither, on the other hand, will it be effective if it ignores the common culture or tries to reverse it completely rather than to purify and direct it. To say this is not to say that education is sheerly conservative anymore than to speak of the transmission of culture means ratifying the antiquated and destructive notion of the teacher as one who pours his own knowledge into students moulded like clay vessels. On the contrary, even the most traditional educations have been to some degree reconstructive. There was always a momentous passage when the tribe did substitute agriculture for aimless food gathering or sails for paddles. Moreover, in cultures like our own where a dynamic of change pervades the whole structure, education may be literally traditional and yet far from conservative. For if society, by choice or necessity puts a premium upon adventuresome and pragmatic qualities and encourages inventiveness and a restless zeal for improvement, then this is what the adult generation will communicate. Although education transmits and conserves at all levels it can simultaneously advance knowledge and reconstruct a civilization's outlook and often does so, particularly at the university level.

The philosopher of education does not, therefore, have to accept the *status quo* unreservedly nor limit himself to rationalizing current practices. But he must realize that education, like politics, is the art of the possible and that the historical context not only determines to a considerable extent what is possible but specifies the range of means available for the pursuit of those broad purposes which are common to all cultures and every age. For the Bushmen of the Kalahari Desert, intellectual power means a remarkable acuity in reading correctly the least signs and portents in the natural world so as to tell with precision from flattened grasses along the trail what sort of beast has passed that way. For a modern urban American the objects about which intellectual maturity plays are quite different, yet in both cultures it would be fair to say that education aims at certain decisive and useful habits of mind and character although the proximate definition and the practical realization of this aim differ greatly. One can conclude that, although certain objectives and procedures of education appear to be universally valid, still they are nowhere perfectly incarnated since no single civilization, however rich and enlightened, can or needs to actualize all human virtualities.

It is for this reason that a pragmatist would seriously err should he propose to establish Experimentalism as the unofficial philosophy of the American public school. For this institution is the organ of a community whose conceptualization of ideals and standards is still rooted in Christianity's ethical and finalistic interpretation of human experience. Since scientific naturalism is not the philosophy of most of the people, it could not reasonably be made the philosophy of their schools. In like fashion, a classical humanist would be deceived about his own times if he were to attempt a reinstatement of the Latin and Greek curriculum as the core of the ordinary American high school. If he contented himself with deploring the disappearance of Greek and the decline of Latin he would be more prudent but too indifferent still to this central fact that the aims and content of the academic phase of education largely reflect that total way of life which older people in a society are handing on to their children.

It is true that to a great extent languages and literatures, philosophies and political institutions in the West have been shaped by the classical tradition and that everyone should have some acquaintance with this tradition. But it is equally true that today a firsthand knowledge of Latin and Greek, the ability to read and write these languages is not indispensable. We would not now assert, as Père Jouvancy did so firmly in 1703, that no man is educated unless he is expert in Greek. This is not to deny the intrinsic value of such knowledge nor its special worth for particular groups. The study of Homer may nourish the patriotic ardor of modern Greeks; the Catholic clergy requires familiarity at least with Latin, the language of ecclesiastical law and of the liturgy; the literary critic can hardly become an exegete of *Finnegan's Wake* or understand a good deal of Western thought unless his knowledge of the classical past is deep and exact. But although the maturation of intelligence remains a prime educational goal, it is not now defined nor sought exactly in the manner of Socrates or Erasmus. The perennial aims of education are somewhat differently concretized in a contemporary American Jesuit high school and in a French *collège*. Mothers' Clubs and Parents' Nights, football teams and proms, mission drives and closed retreats are not indefensible accretions to the main business of a modern Jesuit secondary school even though they were unknown in the sixteenth century. They are partial embodiments of purposes which are as much a part, even if not so central a part, of Christian education in the United States today as is that aim of intellectual eminence whose symbol may be a National Merit Scholarship or that aim of moral eminence which God alone can certify.

As a process, then, education operates as a conveyer of culture and a force both for conservation and for reconstruction. But it is also useful to focus upon the product which this social process effects in individual persons. The familiar definitions which speak of unfolding the full register of man's powers—physical, aesthetic, intellectual and moral—are constructed from this latter point of view. To speak of powers may provoke wrangling since this concept implies a distinctive metaphysical analysis of human nature. But it is easy to see that the newborn infant is largely potential. He may become a decathlon champion, a good pianist, a mathematician, or a gifted mechanic. He may become a criminal or a saint. In any case, he is not actually these things in babyhood and his development toward them can be broadly described as a growth even as the expansion of the seedling to the fruit-bearing tree is a growth. The product of the educational process can consequently be thought of as a progressive development from virtuality to actuality. Physical expansion in size, strength, motor skills and sound health is one sort of growth. The chief concern of the formal educator is, however, for growth along the avenues which lead to intellectual, moral and social maturity. It can reasonably be maintained, therefore, that education adequately considered has three great focal purposes or value-categories and that consequently there can generally be distinguished in any historic educational practice these three phases, not separated but interpenetrating and reciprocally influential: the intellectual, the moral and the social. These correspond to essential facets in man himself. For on the one hand, the central aspects of man's spirit are those of intellectual awareness and the capacity for love and free, responsible choice. On the other, since man is also an animal located in time and space these distinctive spiritual powers are expanded chiefly in and through all his interactions with his natural and social environments.

Philosophers of education, no matter how diverse their metaphysical systems and their conceptions of human nature, are generally in agreement upon two basic pedagogical principles which are correlated with those two central aspects of the human spirit, the cognitive and the volitional. They all insist that learning is primarily the self-activity of the one who learns. It is he who possesses that immanent and radical power of intelligence. He learns when this capacity is actuated and when that happens, his personality is enlarged by the addition of some skill or wisdom. It is true, of course, that the implications of this activity theory can be drawn out very differently. One man will easily grant that listening may well involve true pupil activity. Another may claim, as Dewey sometimes did, that the requisite activity must be overt. But the agreement is at least as noteworthy as the disagreements. Secondly, all theoreticians, like all parents and teachers, know that there is no learning unless there is motivation; that the learner's essential activity is not stimulated at all save by desire, if only by the desire to escape punishment. It is also agreed, despite the immanent character of learning, that there is a place for teaching. For man is a social being whose learning can be made easier and more economical if a teacher guides and illuminates the process of personal discovery much as, to use St. Thomas's metaphor, a doctor by his skillful medication strengthens nature's own restorative powers.

Those three great focal aims of all education seem to have a certain hierarchical order. At least it is noteworthy that most celebrated theorists, from Plato through Rousseau to Dewey, have given primacy of honor to that process of moral education which is energized by the ethical aim of making men good. Although it is also true that these writers have very differently defined the nature and norms of morality.[4] Professional teachers, on the other hand, are often most interested in what may be called the academic phase of education. The term is loosely taken here as a label for the whole process whereby through the acquisition of certain skills and information a young person becomes mature enough to maintain himself in an existence whose purposes he grasps, at least in part, and to cooperate productively in some of the myriad roles afforded by man's many communities. Intellectual development is subsumed under this aim although in one civilization it may be achieved through formal classroom instruction and learning while a rural society may train the head together with the hand as it teaches the secrets of agriculture and handicrafts. The social aims of education constitute a third category because no one can live totally outside society, not even the hermit, and no one can live peaceably and fruitfully within society unless he accepts the minimal responsibilities imposed by a community life. Since most learning goes on in a social context and since a great deal of morality is concerned with interpersonal relationships, socialization is closely linked to growth in the intellectual and moral virtues. It is not perfectly identical with that growth, however, and it receives varying degrees of stress in different places. The demands for purely scholastic achievement have generally been more intense for a French than for an American student but the demands for a sense of civic enthusiasm and for that genial conformity which lubricates the social mechanism are apt to be less.

Reflection upon the distinctive task of adolescence points up from a fresh perspective this same threefold character of education. For the youth is laced into a social context and is engaged there in clarifying his own experience and in establishing a firm ethical sense of his personal identity and goals. But these are distinctively intellectual and moral tasks and their fruits are the intellectual and moral virtues.

Many of the debates which are so easily stimulated by spacious talk about educational objectives might be avoided if a truism were recalled: Education is wider, in concept and in fact, than schooling. Education may include the formal instruction of the classroom or the informal instruction that goes on at home, on the job or through the liturgical life and the ministry of the word in the Church. Men may educate consciously or they may create an environment which has an educational impact independent of their advertence to it. The school's share of responsibility for the complete task of education will vary from country to country. Among Europeans, for instance, the distinction between instruction and the wider if vaguer concept of character formation, between *enseignement* and *éducation,* between *Erziehung* or *Wissenschaft* and *Bildung* is so well-established that until recently the French did not generally apply *éducation* to the school because the concept of that institution was of one limited to provision of academic instruction.[5]

It is significant that this distinction has never really taken hold in the United States for it has never occurred to Americans that these two aspects of education should or can be separated. For them, schooling itself has an inescapable ethical dimension and the classroom teacher educates character for better or for worse. The school may think of its academic function as primary and may concern itself principally with expansion of the power and resources for constructive thought. But Americans tend to regard thought itself as instrumental. One learns to think correctly in order to make better ethical decisions—a viewpoint St. Ignatius would have appreciated. Besides, the school is part of life and life in an evolving world constantly challenges us with the need to choose. The realm of choice, however, of the conscious and free act is precisely the human and moral realm. The most determinedly intellectualistic school does itself violence if it tries to abstract from moral education and cannot completely do so anyhow. For better or for worse, it communicates ethical attitudes, directly or indirectly and provokes ethical determinations. The school which unreasonably exalts high grades and the teacher whose favor can be bought by flattery or lost by a display of independent thinking clearly foster moral attitudes and choice.

But if it is actually agreed that moral and intellectual education are intertwined, even in the school, there is still room for the ancient and acrimonious dispute as to their relative importance. Broadly speaking, there are two polar positions that can be taken on this question of the ultimate purpose of education. According to one view, the overall aim of education both in the school and in its entirety is to make men wise. The most ardent defenders of this opinion are found in the university and this is not surprising. The precious value of the university has always lain in its enlightened defense of the pure pursuit of truth and the advancement of learning. This it can do the more easily because it is neither a Church, which thinks chiefly of men's progress in holiness, nor a state, which thinks chiefly of the practical business of preserving peace and prosperity. Nevertheless, although it may be the university's function to keep alive the ideals of wisdom, any attempt to equate the university's specific goals with those of education in its full range will not go uncontested. The great religious figures have always maintained that the overall purpose of education in this integral sense is to make men good and the common people have generally agreed. A Platonic endeavor to unite these opposed views by equating goodness with wisdom may conciliate the first group but not the second which knows by experience that the two qualities are never identical save in God.

American opinion has always leaned toward the second position although the first finds an ever more respectful hearing as the competition with Soviet Russia grows keener. To award the ethical aim primacy does not, of course, mean depreciating, much less eliminating the edu-

cation of intelligence but only means that this academic goal is not considered ultimate in every order and under every aspect nor an aim to
be achieved apart from or independent of the moral and social development of the individual. The strong moralistic strain in American education, a strain which a Dewey did not create but merely voiced, has its
dangers. The disinclination to define education, even in the school, as
primarily a matter of training intelligence may easily lead to a neglect of
that training. But such neglect is not logically inevitable and the Jesuit
teacher, like any Christian educator, will applaud the attempt to keep
simultaneously in focus both the intellectual and the moral aims and to
award at least a primacy of honor to the latter. *In studiis primum locum pietas obtineat,* said Jerónimo Nadal as he drew up that early sketch
for a Jesuit school program which was noted above. And in a document
which Ledesma worked over at some time before his death in 1575, one
finds this as the first of the rules to be followed by all students in the
Society's schools: "Those who come to the Society's *gymnasia* to learn
their letters should have as their chief purpose the acquisition of virtue
and piety rather than scholarship, although the latter must also be matter
for serious effort."[6] The *Constitutions* of the Society officially enunciate
this duplex aim. It is laid down in the eleventh chapter of the Fourth
Part that schools are conducted for the education of youth in learning
and virtue and this concern for the development of character as well as
intelligence does not seem so novel to an American or British schoolman as it might to many on the continent.[7] Such a concern has been traditional in American education with its demand, as John Adams once
put it, for "the instruction of the people in every kind of knowledge that
can be of use to them in the practice of their moral duties as men,
citizens and Christians, and of their political and civil duties as members
of society and freemen."[8] It is also reflected in contemporary inquires
about the influence of the collegiate years on the students' sense of
values. For such discussions assume unquestioningly that the college
ought to have a beneficial influence in this matter; that its task "is not
only more than vocational but also more than intellectual."[9]

In the light of these general characteristics of all education, some
implications can be drawn for Jesuit schools, particularly for those in the
United States. To begin with, Jesuit education cannot exist as a simple
genus but is necessarily specified by time and place. It will be, for example, sixteenth-century Italian Jesuit education or twentieth-century
American. It must, moreover, share with other agencies the work of com-

municating two visions, neither of them static: that of the Christian Church and that of the political community. For the school, as we noted, is simultaneously situated within both these societies. Ribadeneira was thinking of the second of these when he observed that Jesuits conducted schools *in bonum reipublicae*—for the benefit of civil society. Spanish Jesuit education will, therefore, be as different from American Jesuit education as Spain is from America though there will be points of likeness between them since they are both embodied in Christian schools run by Jesuits. The maintenance of that traditional Jesuit spirit is itself strongly conditioned by the temper of the secular culture. In the fiercely competitive scholastic atmosphere of France, a Jesuit educator once asked whether it were possible for Jesuit schools to hold to their custom of fostering the free creativity of young writers and speakers and of seasoning their work with the customary academic celebrations, festivities and holidays. All these things took time from the grim pursuit of success in the examinations for the university admission. Up till now the question has had less point in America where, if critics are to be believed, there is only too much time and taste for *jeux et fêtes*.

In many nations, especially those still insufficiently industrialized, there has been an oversupply of competitors for the relatively few well-paying jobs and consequently intellectual eminence has been passionately desired and cultivated as the road to affluence. But in the United States, a wealthy country where opportunity is still comparatively widespread, the intense education of an academic elite has not found so much open acceptance. If a Christian school were to imitate in America the full rigor of the French fashion even to excluding the American enthusiasm for crowning heroes whose achievements are not scholastic, it is likely that enrollments would decline sharply and the apostolic purpose of conducting a school would be frustrated. For quite apart from the respective merits of these diverse national attitudes, it is still clear that a school in the United States must actualize its students' intellectual and moral potentiality within the American context. For that is the context, after all, in which the students and teachers are. The phrases of Pius XII quoted before are applicable here: ". . . the work of education, since it must be carried on in a specific environment and for a specific background (*milieu*), must constantly adapt itself to the circumstances of this background and of this environment wherein this perfection has to be obtained and for which it is destined . . ."[10] This truth does not imply, to be sure, an uncritical acceptance of whatever one's environment may happen to affirm. No doubt there is an interplay, in the best of civilizations, of good and bad elements, of the gold and the gray, the vital and the destructive. Consequently there is a need to strengthen the advantageous factors while eliminating the disadvantageous.

But schools can perform this reconstructive work only slowly and partially for they are by nature conservative and practical rather than innovating and theoretical. St. Ignatius was in many matters a great reformer who introduced important innovations into the concept of the work and nature of a religious order. But he was no rebel so far as school curricula went. If the sixteenth-century bourgeois wanted for their sons the insignia of Latinity, that is what Ignatius was willing to provide for the sake of the chance to provide something more than that. One who understands the vital and basic relationship of education to the civilization that supports it and to the historic forces which have shaped that civilization will have a sensitive appreciation of how hard it is to bring the actual a bit closer to the ideal and how modest any success must be. He will, therefore, easily avoid unrealistic criticism. There is little use, for instance, in a Christian educator's complaining of the tension caused by the necessity of responding to several traditions which often enough are not merely disparate but conflicting, that of the Church and that of modern secular society. One cannot unmake the history which produced this tension. Some of it, moreover, is inevitable for it is a quality of any life which strains to synthesize the dimensions of nature and grace. Doubtless in theory there is no place for insoluble conflict between grace and nature since the former builds upon the latter. But there is a hierarchy here, since these are essentially different levels of being, and that supposes some subordination. Subordination, in turn, implies sacrifice and sacrifice is often painful. Consequently, a conflict in practice between the demands of nature and grace is not unknown so long as we are, to use the medieval terms, *viatores*—wayfarers.

There are many other illustrations arguing this need for realism. It would, for example, be unwise for the high school or college teacher to blame his students' inadequacies simply upon the failure of the elementary schools and to demand its wholesale alteration. For while it may be quite true that the root of later weakness is some deficiency in the grades, still there is not going to be a substantial revision of the elementary school until there are substantial changes in civil society itself. Meanwhile the secondary school and college had best do what they can to make up the deficit while acknowledging that the elementary school has certain positive achievements to its credit and deserves help in its business of piecemeal progress and reformation.

A similar inattention to the deposits of history has prompted some critics to deplore the multiplication of Catholic colleges and universities in the United States during the nineteenth and early twentieth centuries. Would it not have been better, they ask, to have concentrated on fewer and stronger institutions or on the establishment of foundations caring for the spiritual needs of Catholic students close by the campuses of the Cambridges and New Havens, the Berkeleys and the Ann Arbors. Imprudent expansion is of course, a very real error but may it not be that these complaints overlook the adamant truth that in history a perfectly unclouded option is impossible. When the Jesuits and other religious orders accepted the invitations of American bishops and opened schools at the four points of the compass they generally did so because at the moment this was the best choice available. When travel was slow, risky and expensive it would not have helped a bishop in St. Louis or California or Chicago or New Orleans, obliged to provide for the education of the sons of his immigrant flock, to know that there were one or two Catholic colleges on the Eastern seaboard in which all the talent the religious orders could muster was grandly focused. Schools were needed at once and right at hand in each of these widely separated cities and they had to be open to as many as possible of the qualified in the rising generation. One could not wait until technology had cast up the transcontinental airline or until the American Catholic community had acquired affluence or until the nondenominational and the public universities had become sophisticated enough to welcome the Newman Foundation. It was immediately necessary for the Catholic people to lift themselves by their own bootstraps. But once these Catholic schools had begun and continued for a century or more they could hardly be plowed under to make way for a handful of pre-eminent institutions. For better or for worse, certain decisions had been made and certain responsibilities accepted which could not be reversed or repudiated.

If we grant, then, that American Jesuit schools must now as always operate within that American civilization which has contributed to their very essence and existence, it will be appropriate to pause for a moment over certain apposite features of that civilization itself. Some of these have already been suggested. All of them are obvious enough and many of them are characteristics shared with other nations. It may be noted, to begin with a point on which there is general agreement, that the American culture has both a baffling complexity and an astonishingly rapid rate of change not only in technology but also in political and social mores. Our schools, consequently, have more difficulty defining their purposes and less success in fulfilling their conserving-transmitting function than has a school in a primitive society where the aims of education are more easily grasped just because they are rudimentary and comparatively stable. We warmly affirm the great focal categories of purpose but determining the intermediate goals which clarify the content of these moral, intellectual and social emphases and inventing means to achieve them is difficult when there is so much to choose from and such dispute about the norms which ought to guide that choice. Indeed, in a day of wide debate over the supposed loss of a sense of national purpose one is not surprised if the schools find it hard to chart a clear course.

Yet it would be agreed that, however educational purpose is defined, it certainly involves a plurality of aims. Most lists of educational goals, whether drawn up by public or nonpublic educators, envision the school as somehow contributing to the cultivation of intelligence as well as physical health and strength; to an effective concern for the public welfare and benevolence toward others; to development of vocational capacities as well as to a personal appropriation of the cultural riches of the past millennia. If the school is church-affiliated it expects to nourish faith and even state-supported institutions are generally presumed to have some minimal care for developing "religious literacy" at least through study of religion as an historical and social factor.

Unless one holds that all these aims are perfectly equal, one must confront the problem of introducing some kind of hierarchical order into their ranks without impoverishing or eliminating any of them. There is always a temptation to solve that problem either by reducing certain elements to the status of sheerly utilitarian means or by elevating some partial and intermediate goal such as good citizenship to the position of an ultimate master value to which all else is ordered while it is itself ordered to nothing. More usually, however, any grouping of the several goals of American education will emphasize the ethical objectives. For King's College, later Columbia, this meant, according to the advertisement announcing its opening in New York City in 1754 that "The chief Thing that is aimed at in this College, is, to teach and engage the Children *to know God in Jesus Christ,* and to love and serve him in all *Sobriety, Godliness,* and *Richness* of Life, with a perfect Heart and a Willing Mind: and to train them up in all Virtuous Habits, and all such useful Knowledge as may render them creditable to their Families and Friends, Ornaments to their Country, and useful to the Public Weal in their generation."[11]

For a good many people two centuries later it may be the concept of an effective person implying, at the minimum, "one who can hold a job, be related to and take care of a family and keep out of jail," which is attractive but the moral strain even in this notion is evident.[12] In any

catalogue of goals a great deal will always be made of the ideal of freedom which is so universally esteemed that a President not given to radical
pronouncements could confidently call it the central concept of our society.[13] This accent on liberty has obvious educational reverberations in
matters of discipline, methodology and curriculum. Because most moral
principles have considerable social relevance, the ethical concern in
American education easily leads to an emphasis upon the ideal of good
citizenship which is itself in a democracy, an exercise of responsible
freedom. Consequently, considerable attention will be paid to the
school's part in preparing children for their social and civic roles. A basic
supposit of these roles is economic self-sufficiency so that a lively vocational interest is also typical of American education and even the accent
on intellectual prowess which gathered force after the second World War
was greatly due to the increased vocational importance of mental skills.

Between the school and the home there is in America so close a
relationship that foreign observers have called our public schools, "folk
institutions." But the parochial and independent schools also invite or
at least endure, parental curiosity about their operations. No doubt a
clerical despot in a church-affiliated school can more easily deroute this
interest than can a bureaucratic despot in a public institution. But the
tenure of the despot is generally uneasy and his success is questionable at
best. Some parents, no doubt, are delighted to unload all responsibility
for their children's intellectual and moral education upon the school. The
more usual pattern, however, finds parents keeping themselves informed of their children's progress and helping out with homework,
attending the powwows of the PTA, conferring with the school's guidance staff if problems arise and, if they are more leisured or more
zealous, lending their energies to the school's fund-raising ventures.

There are two other strains in American education with which
Christians can sympathize provided they are able to interpret these in
accord with their own ideology: its accent on the practical and its accent on the future. Even the strictly academic sphere is pervaded by a
strong pragmatic or instrumental emphasis. Knowledge is not ordinarily
sought exclusively for its own sake but rather because it promises to serve
other purposes. These other purposes are not inevitably crass. A vocational aim is included among them but it is not all-inclusive. What is intended, at least in theory, is the dynamization of education by a noble
sort of instrumentalism. This was suggested in the well-known maxim
of the Northwest Ordinance which the Congress of the Confederation
adopted in 1785: "Religion, morality and knowledge, being necessary
to good government and the happiness of mankind, schools and the

means of education shall forever be encouraged." A St. Ignatius would surely object to equalizing religion and education on the same level of instrumentality. But the Church itself has an instrumental character, for it is a divinely ordained vehicle bringing man to that supernal union which is truly the ultimate goal. The Christian has a definite idea about the content and location of plenary happiness and he finds a radical instrumentalism congenial since for him the whole of human life is finally ordered as a means to that goal of beatific life in God.

This does not imply that either Ignatius or the authors of the Northwest Ordinance necessarily reject Newman's celebrated defense of the intrinsic value of liberal knowledge in the University: ". . . if a healthy body is a good in itself, why is not a healthy intellect?" Nor would Newman for his part deny that even a university education has a valence of utility. "If then a practical end must be assigned to a University course, I say it is that of training good members of society."[14] The two positions are easily enough reconciled provided one does not equate the practical with the purely utilitarian and does distinguish between the overall purpose of education in general and the specific purpose of such distinctive institutions as the liberal arts college or the university. After all, not every one who cultivates the pragmatic function of intelligence subscribes also to that technical form of pragmatism which is identified with relativism in epistemology and ethics and skepticism in natural theology. Nor is every philosopher who values experience automatically an empiricist after the model of Lockean sensism. It can be asserted of Americans, therefore, that they favor an instrumentalistic emphasis and, at the same time, do cherish, as D. W. Brogan once observed, "absolutes in Ethics. They believe that good is good, even if they quarrel over what, in the circumstances *is* good."[15]

The pragmatic strain, however, arouses uneasiness in many quarters. Mark Pattison, a contemporary and acquaintance of Newman, wrote confidently: "Though a useful and practical life may be the end of education, yet . . . the perfection of education consists in the perfection and enlargement of the intellect *per se*."[16] Any indifference to this spirit alarms some people particularly if they suspect that it is joined to the sort of ethical intention that prompted the sixteenth-century Jesuits to put moral excellence ahead of intellectual excellence or Dewey to insist that all knowledge must become a true motive force of conduct. Toward the close of the 1950's, after the surprise of the first Russian sputnik, those who envisioned the school as solely ordered to intellectual development began to get a much better press and to enlist in their ranks people of all sorts, from journalists to college presidents. The older formulation which inclined to put the academic and guidance functions of the school on a nearly equal plane lost some of its appeal.

Among Christian educators there has been for some decades a subtle shift in this whole matter of formulating aims. It is now generally recognized that Newman's concept of an institution whose chief purpose is the expansion of intellectual power provides a necessary and valuable clarification. It does not effect a displacement of the general moral aim of education taken in its wide sense nor a rejection of practical concerns. But it does lead to a wiser appreciation of intellectual growth as a major value in itself and one whose achievement helps fulfill the divine intention by bringing part of creation out of chaos into light. A cultivated intelligence, for instance, contributes to the civilization of character although it is not the same thing as moral virtue. There is a significant difference between knowing chemistry or theology, on the one hand, and supplanting egoism with altruism on the other. Most people would doubtless agree that it is better to be kind than to be erudite. It does not follow, however, that there is small value in erudition. Today, in fact, religious people are more aware, than certain of their predecessors were, that the advancement of knowledge and the maturation of intelligence are themselves a cooperation with the design of Providence quite apart from their ethical and practical values. Institutions which engage in these pursuits find their just and noble rationale in the very nature of that work.

The Christian who argues this position accepts the notion and the reality of intermediate ends. These are goals, as was indicated in the first chapter, which may be ultimate within their own dimension, as the advancement of scientific knowledge is ultimate for the physicist precisely as a physicist, and yet clothed also with an instrumental character when viewed within the total context of life and being. The progress of scientific research, for instance, makes the life of man more rational or at least is capable of doing so. It cultivates that natural soil upon which the action of grace falls and thereby contributes to the eventual coming of the Kingdom of God by disposing men, in some measure, for its reception.

Yet although it is entirely possible to harmonize a concern for intellectual growth with an insistence on the primacy of character formation by invoking this distinction between ultimate and intermediate ends, still it must be granted that there is at least a difference in temperament between those who usually think of education in its broadest range and those who think particularly of the proper and partial purposes of a school. All the great educational theorists would agree with Aristotle that one of the supreme aims of education is to bring to majestic fruition man's potentiality for a rational life, for the exercise of intelligence on the problems of existence itself. Many would agree, too, that this potentiality is the distinctive human quality.

They would not, however, all agree that intellectual virtue is, here and now from every point of view, the highest and best human achievement and that man attains his distinctive human purpose in this sort of fulfillment—that he is made to know and that in this life to know is to be both happy and good. For a number of such theorists, pragmatists as well as Christians, the power of intellectual contemplation, of inquiry and of skill at problem-solving is itself ordered to the responsible exercise of freedom in the interests of the personal and the common good. Pius XI, for instance, certainly esteemed scholarship but his instrumental emphasis is congenial to the American spirit when he observes in the encyclical on education: "Since however the younger generation must be trained in the arts and sciences for the advantage and prosperity of civil society, and since the family of itself is unequal to this task, it was necessary to create that social institution, the school."[17]

In the United States there goes along with the pragmatic outlook a correlative strain of futurism since any instrument or tool naturally looks beyond itself to the work to be done and the product to be achieved. For a century and a half, visitors from abroad have been putting down as typically American this enthusiastic concern for the future.[18] A glance over the world today, however, will keep anyone from concluding that this trait is uniquely American. From China and India to the new African states and the booming economies of Europe a busy dedication to the building of tomorrow is everywhere dominant. But it has, in any event, always been a characteristic of Crèvecoeur's "new man," the American, and it naturally conditions his approach to education. Henry Ford did not really speak for many of his fellow Americans when he judged history to be bunk. Americans are actually very interested in the past, not only their national past but that of Europe, ancestral home of most of them. But they would also ratify the inscription on a statue before the entrance to the National Archives in Washington: "What is Past is Prologue." The American prefers to face forward and so, for that matter, does the Christian.[19]

It must be admitted, by way of a coda, that these positive features of the American faith in education have their corresponding dangers which are the obverse side of the coin. Moral zeal uncompanioned by the wisdom of prudence and a rational grasp of the bases of morality easily veers to a vicious extreme. A wide-visioned instrumentalism can decline to a narrow and even materialistic utilitarianism. The ideal of re-

sponsible citizenship with its implication of rational conformity to just
law and sound standards can be perverted into conformity in the miserable sense of a timid or slothful acquiescence in the thoughtless patterns
of the crowd. License can masquerade as freedom and indifference pretend to be tolerance. A sense of self-righteousness can insinuate itself
into the place of earnest striving for true morality and an enthusiasm
for virtue can be confused with its actual possession. The ideal of individual excellence can be submerged in a fury of socialization just as
social maturity and accountability can be weakened by a destructive emphasis on individualism and intellectual or material self-aggrandizement.
The faith in education can degenerate into a fideism which trusts in the
magical effect of a mere passive passage through twelve or sixteen years
of schooling. Even religion itself can be corrupted by religiosity, superstition and self-interest.

All this is true enough but hardly news to the realistic Christian
educator who knows that a challenge always involves some risk and
that his task is not so much the deploring of evils as the laying hold of
"All that rings true, all that commands reverence and all that makes for
right; all that is lovely, all that is gracious in the telling; virtue and merit,
wherever virtue and merit are found," (Philippians 4: 8–9). These verses,
in fact are the theme of the Christian humanist who hopes that education
will contribute to making persons both authentically human and authentically Christian. But that is a large goal which supposes that one
understands not only what a school requires if it is to be a school at all
but what it also requires if it is to be a Christian school. Concluding re-
flections upon this latter formality are, therefore, in place.

Characteristics Flowing from the Nature of Christian Education

As a religious order within the Catholic Church the Society of Jesus
receives not only its existence but its particular vocation from that
Church. In the final analysis, therefore, it conducts schools because the
Church wishes it to do so and has delegated to it and many other orders
and congregations a share in this task. The Church, in turn, promotes
schools because teaching is integral to its work of making all men holy. It
has always been conscious of this teaching mission but the full range of
that mission has emerged only gradually as the course of history stimulates an ever deeper awareness of the virtualities in the Church's divine
commission to educate. In a world of national lay states the Church has
exercised its right to teach not only religion but every manner of secular

subject in schools of its own and it has tenaciously defended the freedom to do so, whenever this has been assaulted. A classic formulation of this defense was made by Pius XI in the encyclical letter, *Divini Illius Magistri* which appeared on the last day of 1929. The passage in question is preceded by a brief statement of the Church's double title to education—the title based upon the direct teaching assignment received from our Lord Himself (Matt. 28: 18–20) and the title rooted in the very nature of the Church's responsibility for the nurture of those whom it has regenerated through Christian Baptism and who stand to it now as children to their supernatural mother. After these observations, the Pope indicates the freedom and scope claimed by the Church for her work of education.

> . . . the Church is independent of any sort of earthly power as well in the origin as in the exercise of her mission as educator, not merely in regard to her proper end and object, but also in regard to the means necessary and suitable to attain that end. Hence with regard to every other kind of human learning and instruction, which is the common patrimony of individuals and society, the Church has an independent right to make use of it, and above all to decide what may help or harm Christian education. And this must be so, because the Church as a perfect society has an independent right to the means conducive to its end, and because every form of instruction, no less than every human action, has a necessary connection with man's last end, and therefore cannot be withdrawn from the dictates of the Divine law, of which the Church is infallible guardian, interpreter and teacher . . . Therefore with full right the Church promotes letters, science, art, insofar as necessary or helpful to Christian education, in addition to her work for the salvation of souls; founding and maintaining schools and institutions adapted to every branch of learning and degree of culture. Nor may even physical culture, as it is called, be considered outside the range of her maternal supervision, for the reason that it also is a means which may help or harm Christian education.[20]

The Church, in short, wants Christian schools and wants them because in order to be a Christian one must first be a man and the more fully human a man is, the more perfectly Christian he can be. "By the perfect Christian," said Pius XI's immediate successor, Pius XII, "We mean the Christian of today, child of his own era, knowing and cultivating all the advances made by science and technical skill; a citizen and not something apart from the life led in his own country today."[21]

These comments, endowed as they are with a special weight because of their source, direct our attention to certain essential features of any Christian school and therefore of any Jesuit school since the basic inspiration of such a school is Christian just as the fundamental spirit of the Society or any Religious Institute must be that of the Church. Nadal once remarked that Ignatius was not accustomed to speak of the "Spirit of the Society," but rather of its *modus procedendi,* the Society's characteristic manner of action. The spirit must be Catholic; the procedures it animates may have a color and tone of their own.[22]

In the first place, then, a Jesuit school has an optimistic belief in the possibility of what is nowadays called a Christian Humanism. This faith is certainly tempered by a realistic awareness of man's natural infirmities and the historic record of grief and terror which has flowed from them. Nevertheless, this measured optimism (or hopeful pessimism) supports a conviction that the ideal of culture joined to holiness is viable. Pius XII often formulated this conviction and his remarks to an International Congress of Humanistic Studies in 1949 are simply representative. "The Church has affirmed the value of what is human and what is in conformity with nature. Without any hesitation she has sought to develop it and place it in evidence. She does not admit that in the sight of God man is mere corruption and sin. On the contrary, in the eyes of the Church Original Sin did not intimately affect man's aptitudes and strength and has left essentially intact the natural light of his intelligence and freedom."[23] It follows, since the achievements of science and technology, art and philosophy, politics and exploration as well as the maturation of intelligence and freedom are human values, that the Church esteems and promotes them.

No doubt there have been and still are certain sincere, even saintly Christians temperamentally inclined to depreciate human culture either because their personal need is for extreme abnegation rather than for a consecrated employment of these terrestrial fruits or because their passionate preoccupation with the divine reality which this world so inadequately symbolizes absorbs all their energies. A St. Peter Damian in the eleventh century speaks for these fervent but one-sided spirits, whatever their century:

> I spurn Plato, the searcher into the hidden things of nature, who set a measure to the movements of the planets, and calculated the courses of the stars; Pythagoras, who divided the round world into its regions with his mathematician's rod, means nothing to me; I renounce the much-thumbed books of Nichomachus, and Euclid too, round-shouldered from poring over his complex geometrical problems . . . What are the inventions of crazy poets to me? What do I

care for the melodramatic adventures of pompous tragedians? . . .
The Ciceronians shall not sway me with their smooth speech, nor
the followers of Demosthenes convince me by skilled argument or
captious persuasion. Back to your shades, you whom worldly wisdom has defiled! Those blinded by the sulphurous flames of the
teachings of darkness can give me nothing. Let the simplicity of
Christ instruct me, and the true humility of the wise loose me from
the chains of doubt. . . . Teach me that of which the unskilled
throng of dialecticians knows nothing; let wise folly tell me that
which foolish wisdom cannot understand.[24]

The fulness of the Christian tradition, however, is more accurately
voiced in the mild words of the second century martyr, Justin: "The
truths which men in all lands have rightly spoken belong to us Christians."[25] This theme was elaborated by Pius XI, himself both a former director of the Vatican Library and an ardent Alpinist who represented
neither the obscurantism of Peter Damian nor the worldly humanism of
his own Renaissance predecessor, Aeneas Silvius. In the 1931 Apostolic
Constitution on Universities and Faculties of Ecclesiastical Studies, Pius
XI comments that since faith and reason are not only unopposed but harmonious and mutually beneficial, "the Church has always considered it
her duty to assist and promote the cultivation of human arts and disciplines." In support of this thesis, he introduces a rapid review of history
from the great third-century schools, which made of their students both
theologians and civilized men, through the dark ninth century when the
Councils of Rome continued to foster the study of liberal arts and missionaries went into the wilderness to humanize it "by the Cross and by
the plow," to the medieval era of the university's origins and thence
down to recent times. The Pope's conclusion is that the Church fears
neither persecutors nor heretics but only an ignorance of truth.[26]

But if the Church has this sanguine esteem for the forces that genuinely humanize man, yet it is also true that her concern for the work of
schools and teaching is an instrumental one. This point has already been
noted and is inescapable. Since the intention of the Incarnation was to re-
deem men by sanctifying them, the teaching mission of the Church
serves this purpose at every level of its operation. That purpose itself, as
Newman observed in the first of the Parochial and Plain Sermons, "is declared in one form or other in every part of the Scripture. It is told us
again and again, that to make sinful creatures holy was the great end
which our Lord had in view in taking upon Him our nature, and thus
none but the holy will be accepted for His sake at the last day."[27] It is
hardly surprising then, that Pius XI should have defined the proper and

immediate aim of Christian education as cooperation with Divine grace in forming the true and perfect Christian who is, "to use the current term, the true and finished man of character."[28]

No one can consider this a denial of the school's primary dedication, at least at its higher levels, to the specific work of enlarging and enriching intelligence unless he first rejects the distinctions previously noted. For to distinguish sanctity and wisdom is not to deny their reciprocal relationship nor their unity in the living person. To put holiness in first place does not mean a preference for barbarism, if for no other reason than that savagery does not dispose to sanctity. To give primacy to the moral aim is not to make it exclusive. To focus upon the overarching general purpose of all education is not to deny the proximate end secured through the school. Indeed, the work of the school becomes fully intelligible only when it is seen within this wider framework of integral education. As a matter of fact, the conflict between the Christian educator and his critics stems from the fact that they too wish to make men good. But since a scientific humanist or a totalitarian nationalist has his own concept of goodness and his own ethical idealism with its quasi-religious aura, his disagreement with the Christian is passionate and irreconcilable. So true is this that a Christian educator's task of sharing fully the life of his country and his time will become more delicate and difficult if much of that life is dominated by these hostile ideologies with their vexing commingling of truth and error.

For the Christian has, of course, his own distinctive explanation of life's meaning and purpose. This insight afforded by religious faith is the central contribution of revelation to his theory of education. If it were ever possible for a school to prepare people for life in the sense of providing them with all the knowledge they would need and with behavioral reactions equal to any future moral demands, it is scarcely possible now. Much of what is learned in school today is obsolete by the time one reaches middle age and genuine ethical and religious maturity is required for contending with the novel tensions of a civilization marked by radical change and crisis. The maximal possibility and minimal necessity is twofold. On the one hand, young persons must acquire the tools for continuing their own education. On the other, they need a personal realization of that religious interpretation of human life and history which will stabilize them amid vicissitude and also provide those firm value standards which preserve men from subjectivism in their use of freedom without diminishing their creative response to human problems. Thus armed they may with grace achieve in their own persons a living synthesis of all that is best in the teeming flow of experience.

Without this grasp of encompassing goals, dynamic yet unshakeable, a coherent philosophy of life and hence of education is hardly possible for there cannot be order without a rational organization of means to an end clearly seen. Christianity, of course, is not the only system to provide a world-view but the Christian school believes that the vision it serves is the only adequate one.[29]

Left to itself humanism inclines to narcissism and Christianity gives it what it needs—the form, the force, the direction provided by a sense of purpose which gathers human energies up and focuses them beyond themselves not upon an abstract ideal but upon a Person in whom all that is valid in any ideal is perfectly realized. This may seem general enough but a full-fledged study of Christian education would draw out its detail and application. When this work of elaboration is accomplished, certain nuclear themes or emphases will order the heap of individual items which constitute the daily school experience even as bits of tile compose a mosaic. The Christian position will, for instance, appear as everywhere a center position because it will aim at synthesizing what is valuable in the extremes of right and left. Thinking of the human person as a vital and dynamic composite of body and spirit it will reject the unilateral stress both of materialism and angelism. There will be neither a Buddhistic negation nor a naturalistic idolatry of nature; neither a contempt for human powers nor an excessive confidence in them.

The summit of human life will be fixed, indeed, in that central relationship of love between God and man. Since this love flowers from the reciprocal operations of mind and will, one may say that the human person appears as supremely himself in these spiritual activities. At the same time, this vocation to affective union with God characteristically employs the full human register of corporeality and sociality for its realization. Love manifests itself in the bodily word and gesture and validates itself pre-eminently in a social context. "For he who loves his neighbor has fulfilled the Law." (Rom. 13:8). Or as St. Thérèse of Lisieux put it: "We only love God in so far as we practise love of our neighbor."[30] John Dewey once called education the art of "giving shape to human powers and adapting them to social service" and although his perspective was strictly temporal and his language rather gray one finds here a certain affinity with a Christian ideal.[31] For that love of God which is the core of Christian life is pre-eminently embodied in an altruism which is indeed a "social service."

The composite nature of man is verified not only in his purest religious aspirations but also, to take another instance, very typically in that manual work which is so distinctively human. If men require a social and material milieu in which to incarnate their faith and love they also need these for sustaining their life through a labor which employs together the head, the heart and the hand. So the farmer wills to actualize the plan he has conceived and out of an acre of underbrush he makes a garden. Conscious of this human composition, a Christian education will avoid alike the extreme of an intellectualism which scorns the creativity of work and generous fellowship and a utilitarianism which ignores the spirit's aspiration for pure wisdom. It will not pretend that it is easy to break out of our individual solitude nor deny that much work is toil and that lethargy, sloth and limitations of talent always make intellectual growth partial and painful. But neither will it settle for something less than a truly human growth, at least as an ideal, simply because this is difficult to achieve. The Christian, as Père de Lubac observes, must avoid both the mystical or celestial illusion and the positivist or terrestrial illusion. "We do not want a spiritual life in a dream-world, nor an eternity which is not prepared for us by time. But neither do we want a closed humanism, an 'inhuman humanism.' 'Nothing but the earth' is the cruellest of all illusions."[32]

A Christian pedagogical creed contains therefore a number of affirmations which are as invigorating as they are formidable. Most of them have already been suggested and in the chapters to follow we shall summarize some of the specific objectives and procedures that have been subsumed under these articles in one tradition of school practice. There is, to begin with, the central esteem for the reality and value of the human personality. There goes along with this a recognition of the fact that the human person, by reason both of his nature and his actual situation, is a combination of contrasts and tensions between matter and spirit, individuality and sociality, the aspiration for the good and liability to sin and error. In the two chief phases of formal education, therefore, there is a correlative acknowledgement of strength and limitation. In intellectual education, the Christian teacher asserts the splendor of the human mind without worshipping it. He defends a realistic view of knowledge for he believes that he can indeed know things as they are but he is not a rationalist for he does not think he can know all things or even any one thing exhaustively. In his work of moral guidance, the Christian teacher acknowledges man's aspirations for holiness and his physical capacity to avoid evil while confessing at the same time the moral incapacity, apart from grace, for a sustained fidelity.[33]

Upon this belief in the worth of human personality, Christian education grounds its dedication to culture and wisdom and the full exercise of intelligence. The Christian teacher and his students ought logically to welcome all the values of philosophy, art, science and technological achievement while their theological insight discovers for them the design which unifies this brilliant manifold.

Finally, the Christian educator esteems human freedom and, if he is true to his own ideals, he will always seek to nourish it, mindful of the words of St. Paul: "You have been called to liberty, brethren" (Gal. 5: 13). Human persons are summoned to elect a love of God steadfast enough to bring them at last to direct and eternal confrontation and union. But such a vocation and goal presuppose not only consciousness but freedom, since choice and love are impossible without liberty. And because freedom requires the guidance of intelligence, the Christian teacher has here an additional reason for valuing intellectual formation as well as discipline in the orderly practice of liberty so that love may be embodied in service.

These orientations provide a foundation for all Christian schools and beyond them there is little that is common everywhere at every time. To put them down is not, of course, to claim that Christian schools always achieve these ideals to any definitive extent but simply that these are the ideals. The pages which follow summarize the fashion in which one educational tradition has tried to translate these great commitments into practice, into the choices, accents and nuances characteristic of its school work.

NOTES: CHAPTER IV

1. Pius XII, "To the Union of Italian Teachers," Text of an Address, September 4, 1949, *The Catholic Mind,* 48 (September, 1950), 572.
2. Pius XI, "Christian Education of Youth," *The Catholic Mind,* 28 (February, 1930), 63. This celebrated encyclical, often referred to in the customary fashion by its opening words, *Divini Illius Magistri,* was issued on December 31, 1929 and is available in a number of pamphlet editions. These later editions make a few verbal corrections in the earliest English version and these are incorporated here without further note.
3. This is a fact commonly observed by educational theoreticians in every tradition, from the pragmatic to the scholastic, although not infrequently overlooked outside their ranks. It is put succinctly, for instance, by Christopher Dawson, *Understanding Europe* (New York: Sheed and Ward, 1952), p. 292: "Taken in its widest sense education is simply the process by which the new members of a community are initiated into its ways of life and thought from the simplest elements of behavior or manners up to the highest tradition of spiritual wisdom."
4. In the *Republic,* Plato's theory of education is set, as Nettleship observed, in the wider context of his search for the nature of the morally

good life and Jaeger remarks that for the Socratic-Platonic tradition, the religious duty of caring for one's soul is the central educational concern. See Richard Lewis Nettleship, "The Theory of Education in Plato's *Republic*," *Hellenica: A Collection of Essays on Greek Poetry, Philosophy, History and Religion,* ed. by Evelyn Abbott (2nd ed.; London: Longmans, Green, 1913), pp. 61 ff. and Werner Jaeger, *Paideia: The Ideals of Greek Culture,* trans. Gilbert Highet (New York: Oxford University Press, 1943) II, 39, 376 n. 65. The Greek and Roman exponents of the popular rhetorical culture shared this conviction of the primacy of the moral aim. Isocrates subscribes to it and Quintilian, in the classic definition of the orator which he had from Cato, *vir bonus dicendi peritus,* sums up the thesis that only the good man can be truly eloquent. He further concludes that, if one must choose, it is better to be good than to be gifted. See Aubrey Gwynn, S.J., *Roman Education: From Cicero to Quintilian* (Oxford: At the Clarendon Press, 1926), pp. 230 ff. The theme is, of course, commonplace among Christian educators, whether Catholic or Protestant. Writing of Sturm, the sixteenth-century Lutheran schoolman, Bolgar says: "In his eyes, as in the eyes of all the great Protestant educators of the period, a teacher's first duty was to inculcate sound religious and moral principles. Once this Christian outlook had been firmly established, it was then to be bolstered by carefully selected material drawn from the classics, and the arts of expression were to be very fully taught. Since Latin was the learned language of the time, that meant the detailed teaching of Latin." *The Classical Heritage and Its Beneficiaries, op. cit.,* p. 350. In the *Émile,* Jean Jacques's general purpose is seen to be the bringing up of his charge in such wise as to keep his "heart from vice and from the spirit of error." For John Dewey, problems of human conduct are the central problems of life and he makes the education of intelligence instrumental to character formation as when he argues in *Moral Principles in Education* (Boston: Houghton Mifflin Company, 1909), p. 2, that the chief business of the teacher is to see to it that the greatest possible number of ideas acquired by young people are so acquired as to become true motive forces of conduct. To make moral formation the prime educational goal is not to make it the only aim or to deny that particular institutions may have as their chief purpose one of the intermediate goals—the school may have a primarily academic function and the gymnasium be chiefly concerned with physical development.

5. Edmund J. King, *Other Schools and Ours* (New York: Rinehart, 1958), p. 9. Relevant here is an observation of Tad Guzie, S.J., *The Analogy of Learning: An Essay Toward a Thomistic Psychology of Learning* (New York: Sheed and Ward, 1960), p. 18 n. 2: "St. Thomas, too, uses the word *educatio* (to my knowledge) only in reference to the 'education' of a child to a proper moral character."

6. Both these documents are in the *Mon. Paed., op. cit.,* For Nadal's remark, see p. 89 and for Ledesma's, p. 299. Farrell, *The Jesuit Code of Liberal Education, op. cit.,* has full analyses of these treatises.

7. In the previously mentioned "Instruction" drawn up for the educational

work of the American Jesuits and approved by the Father General John Baptist Janssens in 1948, the general aim of this educational endeavor is thus formulated (using the consecrated expressions of the *Constitutions*): ". . . To bring our neighbor to the knowledge and love of God. Our first care, therefore, must be to see that our students acquire, along with learning, the moral virtues worthy of a Christian and in all our schools the moral and religious instruction of the students according to the Church's principles and directives must hold first place." *Instructio Pro Assistentia Americae de Ordinandis Universitatibus, Collegiis, ac Scholis Altis et de Praeparandis Eorundem Magistris, op. cit.,* p. 13. It may be noted, however, that all the major disciplines, languages, mathematics, science and social studies actually receive a larger share of class time than do the courses in religion or theology.

8. Quoted in Ellwood P. Cubberley, *Public Education in the United States* (rev. ed.; Boston: Houghton Mifflin Company, 1934), p. 90.

9. David Riesman, "The Influence of Student Culture and Faculty Values in the American College," in G. Z. F. Bereday and Joseph A. Lauwerys (eds.), *Higher Education: The Year Book of Education 1959* (Yonkers-on-Hudson: World Book Company, 1959), p. 389. Riesman is here commenting on Philip E. Jacob's *Changing Values in College* which summarizes many of the surveys and studies made on the question of the moral impact of the collegiate years.

10. See chapter II, note 29.

11. Quoted in Cubberley, *op. cit.,* p. 265.

12. The phrase is found in quite a different context, in a review by the psychologist, John Dollard, of *The Ineffective Soldier* in *The New York Times Book Review,* June 21, 1959, p. 1.

13. Dwight D. Eisenhower quoted in *The New York Times,* May 15, 1959, p. 14. The remark was made in a speech at a symposium held in New York City on May 14, 1959.

14. John Henry Cardinal Newman, *The Idea of a University: Defined and Illustrated* (New York: Longmans, Green and Company, 1925), pp. 162, 177.

15. D. W. Brogan, *The American Character* (New York: Alfred A. Knopf, 1944), pp. 131–32.

16. Mark Pattison, *Essays* (Oxford, 1889), I, 432, quoted here from Henry Tristram (ed.), *The Idea of a Liberal Education: A selection from the Works of Newman* (London: George G. Harrap, 1952), p. 210.

17. Pius XI, "Christian Education of Youth," *The Catholic Mind, op. cit.,* p. 83.

18. The American vision of the golden future is suggested, for instance, by the motto on the Great Seal, reproduced on every dollar bill: *Novus Ordo Seclorum.*

19. Observers from other countries believe that the ideals of American life and education are not simple mirages. Julian Marias, a Spaniard, writes: "In the United States . . . is a way of life that is clearly defined by virtue of having a definite *form,* that is to say, by being channeled into a system of solid and effective norms that do not impede movement and change, but on the contrary permit them, just as the river bed is what

makes possible the rapid flow of the waters. These norms result in a
general moral level that is not surprising if one has any appreciation of
the basic conditions requisite for effective coexistence: kindness taken
for granted, at least relative love for one's fellow man, pleasure in dealing with him, a predisposition toward benevolence, infrequency of
envy to a degree that it is possible to live without taking it into account
(although, as is obvious, it *also* exists here, as do the rest of the sins and
defects of this world); mutual confidence, veracity, and understanding.
And finally those things that are at one and the same time the basis and
consequence of all this: the primacy of the private over public life,
limited preoccupation with politics, widespread good health and well-
being—not only economically but in everyday life—and participation
in a gigantic historical enterprise of which the Americans, without too
much or perhaps even enough rhetoric, are more or less cognizant."
"From Spain," in Franz M. Joseph (ed.), *As Others See Us: The United
States Through Foreign Eyes* (Princeton: Princeton University Press,
1959), p. 28.

20. Pius XI, "Christian Education of Youth," *The Catholic Mind, op. cit.,*
pp. 65–66.
21. See n. 1, *supra.* Some sentences of a distinguished Catholic scholar
sum up the points made in our text here: "The Church . . . never aimed
to teach for the sake of teaching. The true aim of the Church has always been to *educate,* and, more precisely, to educate men in view of
their eternal salvation. Naturally, since teaching is part and parcel of
all education, the Church has always had to teach. Even today, when
missionaries set up a chapel, they open a school at the same time. The
reason for this is simple enough. Before making Christians, missionaries
have to make men . . . Yet when all is said and done, the main-spring
of this tremendous teaching activity has always been the will to save as
many souls as possible. In short, the teaching work of the Church has
always been subservient to a higher aim, namely Christian education."
Etienne Gilson, *The Breakdown of Morals and Christian Education*
(Toronto: St. Michael's College, 1952). The passage in question is on
the tenth of the unnumbered pages of this booklet.
22. "Unde P. noster Ignatius non solebat dicere: spiritus Societatis, sed
modus Societatis procedendi," This is from the *Ordo Studiorum* which
Father Farrell believes must have been drawn up by Nadal in 1565
when he was rector of the Roman College. *Mon. Paed., op. cit.,* p. 125.
23. Pius XII, "On Humanism," An Address to members of the International
Convention of Humanistic Studies, September 25, 1949, *The Catholic
Mind,* 48 (May, 1950), 317. The Pope prefaced the remarks quoted
here with the acknowledgement that there had been in the Church, at
various periods, "fleeting opinions" of an anti-humanistic sort but suggested that these are not to be taken into account in looking for the
true mind of the Church.
24. St. Peter Damian, "The Book of 'The Lord Be With You'," chapter 1,
quoted here from *St. Peter Damian: Selected Writings on the Spiritual
Life,* trans. by Patricia McNulty (New York: Harper and Brothers,
1959), pp. 54–55.

25. Justin Martyr, *Apol.,* II, 13. The quoted sentence from this Second
    Apology is found in *Writings of Saint Justin Martyr,* trans. by Thomas
    B. Falls as one in the series, "The Fathers of the Church," (New
    York: Christian Heritage, Inc., 1948), pp. 133–34.
26. Pius XI, *Deus Scientiarum Dominus, Acta Apostolicae Sedis,* 23 (July,
    1931), 241, 244–45.
27. John Henry Newman, "Holiness Necessary for Future Blessedness,"
    Parochial and Plain Sermons (London: Rivingtons, 1882), I, 1.
28. Pius XI, "Christian Education of Youth," *The Catholic Mind, op. cit.,*
    p. 89.
29. The importance of some objective and inclusive framework within
    which to view life and pursue its aims was effectively put by a person
    working with a British committee studying the concept of Christian
    education: ". . . the people whom I meet in the suburbs of the great
    city in which I work, even the products of grammar school fifth forms,
    show some very real deficiencies: an incapacity for objective reasoning;
    a reliance on three basic principles: 'What I like is beautiful; what I
    think is right; what I do is good'; an incapacity for awe or reverence
    before the natural world or before persons; an inability to relax, to
    have leisure in the Biblical sense of 'being still,' or to reflect upon
    their lives; and an incapacity for creative suffering, despite much pain
    and anxiety. The people who are most likely to get 'lit up' are those
    who have a firm hold on some 'end' of man—whether Marxist, Chris-
    tian or other." Quoted in W. R. Niblett, *Christian Education in a Sec-
    ular Society* (London: Oxford University Press, 1960), p. 15.
30. Quoted here from Hans Urs von Balthasar, *Thérèse of Lisieux,* trans.
    Donald Nicholl (New York: Sheed and Ward, 1954), p. 4.
31. John Dewey, "My Pedagogic Creed," first published in 1897 and re-
    printed in *Education Today* (New York: C. P. Putnam's Sons, 1940),
    p. 16. Another characteristic formulation of this dominant ethical con-
    cern is found in Dewey's argument that education should provide stu-
    dents with an "opportunity to shift the center of ethical gravity from
    an absorption which is selfish to a service which is social." *Ethical
    Principles Underlying Education* (Chicago: The University of Chicago
    Press, 1903), p. 17. It is difficult not to see in such passages the influence
    of Dewey's early religious upbringing in a devout Protestant household.
    For a study of the effects of this upbringing on the thought of his first
    professional years see the essay by John Blewett, S.J., "Democracy as
    Religion: Unity in Human Relations," in the volume edited by Father
    Blewett, *John Dewey: His Thought and Influence* (New York: Ford-
    ham University Press, 1960), pp. 35–58.
32. Henri de Lubac, *The Discovery of God,* trans. Alexander Dru (New
    York: P. J. Kenedy and Sons, 1960), p. 179.
33. This paragraph owes a great deal to the wonderfully rich little book of
    Peter Lippert, S.J., *The Essence of the Catholic* (New York: P. J.
    Kenedy and Sons, 1930). This is an anonymous translation of three lec-
    tures delivered to Catholic students at Heidelberg in 1922.

PART TWO

THE CONTENT OF THE IDEA

CHAPTER V

THE EDUCATION OF INTELLIGENCE

*Through the merits of Jesus Christ, Thy Son, do
Thou grant us most merciful Father the grace of
Thy Holy Spirit so that our minds may now be
enlightened by these liberal studies which henceforth we may employ for Thy honor and for the
benefit of Thy Church and ourselves.*

Prayer before Class in
Sixteenth Century Jesuit
Schools of France[1]

On the threshold of the *Ratio* of 1586 it is laid down that the Society of Jesus must be fortified by two chief supports: an ardent zeal for
holiness and genuine learning. Everything in the *Constitutions* pivots
upon these foundations, this Preface observes, because piety which is
not companioned by learning is almost useless for the service of God
and one's fellow man.* Nor is it enough to have a smattering of erudition. It is excellence that is required according to the authors of the
document who thus anticipate by four centuries a popular academic
cliché: *doctrinam, non vulgarem illam, sed excellentem quandam desi-
derant.*[2] We should naturally expect, therefore, that a community in-
vigorated by this twin concern would have some distinctive convictions
about the pursuit both of virtue and of wisdom, about the education of
intelligence and of character. In these three final chapters we hope to
disengage those convictions from the somewhat distracting matrix of
rules which form the surface of the *Constitutions* and the *Ratio*.

---

* It should, perhaps, be noted that the Latin *pietas* has no implication of
pietism or anti-intellectual and affected devotion. It means fidelity in thought
and action to all the obligations flowing from one's most fundamental relationships—to parents and to country, for instance, and to God above all.

117

Guide Lines

This business of disengagement requires caution, discrimination and adaptation or transposition. It requires caution if we are to avoid reading our own notions into those laconic pages or deciding that a recommendation is valid simply because it agrees with one of our own or that it is perennial if it fits a contemporary problem. In the summer of 1961, the journalist William S. White wrote sharply about college youth and maintained that were he a trustee of some institution of higher learning he would put "a couple of additional courses into its curriculum. One of these would be instruction in manners."[3] Jesuit teachers recalling that the *Constitutions* insist upon students acquiring *Christianas costumbres*—the conduct worthy of a Christian—along with their letters will be inclined to see in White's article a contemporary echo of their own concern for humane behavior.[4] Good manners are not the whole of morality but they are the product of an altruistic conquest of egoism which is basic to morality and so they have been cultivated by all substantial educational traditions including the Jesuit. Father Manare's detailed rules cited in Chapter III were only one embodiment of this concern.

The modern reader who picks up a discussion of programmed instruction comes upon contemporary psychologists insisting that effective learning requires careful organization of subject matter into a logical sequence with small, discrete steps built deliberately one upon the other and freedom for the learner to progress through this sequence at his own rate with his learning responses immediately corrected when wrong and reinforced, perhaps by a reward, when right. The student of the *Ratio* finds all this remarkably familiar. He knows that the *Ratio* systematized the curriculum so that students might proceed securely from mastery of one element of Latinity to the next. He remembers that under this plan a student could be promoted as soon as he was ready for it and that the apparatus of the *concertatio* provided as vigorous a correction of error and reward for accuracy as does a boxing match in which one contestant fails to keep his guard up. The simplest form of *concertatio* found pupils paired off as rivals and able to score victories over one another by immediately correcting faulty responses to the teacher's questions. This "honest rivalry" is warmly recommended by the *Ratio* precisely because it was considered a great incentive to learning.[5]

These agreements, apparently so felicitous, need to be approached with some reserve. If you are looking for perennial elements in the Jesuit tradition, it is not a bad idea to search out the current problems for which that tradition has an answer. Questions that appear century after century probably point to issues which are universal and for which timeless principles would surely be desirable. Still, fashions change and if today you extol the graduated organization of discrete portions of subject matter as a characteristic of Jesuit education possessing perennial validity since it answers a contemporary question and squares with contemporary opinion, you may find that this opinion has changed by tomorrow and the whole question has evaporated. Rousseau thought that the ideal learning situation called for a one-to-one ratio of teacher to pupil. Dewey, on the contrary, believed that learning like life calls for a larger society than a twosome. The advocates of programmed instruction are currently praising "teaching machines" because they approximate that one-to-one ratio which is once again presumed to be ideal. It is wisest, perhaps, to conclude that when a thesis of sixteenth-century Jesuit educational theory fits the mood or the problem of our day this may indicate that it is an essential rather than accidental element but does not conclusively prove it.

In the second place, an inquiry into the fundamental Jesuit tradition calls for some discriminations. In the *Constitutions,* for instance, it is necessary to distinguish what is said about the education of Jesuit scholastics from what is recommended for schools open to the general public. Historically the academic program for lay students does seem to have been influenced by the program devised for scholastics if for no other reason than that there were, as Nadal noted, elements common to both.[6] Besides, the scholastics' program was designed before that of the externs. But this does not mean that the principles governing the first case can be directly applied to the second. The dominant aim in the education of scholastics was the pragmatic one of preparing apostles of Christianity. Naturally speaking, the two requisites of an effective apostle are knowledge of the doctrine he intends to expound and the ability to present it persuasively. The Jesuit *Constitutions* underscore both of these.[7] St. Ignatius proposed for the scholastics a curriculum which would particularly develop the arts of communication and a sound knowledge of theology. He himself was not interested so much in making scholars as in making effective preachers, although in subsequent generations the members of his Society would come to a clear appreciation of the natural and supernatural values of scholarship itself and its exercise in teaching and research. But in any case, recommendations for the making of a sixteenth-century preacher will not have much applicability to a twentieth-century American high school.

It is equally necessary to separate the permanent elements of

Jesuit practice and theory from the Renaissance setting in which they were at first encased. The Ignatian directives for students which advise them to take notes at lectures and to review the material afterwards with one another are certainly sound, although somewhat obvious, even if still easily forgotten by more than one listener slumped in his seat at a lecture.[8] What is most significant in these rules, however, is the basic conviction of which they are one expression, the conviction that students must activate themselves at all times. It may not be necessary, in a day when textbooks are common, to repeat a lecture with a classmate but the mutual intellectual give-and-take of students in discussion with one another is always to be encouraged. The general characteristics of the educated man, as St. Ignatius set them out in the Preamble to the Fourth Part of his *Constitutions,* add up to the portrait of a person who knows something and can use what he knows. This ideal is permanently valid, though it is no longer true that skill in Ciceronian Latin is a significant tool for the use of one's learning.

This sifting process must be applied both to procedures and objectives. The *Ratio,* we can say, aims at developing men of intellectual culture. Now this is a universally admirable goal but much too general to be meaningful. When the sixteenth-century editors of the *Ratio* went on to specify it they did so in the usual Renaissance terms of Latin eloquence.* The aim then became much more exact but lost its universality. It is a concept of culture which looks backward to certain mediterranean classics as absolute models of expression and it has less relevance for our own times when the dominant model of intellectual culture is that of a scientific learning which looks so far forward that today's textbooks are obsolescent almost as soon as they are published. Still it is true that admission to a good college currently requires good performance

---

* It should be noted that "perfect eloquence" had wide and admirable connotations for Renaissance educators. It was supposed that one necessarily developed character and intelligence in achieving this eloquence. Every age makes confident assertions of this sort for its favorite intellectual pursuit. Some of our contemporaries claim as much for science as the Renaissance did for rhetoric. C. P. Snow, for instance, has remarked: "The scientists I have known . . . have been in certain respects just perceptibly more morally admirable than most other groups of intelligent men." ("The Moral Un-Neutrality of Science," *Science,* 133 (1961), 256). A social scientist, George A. Lundberg, writes: "The unifying discipline of modern education lies in modern science . . . in the fields where it has been tried, science has superseded theology and philosophy as the acknowledged authority." (*Can Science Save Us?* New York: Longmans, Green, 1961, p. 75). These are not isolated instances.

on the verbal items of standardized examinations. It is therefore quite defensible to conclude that developing the arts of communication and *eloquentia perfecta* are still essential tasks of the secondary school even though the form and content of eloquence changes from epoch to epoch and nation to nation. Since good procedures, moreover, are procedures adapted to the end they serve, it is reasonable to suppose that methods devised by early Jesuit schools for securing that Renaissance aim of Latin culture will need to be carefully scrutinized and refined even when they are adopted today.

Finally, to repeat a theme rung often enough already, it must be remembered that even when objectives or procedures of the *Ratio* of 1599 are adopted they will probably need first to be adapted. Certain principles of sixteenth-century Jesuit education may be applied to our contemporary school actualities but they will usually require transposition into a new key. The Jesuit schools of the late Renaissance, like all schools of that era, not only accented Latin studies but did so for a purpose quite different from that commonly assigned to the classical curriculum today. They sought a facility in the actual use of Latin as a medium of communication in letters, speeches and even conversation.[9] That this was the purpose of Jesuits themselves in learning Latin is clearly indicated by one of the little essays in the *Ratio* of 1586. The six Fathers who wrote that page believed that all young Jesuits should have some experience teaching in secondary schools. For, they said, Latin is widely employed in all the apostolic ministries of the Society and a man can scarcely acquire real fluency in it unless he has at some time taught it. If he has never been master of a class in grammar or literature he may later make shocking blunders in pronunciation when he preaches Latin sermons or he may find himself tongue-tied when he has to converse with prelates from another country.[10] The lay students in the Jesuit colleges could not have entertained these precise aims but there was still a certain place for Latin skills in the professions and business towards which those sixteenth-century boys were straining. In the first Jesuit schools, then, the Latin if not the Greek authors, were read in order to acquire good style rather than for an understanding of that ancient world which was the source of so much of Europe's philosophical and political tradition. No doubt some information about classical civilization and history was introduced but only to supplement or facilitate the attainment of that primary objective.

The question of Latin's place in the curriculum of contemporary secondary schools, even of strictly academic ones, is so prickly as to have no fully satisfactory solution. But in any case, no one supposes that when

Latin is prescribed it is to be approached in the manner of a junior Foreign Service officer studying the language of a nation to which he is being freshly posted or a prospective tourist enrolling in a Berlitz class. In Jesuit high schools, Latin is not now usually taught either with a strictly functional aim or by predominantly direct methods. The textbooks are no longer written in Latin nor are the classes normally conducted in Latin. What is generally sought is a formal, analytic knowledge of the language marked by mastery of its basic generalized rules and patterns and mastery of the verbal forms most serviceable for reading a few selected authors. The reading knowledge aimed at has not generally been that of a sight reading but of a direct reading which has been prefaced by careful study and exercise in translation. This is not, of course, the only possible objective. One might aim at developing ability to gather meaning from a page of Latin without translation or analysis. One might emphasize a speaking knowledge within the limits of a small vocabulary or a study of classical culture based upon wide reading of Greek and Latin literature in translation. The formal approach, however, stresses the reading of a limited number of original texts accompanied by a good deal of written work, particularly in Latin composition. This orientation has generally characterized the Latin course of a Jesuit high school. In recent years, it has sometimes been modified in American schools by the introduction of methods that are characterized as "functional." But in this context the term "functional" does not mean teaching Latin so that it may function as a tool for daily living. What seems to be meant, rather, is an easing of access to the classical Latin texts by a gradual introduction to Latin grammar in which usages are presented in terms of their syntactical function rather than as abstract principles. To this there may also be joined some employment of the so-called "army method" of aural-oral language teaching through practice in easy Latin conversation and relatively wide reading of simple texts.

What is the purpose of the Latin course, howsoever it be taught? It is usually said that the study of Latin, if continued long enough—during all the four years of high school, for instance—and in such fashion that the necessary steps are mastered and there is no crippling recourse to "trots," will issue in certain habits developed by the intellectual discipline of the subject and in certain humanistic insights developed as students become acquainted with the psychology and politics of imperialism in Caesar, or with the themes of government and the citizens's responsibilities in Cicero's duel with Cataline, or with the themes of suffering and vocation as these are dramatized in the epic of Aeneas. These objectives have been sharply attacked, to be sure. Several decades ago, in fact, the very notion of mental discipline was judged a mischievous delusion. It is fair to say, however, that many contemporary psychologists would grant that given equally skillful teachers and equally favorable factors of motivation and milieu some subjects will develop intellectual skills more fully than others because they call more fully into play certain significant mental operations such as abstraction from particulars and subsequent generalizations toward universals. It would not ordinarily be claimed that the college student's intelligence is, for example, just as effectively enlarged by a survey of the history of education as by a stiff course in mathematical analysis or nuclear physics or epistemological theory provided the teaching is equally competent in all cases. The operations of perception, conception, discernment of relationships, inductive and deductive reasoning appear to be not only those chiefly required in the more significant areas of our lives but also to be better nourished by the more rigorous academic disciplines. If formal analytic language study is itself such a discipline, then one of the values claimed for it seems reasonably well established.[11]

Yet it is true that other subjects may be quite as effective at generating desirable intellectual habits and also more immediately relevant to the needs of our own time. The traditional humanist may counter this challenge by maintaining that the study of mankind through literature and philosophy is always more humanizing than the study of matter through the physical sciences and that, so far as classical studies are concerned, people of the West need to know something of that mediterranean civilization in which are the origins of much of the modern world, both East and West. A disillusioned teacher might then object that such wisdom is hardly acquired by painfully decoding a few Latin authors and that in the time allotted one could learn far more about our classical heritage through an ambitious program of reading in good translations. The defender of Latin retorts that in this case the intellectual habits supposedly elicited by formal Latin study will have been lost. The rest of the academic establishment then promptly offers to make sure that these very habits are developed through study of French, social science, chemistry, mathematics, modern literature or whatever discipline it may be that the speakers themselves favor.

There is no need to attempt a conciliation of the disputants in this matter since the purpose of reviewing the question here is simply to indicate that even if Latin is given a balanced position in a contemporary high school or college curriculum it will not be for exactly the reasons that won it a practical monopoly of the sixteenth-century school day. Its cultural potential as a humanizer of intelligence will be heavily under-

124 JESUIT EDUCATION

scored. The value of some first-hand acquaintance with that antiquity which partly created our own civilization will be more strongly emphasized. And given these changes in objectives certain correlative modifications in methodology will be expected. The principles of adaptation and transposition will clearly have been busily at work although they may have scarcely been recognized.

They are at work on even higher levels of generalization. The student of Jesuit education might, for instance, prescind altogether from the question of Latin and simply observe that what is truly essential in the Jesuit concept of secondary schooling is insistence on mastery of skillful communication or the development of mature style and that what is essential to the Jesuit concept of the liberal arts course is mastery of the habit of philosophical thought. But the Renaissance definition of both these matters was quite different from ours. For the sixteenth-century Jesuit pedagogues, good style was good Latin style and good Latin style was that which imitated Cicero as perfectly as possible—used his phrases in the way he used them and with the same rhythms. It was debated, in fact, whether one should employ the word *passio* since Cicero used only *perpessio*. But because *passio* was dear to Christians as the term designating Christ's redemptive suffering, Edmund Campion, the English Jesuit martyred under Elizabeth I, said that he would throw all of Cicero in the Tiber rather than surrender this word.[12] The modern objection to the Renaissance concept of style is more radical. Nowadays it is generally supposed that an adult writer will have sufficiently mastered his tools to use them in his own distinctive way. In his apprenticeship years, of course, he will have studied models, consciously or unconsciously, for everyone builds upon his predecessors. But the ideal toward which our embryonic rhetoricians work is not that of writing as much like Hemingway as possible. Second-raters may do this in fact but even they would not admit it since they too hold that the style is the man. All educated persons aim to speak and write correctly, of course, since they want to be heard but they wish also to speak with their own voice and intonation.

The concept of a philosophy course in the sixteenth century appears also to have embodied a distaste for the path of any individualism. A Jesuit teaching philosophy in the Roman College at that time sought to entice his auditors by telling them that the ancient thinkers had solved every philosophical problem and all that remained to be done was to gather in leisure the ripe fruits won by the industry of Greece.[13] As one reads the *Ratio's* prescriptions for the philosophy curriculum one finds that Aristotle is as dominant here as Cicero was in the middle school. Twentieth-century Jesuit philosophers certainly esteem the achievements of the Aristotelian-Thomistic tradition and would wish to have an exact familiarity with its sources. But they find odd indeed a concept of philosophy which supposes that all problems and solutions are two millenia past or which defines the philosopher's work as a literal rethinking of Aristotle's thought. They would judge it more important to emulate classical philosophy's spirit of profound and free inquiry than simply to master its conclusions. Even if one affirms, therefore, that the Jesuit secondary school aims to cultivate habits of style and that the Jesuit arts course aims to cultivate powers of reflective thought one must recognize that neither of these aims is specified today precisely as it would have been by the authors of the *Ratio*.

In summarizing the Jesuit tradition relevant to the education of intelligence we have first to recollect these guiding admonitions of caution, discrimination and adaptation. This done, we must review the response of that tradition to three basic questions. What are the school's broad intellectual aims? What does it propose to teach in order to achieve these aims? And how does it propose to teach the disciplines it has chosen? Under each of these headings, principles or recommendations are looked for which will be capable, at least after smelting the Renaissance ore, of transposition to any historical context. It will also be necessary to point out the aspects of the total school experience to which these principles do not extend or for which they are inadequate. In this connection it will be remembered that the integral theory of a Jesuit school includes a great deal more than the family accents under examination here and that the full Christian concept of education enfolds principles applicable to those many areas left untouched by the editors of the *Ratio* of 1599.

The Question of Aims

The most remarkable aspect of the discussion of objectives in the early Jesuit educational documents, the *Constitutions* and the *Ratio,* is that it is practically non-existent. A few broad focal values are summarily indicated and these are, of course, significant. Once they are enunciated, however, all subsequent attention is turned to matters of policy: school organization and procedures. This is also significant. It suggests that were twentieth-century Jesuit schoolmen to follow the example of their sixteenth-century predecessors they would be found devoting most of their time to consideration of ways and means, to the use of teaching machines and educational television, perhaps, or to innovations in class scheduling and experimentation with class size. At least the men of the sixteenth century appear to have felt that there was no great problem about recognizing ultimate objectives and that their real task was to devise means for securing those general goals universally esteemed.

In any case and for whatever reason, St. Ignatius and the authors of the *Ratio* certainly handled the issue of educational aims expeditiously. Some people today would applaud this procedure because they have themselves become impatient with lengthy discussions about the purpose of the school. There are a number of reasons for this discontent. For one thing, those discussions are often positively global. When people talk about the aims of education they are usually talking about the aim of human existence. For them, as for Socrates, it is really the quality of life that is under inquiry and if they complain about current objectives or call for new ones it is the quality of life at present which they are indicting. In the second place, just because the angle of vision is thus all-embracing, the aims of the school are multiplied in order to account for every value contributing to a fully human and satisfying life. If the statement of aims is not rich and even grandiose, it will not do justice to the vision of a complete human experience. On the other hand, the more vast and encompassing the charter of goals, the more stupefying it is and the more clearly impossible of realization.

The catalogue of a twentieth-century American Jesuit school or university will marshal a legion of aims even more dazzling than those lined up by public institutions since here the purpose is not merely to nurture a man of culture and a perfect citizen but a saint as well. "Jesuit education," says one high school bulletin quite typically, "seeks to develop every part of the human personality . . . to produce men whose minds have been liberated by a broad knowledge of various subjects . . . [with] the character to act reasonably in accord with . . . conviction . . . leaders, mature men who will lead the way in the future in religious, intellectual, and social activity." Yet it would be uninformed to criticize a statement of this kind for its exaltation and optimism. Nowadays both the American mind and that Christian inspiration which found voice in Pius XI's encyclical on education are convinced that educational goals must be thus spaciously conceived. It is as though men today realize that only such generous ideals adequately acknowledge the range of human potentiality and that only by shooting for the stars are they aiming at a worthy target.

Besides, these objectives, though vast and rather vague, are certainly unexceptional. What school administrator would ever admit that he was not ardently tracking after excellence? But by saying so much, these current statements may seem to say very little that is directly relevant to humdrum school realities and the case will be made worse if the prospectus is packaged in jargon. Consequently it is not surprising to find a Dr. Conant remarking:

> When someone writes or says that what we need today in the United States is to decide first what we mean by the word "education," a sense of distasteful weariness overtakes me. I feel as though I were starting to see a badly scratched film of a poor movie for the second or third time. In such a mood, I am ready to define education as what goes on in schools and colleges.[14]

Other writers equally jaded will dismiss all discussion of aims either as unnecessary because we are all in agreement anyhow or as useless because the traditional broad-gauge objectives are not really possible goals or end products of what is actually done in the classroom.[15] They believe we should content ourselves with proximate aims clearly determined such as scoring well on a College Entrance Examination or making the Dean's List.

It is not true, however, that advertence to basic aims is pointless or that there is any general consensus about all of them. An effective education like a mature personality needs to be dominated by a sense of purpose which gathers up and focuses all the energies expended on the more limited secondary goals which aim at producing merely the good humanist or the skillful physician or the prudent business manager. The strength of Soviet schooling is due in part, no doubt, to the firm sense of direction imposed upon it by Communist emphasis on its own version of humanity's long-range goals. In the United States, the discussions after the Second World War about the national purpose, its character and possible loss, suggest that there has been a good deal of dissatisfaction with theories of life and education which are steered only by delimited proximate aims. A Christian school, moreover, will find it increasingly necessary to spell out its basic convictions if the pluralistic society in which it is situated becomes more fragmented and secularized. In such a society everyone will agree that literacy and the intellectual and ethical maturity needed for wise choice are essential aims but not everyone will agree that development of the religious dimension of life is equally indispensable and much less will they agree about the total content of ethics or Catholicism's claim to be the True Faith.

In the *Spiritual Exercises,* the dominance of Christian purpose is inescapable and it was equally so in the lives of St. Ignatius and his sixteenth-century followers. Nevertheless, their educational documents contain no reflective considerations of such matters as the nature of a truly liberal Christian education or the aims of Christian character formation.

Of course, these documents are practical rather than theoretical whereas the charting of broad objectives is usually done in essays on theory. But it is interesting that the early Jesuit school planners should so easily have dispensed with all the vast, as well as rather cloudy and insoluble questions, and gotten speedily down to brass tacks. The earliest materials preserved in the *Monumenta Paedagogica* show them concentrating firmly on mundane problems: how many Jesuits will be needed for a new foundation; how much endowment; how many classes and sections should there be. Father Ledesma, whose work so strongly influenced the *Ratio,* defended his tireless zeal for minute detail by remarking (with some inaccuracy in the actual reference) that he was handling practical matters, "and in practical matters, as Aristotle says in the First Book of the Ethics, universal principles are not so useful."[16] So it happens that in medicine it's not enough to say keep the patient warm but one must be told, continues Ledesma, just how to make a plaster for the sick man. Nor can the architect stop with calling for a pleasant and commodious building. He has to specify the exact measurements of doors, windows and rooms.

Father Ledesma and his successors were certainly conscientious architects and were not given to enunciating universal principles. Had they been physicians they would probably have recommended the exact brand of mustard to fill the plaster. They pointed out, of course, the broad aims they were after but even this was done as concretely as possible. They did not, for instance, assign to the school any such total accomplishments as development of a thoroughly cultured personality or of the power of critical thought. They described the business of the school as the study of letters and this in a context which further specified it as the study of Latin with some Greek. This fondness for defining aims operationally was quite Ignatian. The founder himself defined the purpose of the Society as to travel all over the world, preaching, hearing confessions and working for souls.

In the first chapter of his plan for the curriculum of the Roman College, Ledesma begins with a capsule statement of aims. Both civil and religious society, he notes, find that schools of letters (that is, secondary schools) are essential for a decent human life, for the right governance of the state, for the enhancement and maturation of intelligence itself and, above all, for teaching, defending and spreading the faith and conducting mankind more securely to heaven.[17] Then he gets on to procedural matters and to blueprints for the organization of a school of this sort. He was living, after all, at a moment when most Europeans still believed in the Christian view of human destiny and accepted the common scholastic theses on the existence and nature of the human spirit as essentially non-material and endowed with self-consciousness and freedom of choice. He and the authors of the subsequent versions of the *Ratio* could devote themselves to eminently practical tasks because no speculative uncertainties clouded their vision of ultimate goals. There were advantages to this situation. Most of the school problems that vex any age are actually technical ones of this concrete sort. His philosophy of human nature may help an educator decide whether or not to teach French. But if he does elect to develop fluent French speakers it really won't matter, so far as availing himself of the best techniques goes, whether he holds man to be a spirit temporarily imprisoned in corporeal sludge or a composite of material and spiritual principles or so essentially continuous with the infrahuman material world that thought is only a secretion of his brain. It is possible that extreme religious convictions could have a negative effect upon classroom procedure. A fundamentalist sect, for example, might proscribe all mechanical devices like tape-recorders and language laboratories. But aside from these fringe cases, once a curriculum has been chosen, most problems are approached by everyone in more or less the same manner. A teacher may be a Platonic believer in learning as reminiscence but this is not likely to inhibit his use of effective teaching methods worked out by his Aristotelian neighbor.

The educational tradition to which Ledesma and the *Ratio* belong subscribed implicitly to the position that formal schooling, like politics, is just this kind of art of the possible and that schoolmen's chief problems are ones of practical policy, that is, of the ordering of promising means to possible goals. The Catholic theoretician needs to salt his work with this emphasis since he is naturally apt, as James Collins noted, "to be embarrassingly rich in general recommendations which he does not know how to make concretely applicable to the particular shape of the problem confronting the practical man."[18] Neither St. Ignatius nor Nadal and Ledesma nor the multitude that had a hand in shaping the definitive *Ratio* suffered from this deficiency, at least so far as the shape of the sixteenth-century problem was concerned.

Still there are disadvantages in handling philosophical issues too summarily or in confining oneself almost exclusively to procedural details. Such a concentration will produce, as it did in the *Ratio,* an organization of the school in terms of a curriculum whose contents are remarkably well clarified and integrated. The price, however, is that of some impoverishment of the concept of education and the risk of quick obsolescence. In the long run, it is the statement of general goals which outlasts the program of specific means. Modern Jesuit educators would like to emulate their predecessors' enthusiastic search for effective techniques while at the same time sustaining realistically a more profound and subtle reflection upon the broad aims of the whole enterprise of Christian secondary and higher education. A goal without technique is like a car without gas; technique not clearly related to an ultimate goal is like a journey without a destination.

The *Ratio* and the *Constitutions* advert, of course, to ultimate goals but this is done in stenographic formulations which are often oblique. These statements yield, however, four theses which add up to a fundamental position on the purposes of education. There is, in the first place, recognition of a triple educational aim or three positive values which the school is expected to nurture: growth in intellectual, in moral and in social maturity. Secondly, these three dimensions or aims are seen as interrelated. The moral purpose, however, is given primacy—at least in theory. For as will be noted later, the *Ratio* says very little about guidance and character education and assigns to formal religion teaching, which for Christians is closely linked with moral development, only an hour or two of the week. Finally, all the elements of the curriculum and of the whole school life are seen as ultimately instrumental. They are not themselves the final goals but rather tools for perfecting the true Christian whose love of God will be translated into service and thereby harvest redemption for himself and for others.

St. Ignatius's own recognition of the triple aim occurs when he is speaking of the formation of young Jesuits since this is the context in which he envisions the full range of education. His prescriptions for schools open to the public are chiefly concerned with administrative matters but when he speaks of the education of the Jesuit scholastic the reader is conscious that this is done against the background of the integral Christian ideal. Those who enter the Society of Jesus, says Ignatius in the Preamble to the Fourth Part of the *Constitutions,* should be men of upright conduct and possessed of sufficient learning for a life of service. There are not, however, many persons who are thus both good and well-educated and also prepared to sign up for the apostolic labors of the Society. Therefore, the Founder concluded, "All of us who desire to preserve and augment the Society for the greater glory and service of God our Lord have thought it wise to adopt another procedure. It is this: to admit young men who because of their good morals and ability give hope of becoming both virtuous and learned in order to labor in the vineyard of Christ our Lord."[19]

The threefold aim of *probitas, eruditio* and *officium* can be deduced from this prescription since young men will not be of a mind to devote themselves to the ministry unless their growth in character and science has included a corresponding development of an apostolic social consciousness. One of the interconnections between the intellectual and moral dimensions of education is indicated in the same Preamble. St. Ignatius is sketching the outlines of the scholastics' formation and he observes: "After the proper foundation of self-sacrifice has been laid, and after the required growth in virtues, they must be trained in letters and in the manner of employing them, as a help to know and serve better God, our Creator and Lord."[20] There is an echo here of St. Thomas's answer to those who had objected that learning is a threat to piety since knowledge, as Scripture says, vainly puffs up. The text, replies St. Thomas shortly, applies when knowledge is without love.[21] Because Ignatius had a decidedly instrumentalistic view of education he always coupled learning and goodness. He was interested in getting educated men to work for the betterment of others and erudition is not enough for this purpose. If education is to be employed generously, a man has to be both good and learned. If he's not educated, he can't help his neighbors as effectively as he might. If he's not good, he won't help them or at least he can't be relied upon to do so consistently.

Elsewhere, speaking of the aims of the schools opened for non-Jesuit students, the Fourth Part of the *Constitutions* adverts only to the intellectual and moral objectives. Schools, it says, are for building up knowledge and morals.[22] Since virtuous action is generally concerned with interpersonal relationships and social responsibilities, however, the third objective is implied in the second. In recent times, Jesuit legislation has made this social emphasis explicit. "Since the purpose which the Society proposes to itself in conducting schools," says the *Epitome,* "is to bring the neighbor to a knowledge and love of God, our first concern in the education of youth should be to see that our students acquire along with letters the habits worthy of Christians. Men should be formed who are not merely cultured but authentically Christian in both their private and public lives and willing and able to live every day apostolically." A bit further on, under the same Tenth Title of the Fourth Part of this *Epitome,* it is urged that students be formed as integral Christians, not only charitable, chaste, industrious and courageous but also urbane, and that they be prepared for their civil obligations as Christian citizens according to the specific needs of their age and nation.[23]

The documents which preceded the *Ratio* often repeat the themes of the *Constitutions* on this point of broad objectives. Nadal in his *De Studiis Societatis,* began with the comment, noted in Chapter IV, that all details should be so arranged as to give pride of place to character formation in the schools. This is a thesis which found an echo in twentieth-century Progressive Education. For "three fundamental principles underlie and guide modern education," said William H. Kilpatrick summing up the tenets of Progressivism in his old age. "The first is that education must aim primarily at character-building, not simply at acquiring subject-matter."[24] The "Rules to be Observed by All Who Frequent the Schools of the Society," which are associated with Ledesma, made the same point. One must work hard for scholarship, but realize that moral virtue is even more important. "Let them strive to cultivate intelligence by every branch of learning yet even more earnestly seek the enlightenment of perfect wisdom which is the product of the fullness of virtue."[25]

In the definitive *Ratio* of 1599 many of the thirty sets of rules begin with a statement of the twofold aim, academic and moral, and they generally indicate that the former subserves the latter. The provincial, whose rules stand at the head of the list, is reminded in the first of them that the Society aims to teach all appropriate disciplines in such wise as to bring students to the knowledge and love of God and that it is his business to see that this objective is attained. The rector, whose rules come next, is instructed to have a care first for the religious and moral training provided in his institution and only then to administer the other functions of the *collegium* or the university. The general prefect of studies, who oversaw both the higher faculties and the secondary school, is told that he is to be the rector's *instrumentum* for so organizing and administering classes that students make as much progress as possible in virtue and in the liberal arts. The first rule for the high school principal (prefect of lower studies) introduces a surprising modification by giving an edge to the academic aim. For it is his task, he is to understand, to work hard at running a school in which students develop character *no less* than proficiency in their studies, which would seem to put that proficiency first. The Scripture professor is admonished to lecture with piety, learning and sobriety so as to strengthen faith in God and sound morals. The professor of scholastic theology must be adept in the subtleties of theological reasoning and this skill must support orthodoxy and devotion. The professor of philosophy finds that his discipline's intrinsic merits are rather ignored. He is advised, instead, that the arts and natural sciences, which comprised the philosophical curriculum in a day when rudimentary physics was subsumed under cosmology, are chiefly valuable as preparing the mind for the study of theology. He should so teach philosophy, therefore, as to prepare students for theological studies and to stimulate them to love of God. The masters in the secondary schools are expected to see to it that the adolescents whom they teach acquire along with literary skills the virtuous character looked for in a Christian.[26]

These firm formulas betray no sense of uncertainty but they may leave a modern reader with some misgivings. Yet if he has a sense of history, he will not be surprised to find that moral aim emphasized because, as the preceding chapter noted, this is customary among those who reflect upon life or education. It is not simply the accent of believers in a religion. Thoughtful men who have rejected Christianity and disagree sharply among themselves on specific ethical issues, still assert the prime importance of moral goodness as they understand it. So Lawrence of Arabia said that "one of the sorest things in life is to come to realize that one is just not good enough" and John Dewey maintained that problems of human conduct are the central problems of life.[27] Moreover, it was usual not so long ago for most men to envision this moral aim within a religious context. Students of American education will ratify the comment of D. W. Brogan: "American education began as a preparation for the next world. It was designed to make good Christians, not good citizens or subjects; the greater, it was assumed, included the less." Horace Mann himself declared that educators and friends of the public school should aim to train children "up to the love of God and the love of man; to make the perfect example of Jesus Christ lovely in their eyes."[28]

But although a strong accent upon ethical and religious purposes in the Jesuit documents is not surprising, it may be confusing to see that once this twinned goal of progress in knowledge and in virtue has been proposed nearly all the subsequent material is devoted solely to the academic advance. Of the seventeen chapters in the Fourth Part of the *Constitutions,* only the sixteenth is concerned with what we would call character formation. Since this Fourth Part is not intended as a systematic account of a school's work one cannot deduce much from its relative neglect of the school's guidance function. It is more remarkable to find that the *Ratio* does not even have a separate treatment of moral education but merely scatters a few elementary hints here and there as it outlines classroom procedures. The puzzled reader may wonder just which aim really is primary. Theoretically the question is an open one since no general answer can be derived from analyzing some immutable essence of the school-as-such. For there are educational institutions like graduate schools which certainly have intellectual development as their nearly exclusive goal and others, like novitiates, which are chiefly concerned with character development. It is at least possible to conceive of an ele-

mentary or even a secondary school as intending equal attention to both
purposes.

The *Ratio* does not tell us how the apparent ambiguity created by
giving the moral aim a primacy and the intellectual aim the lion's share of
attention is to be resolved. Perhaps the editors were unaware of any ambiguity. No doubt they would have said that the overall goal both of life
and of education, understood in that full sense which makes it cotermi-
nous with life, is certainly holiness but the proximate aim pursued by
the school is the civilization of intelligence. This work has of itself considerable moral resonance since, other things being equal, moral maturity
presupposes and is nourished by intellectual maturity. The savage is not
usually a promising candidate for sanctity. The whole matter was put
succinctly by Suarez, that outstanding Jesuit theologian of the era in
which the *Ratio* was fashioned. The education given in Jesuit schools, he
noted, has two purposes: progress in learning and in morals. "The relation between these two is such that knowledge is, as it were, the proper
material of this instruction and the proximate effect of the schools. Nevertheless, the principal aim is moral excellence."[29] Some practical questions
remain, however, since presumably both the proximate and the principal
aim are to be ardently pursued by teachers and students alike. In the next
chapter we shall have to examine what the sixteenth-century Jesuit tradition actually proposed by way of character education. For the moment it is enough to notice that while this tradition knew that the intellectual and moral aims can become competitive and that too much zeal
for study may, as St. Ignatius remarked, cause spiritual deterioration, it
maintained that this ought not happen but that, on the contrary, wisdom
and charity should be partners.[30]

Scholars might suspect, however, that the partnership is bound to be
uneasy so long as you hold that it is more perfect to love than to know and
that study and learning are instrumental to growth in holiness. Do those
formulations of the *Ratio,* it may be asked, allow for adequate acknowledgement of the intrinsic value of the intellectual life and the due autonomy of learned pursuits? It is true, like Ignatius himself, they do not
clearly affirm these values but neither do they deny them and later generations have made them explicit. When the Plan for Higher Studies
in Jesuit Seminaries, issued in 1954, turns to the philosophy course
it begins with a clear statement of the nature and dignity of this discipline
in itself and only thereafter observes that philosophy is, besides, a necessary preparation for theological studies.[31] This is an addition to the view
of the *Ratio* of 1599 which characteristically considered philosophy simply as theology's handmaid. That earlier *Ratio* does not clearly advert to

the inherent worth of research, inquiry and the educated mind because it concentrates so strictly on organization and procedural details. Still, even here the Rector is warned to arrange his other duties so as to be able to foster academic affairs and he is told not to grant exemptions from academic functions nor to employ Jesuits who are in studies in non-academic business. This is at least a practical recognition of the importance of things intellectual.

In the *Ratio* of 1586, moreover, there are oblique testimonies to the value of a mature mind capable of continuing a process of self-education. At one point, for instance, the length of the theology course is being discussed: ought it last for four or five years? The authors of the *Ratio* review the arguments for five years and then those favoring four and remark: "It is much better to embark upon a solid program of reading than to extend the time of the course . . . good reading habits are desirable in themselves and if they are acquired no extension of time will be necessary since materials not useful or less necessary can be omitted."[32] The students of theology are also advised to judge for themselves which of the lecturers' remarks are worth noting down since this exercise of choice promotes comprehension as well as overcoming the auditors' passivity.[33] Long hours in the philosophy classroom are criticized, for when students are deprived of opportunity for individual and private study they are perforce reduced to parroting what they've heard.[34] Nowadays, these hints seem rudimentary enough since clear appreciation of the importance of mature habits of inquiry and criticism is commonplace. A contemporary statement of the full philosophy of a modern Jesuit school would be explicit and detailed in underscoring the prime aim of developing students possessed of sufficient intellectual strength and curiosity to continue their education throughout life. This emphasis, however, would harmonize with those early documents since it does not contradict but only clarifies and enlarges them. It is true that St. Ignatius probably esteemed the intellectual virtues chiefly for their utility. Still, this did not prevent him from appreciating an educated intelligence and knowing what its development required. One of his traditional sayings ran this way: The ability to anticipate what should be done and to evaluate what has been done is the soundest guarantee of successful action. This sounds like a description of scientific procedure and might be hung as a motto in any laboratory or administrator's office.[35] He reminded the young Jesuits in studies that the pursuit of learning demanded almost the whole man and that if they gave themselves to it with the sole intention of serving God they would be offering homage greater than had they concentrated instead on prayer and mortification.[36] Most significantly, he believed in the fundamental concept of a Christian Humanism, in the possibility of synthesizing the temporal and the eternal. Moreover, he provided the basic formula for such a synthesis in his principle of instrumentality which sees all temporal values as ultimately subserving the master-value or eternal purpose. It was easy enough to enlarge that formula later by explicit recognition of the native goodness of the academic disciplines, of research and of the vigorous life of thought.

On Designing a Curriculum

In Utopia the educators' beliefs about life and destiny are faithfully mirrored in their choice of school programs and teaching methods. In the imperfect commonwealths known to history these choices always involve compromise. Christian schoolmen, for instance, have never yet found that the curriculum required or permitted by their civilization corresponded fully with their ideal. Sometimes, in fact, they themselves have hardly understood all the implications of that ideal. At any moment a teacher has only a certain number of limited options. Origen could not have chosen to synthesize the perspectives of Christian faith with those of twentieth-century physical and social science and the twentieth century cannot exactly duplicate his harmony of Hellenic and Christian wisdom. The decisions made by the editors of the *Ratio* as to what they would teach and how they would teach it, did reflect their Christian world view to some extent but only imperfectly if not murkily. An analysis of their recommendations may precipitate some general principles but one must not expect too much. The *Ratio's* curriculum could hardly have been constructed from materials not available to the sixteenth century nor according to a totally original blueprint.

Nevertheless, a good many disputes about the nature of Jesuit education focus around the relative importance of these concrete directives simply because they are so obvious that it is tempting to conclude that the essence of Jesuit education is to be identified with them. If this were so, the Jesuit tradition would be a rather modest and somewhat dated scheme chiefly for teaching the ancient classics through careful "prelections," copious written and oral exercises, systematic repetitions and plentiful exploitation of boys' competitive instincts. It is more reasonable to suppose that the tradition is actually richer if less tangible than these precise prescriptions of the *Ratio* although some elements of that tradition are certainly implied by those same prescriptions.

To begin with, the historical process, which evolved the *Ratio*, itself embodied two instructive attitudes. It showed, as was noted before, that the early Jesuit educators knew that practical problems are solved by taking empirically determined facts into account and that the solutions themselves must be open to subsequent modifications in the light of experience. They tested their ideas in daily action and thereafter developed, qualified or abandoned them on the basis of what this contact with experience had taught. A procedure of this sort will seem somewhat uninteresting precisely because it is tentative and commonsensical. The extreme rationalist, whether of the academic or bizarre sort, will spin an exuberantly original theory right out of a few *a prioristic* convictions and in the process rise so far above the actualities of the school as to disappear into the clouds. The men who constructed the *Ratio* had, on the contrary, a strong experimental bias and carefully reviewed what the past had accomplished. They weighed its current applicability, checked by practice what they thought they could use and moderately reconstructed the future by moderately innovating since as Christians they naturally looked to the future even when they taught the literature of antiquity.

They did hope, it is true, that the *Ratio* which was finally fashioned would remain stable for a long while and in this they were too sanguine. But in a more general sense their very optimism constituted, along with their experimental outlook, a healthy orientation for people tussling with questions of school organization. It has been suggested that this optimism owed something to the sixteenth-century Jesuits' controversy with Calvinism.[37] In praising the humanities, it is said, they were actually defending the possibility of a harmony between faith and reason and were implicitly asserting that human nature is not essentially corrupted by the Fall and that pre-Christian artists were capable of works worthy of admiration. This optimistic willingness to seize the good wherever it is found is the radical lesson taught by that pervasive zest for Cicero and Aristotle. When contemporary Jesuit educators devote themselves to critical study of modern literatures and to the natural and social sciences, they are, therefore, true to the authentic spirit of their tradition.

Empirical and optimistic attitudes of this sort, though advantageous, do not themselves constitute general principles for designing a curriculum. If we make explicit, however, the theory concretized by the regulations in the Fourth Part of the *Constitutions* and the *Ratio* a number of such principles will appear. They may not recommend themselves to everyone but at least they have a vitality independent of their historical context.

The first of these is surely that thoroughly Ignatian principle of instrumentalism which requires that disciplines be taught and methods be employed insofar as they are useful for attaining the school's overall purpose; in this case for achieving Christian intellectual and moral maturity: *profectus in litteris et moribus.* To the actual instruments or academic disciplines it does not deny value but only sovereignty. "Among objects in themselves lovable," said St. Thomas with his tranquil lucidity, "some are loved solely for themselves and never for anything else—thus happiness which is the last end—while others are loved for their own sake, in that they possess some intrinsic worth, and also because they serve the purpose of conveying us to a more perfect good—thus are the virtues lovable."[38] It is in this spirit that the Jesuit educational tradition cultivates the intellectual virtues. A single passage from St. Ignatius's *Constitutions* shows that instrumentalistic principle of determination being applied to the question of the curriculum intended for Jesuit scholastics and indicates the curriculum actually decided upon as well as such secondary principles as that of assigning more time to the more important subjects and that of adaptation:

> The end of the learning acquired in this Society is, with the help of God, to aid the souls of its own members and those of their neighbors. This, therefore, is the criterion to be used in deciding, both in general and in the case of individual persons, what subjects members of the Society ought to learn, and how far they ought to progress in them. To speak in general, the humane letters of the various languages, and logic, natural philosophy [Aristotelian physics] moral philosophy, metaphysics, scholastic theology, positive theology, and Sacred Scriptures are helpful. These are the branches to which those who are sent to the colleges should apply themselves. They will devote themselves with greater diligence to the parts which are more helpful for the end mentioned above. Furthermore, account is to be taken of circumstances of time, place, persons, and other such factors, according to what seems best in our Lord to him who holds the chief responsibility.[39]

It is not really surprising to find this utilitarian accent governing the studies of Jesuits themselves since by profession they aimed to order everything to their apostolic purpose. Thus in a celebrated letter which Polanco wrote in the name of Ignatius to advise Father Lainez on direction of the scholastics in his charge, the point is made a dozen times that Jesuits acquire learning so as "to be of benefit to their neighbor."[40] Whatever is "necessary" or "useful" for making a man fit for the service of God and the neighbor will be included in his course of studies. The classics are read because mastery of the languages in which they were written will help to an understanding of the Scriptures and is also a good mental gymnastic toning the mind up for philosophy and theology.[41] Elsewhere Ignatius advised preachers to employ all suitable rhetorical devices for increasing their effectiveness and so the early Jesuits mastered the resources of Renaissance rhetoric. Even theology was studied not for itself but because it was the most appropriate means for achieving the goals of love, knowledge and service of God: *ad eum finem medium magis proprium.* Everything else was studied because it made for a good apostolic person and prepared the mind for theology: *artes vel scientiae naturales ingenia disponunt ad theologiam.*[42]

When it came to working out the curriculum for schools open to the general public, this pragmatic bent was still evident although now the ultimate purpose was the universal Christian one of knowledge and love of God without the distinctive specification this receives in a religious order. The proximate purpose often assigned to various studies was that of usefulness for secular life. The Fourteenth General Congregation of the Society, which met from November, 1696 to the following January, pointed to the ultimate goal when it said that "care must be taken lest the study of humanities languish," for among other benefits the teaching of these disciplines provides occasion for educating youth to devotion and sound character.[43] The proximate aim of utility is suggested, to take one instance, by the first rule for Professors of Rhetoric in the *Ratio* of 1599 which observes that eloquence is *not only* useful but also an attractive accomplishment. The *Ratio* of 1586 recommends study of mathematics and science as useful for civic life, *in rempublicam utilitates,* where they contribute to medicine, navigation and agriculture, and also as helping to an understanding of points in theology, poetry and history.[44]

It is worth noting in this whole matter that anyone who sets up a curriculum is guided by some general principle of instrumentality. The secular humanist may be outraged by talk of religious goals but it is the goal itself he dislikes, not the practice of ordering curricular contents as means to an end. He himself would devise his own school program to attain the ends he esteems. A sociologist may study Latin literature in order to understand better the society which produced it. A genuine aesthete might read it simply to fashion his own spirit after that classical image. The authors of the *Ratio,* on the other hand, would have been in basic, if somewhat unlikely, agreement with Somerset Maugham when the latter remarked in *The Summing Up:* "The value of art is not beauty, but right action . . . If it is to be anything more than a self-indulgence and an occasion of self-complacency, it must strengthen your character and make it more fitted for right action."[45] The Jesuits aimed to teach the classics in such a way as to make them, in a famous phrase of Jouvancy, the "Heralds of Christ—*Christi praecones*," whose words would instill salutary sentiments in youthful hearts.[46]

Jesuit teachers today may suspect that this is risky moralism, especially when they note that Père Jouvancy goes on to advise his readers to sprinkle their instruction with lively anecdotes which will keep the students from growing bored and will serve to conceal the *ars Christiana*. But as we have noted often enough heretofore, the principle of instrumentalism does not require denial of the native value of the discipline itself nor does it canonize a clumsy proselytizing. In fact, the *Constitutions* and the *Ratio* recognized the innate humanistic power of the various studies in literature, science, mathematics and philosophy. For it was this that they had in mind when they praised those studies for their nourishment of intellectual talent. The instrumental approach does, however, solve the extreme antinomy between studies which are considered liberal, in the sense of strictly disinterested, and those which are useful. For it reminds us that all studies ought to have a certain utility. The sixteenth-century Jesuits had a liberal interest in Latin as their passionate devotion to Cicero proved but they also assigned a pragmatic purpose to its pursuit: it cultivated the mind and prepared students either for theology or for that effective power of communication which men of affairs always need. Eloquence and philosophy, said Perpinian, a distinguished Jesuit pedagogue of the day, are the wise man's tools, *instrumenta*.[47]

Two other antinomies which the instrumental principle dissolves are those between conservation and innovation and between formation and information. If you select for your school whatever contributes to certain clearly understood broad purposes, you will know that you can hardly form intelligence without intussusception of appropriate information. At the same time, there is a clear difference between those gradgrinds who want education chiefly to enlarge the fund of factual knowledge and those who want it chiefly to develop certain operative habits. The Jesuits aimed to have their students acquire a masterful skill in the use of Latin. A modern educator might want his students to acquire the permanent habit of thinking according to scientific method. In each case, information, though not condemned, is reduced to second place. This is a defensible position which need not be converted into sharp opposition between knowing *how* and knowing *what*. In similar fashion, a schoolman aware of historic process knows that without innovation there can ultimately be no conservatism. If successive generations wish secondary education, for example, to continue developing power of self-expression they must be prepared for some innovations in technique and materials for they cannot achieve the basic objective if they use only the tools of past generations.

This manifests once again a second general principle of curriculum design which Ignatius underscored and the authors of the *Ratio* and their successors have constantly employed. It is that familiar principle of adaptation. St. Ignatius was not afraid to have his schools do what was being done in striving for perfect Latin eloquence but he wanted even that curriculum sufficiently adapted to make it a means to his purposes. Those authors who, like Terence, could not conceivably be converted into heralds of Christ were simply dropped. And the principle of adaptation was presumed to be always operative. "Although the order and hours devoted to these studies may vary according to the regions and times of the year," wrote Ignatius, "there should be such conformity that in every region a procedure is used which is there judged most expedient for greater progress in learning."[48] Adapt, in other words, so long as your adaptations promote the final end-in-view. In the *Ratio* of 1599 there is nothing about experimental work in science. This was natural enough. Not until the eighteenth century were there any lectures accompanied by experiments in American colleges. The *Ratio* of 1832, however, brought science up to date, recognized the need for experimentation and considerably diminished the monopoly of Latin in particular and literary studies in general. In doing so it was obviously loyal to the Ignatian principles.

The Content of Formal Schooling

In 1571 Pope Pius V granted teaching privileges to the "Preceptors of the Society of Jesus, those teaching the Humane Letters as well as those teaching the Liberal Arts and Theology."[49] This formula indicated the three focal subject-matter areas in which the sixteenth-century Jesuit schools actually elected to provide instruction. If, to begin with, we examine the program at close range we will find these three familiar "Faculties" so organized as to follow one another chronologically for it was held that they were logically interdependent. The Faculty of Humane Letters, or studies in language and literature, had its five classes and these included, according to the *Constitutions,* grammar, poetry, rhetoric and history among the subjects taught. The Faculty of Arts or Natural Sciences gathered in logic, "physics," metaphysics and mathematics. The Faculty of Theology taught not only scholastic and positive theology but Scripture and Biblical languages. Together these faculties

142 JESUIT EDUCATION

amounted to the *Ratio's* concrete answer to the question of a curriculum for general or liberal education. After one had learned to read and write, he should strive to master the tools of mature self-expression. Next he should acquire through study of the liberal arts an increased facility in analysis and prudent reflection as well as some acquaintance with the disciplines grouped under this category. After concentrating on words, so to say, he should concentrate on things. Finally, he should crown it all with theology, the systematic study of God's vision of reality, though admittedly this faculty was also a professional one. Some of the materials taught in Humane Letters would be found today at the level of the secondary school and some in the junior college. The Faculty of Arts may be loosely identified with the upper years of a modern college course although its mathematics and science program was inevitably more elementary than the programs in our high schools. The Faculty of Theology is identified in its fullness with seminaries although some continental and American universities have chairs or departments of theology and all American Catholic colleges have an undergraduate theology course.

If we now back off a bit and try for some perspective on this curricular scheme, we will notice that the first two faculties reflected very strongly the characteristic cultural concepts of their time. In theory, at least, a school may construct its curriculum entirely from yesterday's materials in an obstinate mood of excessive traditionalism. At the opposite extreme, it might appraise the surrounding civilization critically and weed out all but the seedlings of the future which it would then tend exclusively. This is risky because the gift of prophecy is needed to identify those harbingers of tomorrow. Actually, the curriculum-builder generally follows a third path and prescribes, with or without modification, the cultural materials currently esteemed by his civilization. In the sixteenth century there were significant developments in science, economics, politics and vernacular literature already at the threshold. The common culture, however, usually lags comfortably behind the frontiersmen and it is the common culture which normally governs what most schools will impart. Jesuit missionaries in the sixteenth and seventeenth centuries were exploring South American jungles, canoeing down the Mississippi and penetrating the forbidden cities of China, Japan and India but the Jesuit rhetorician, Nigronius, acted characteristically when he decided to model his description of a garden upon a choice page from Pliny rather than upon some real garden.[50]

Since parents, teachers and pupils all expected a concentration upon classical studies certain other disciplines were given short shrift. Today the importance of history is universally recognized. It not only forms a dominating field in itself but every other subject, including science, gives serious attention to its own historical dimension. In the *Ratio,* however, history is either bypassed or brought in obliquely. The Professor of Scholastic Theology is advised in his Ninth Rule to treat controverted points by the scholastic rather than by the historical method. In the humanities course some history was encountered when selections from Livy, Sallust or Caesar were read, but it was the history of ancient Rome. The *Ratio* of 1832 considerably rectified this situation by adding a whole set of rules for the Professor of Church History. These not only bricked up some gaps but included a firm recommendation of the critical method which was to be used without prejudice or exaggeration.[51]

In practice, the vernacular was so thoroughly ostracized that it was not even used as the classroom medium once the students knew enough Latin to follow the teacher in that tongue. There were two reasons for this. In 1599, as we noted before, the bulk of the great vernacular literatures in English, French, German and Spanish had yet to be written and consequently could hardly have formed a curricular staple. In the second place, as Herman points out, Renaissance educators had a common persuasion which can be summed up in a series of interlocking equations. The aim of the humanities is to insure intellectual culture; intellectual culture is perfect eloquence; eloquence is mastery of Cicero's language, style and cadence.[52] So one finds in the Jesuit education documents, from the very outset, that prevalence of Cicero: *recitant Ciceronis epistolas; per tres quartas docet Ciceronem; repetit Ciceronem; recitant Ciceronem de officiis; transcribent cotidie lectionem Ciceronis futuram.* The purpose of all this was, as Nadal put it, to acquire a Latin style free of any blemish of solecism or barbarism.[53]

In the Arts faculty Aristotle enjoyed a similar hegemony since, as the Rules for the Professor of Philosophy in the *Ratio* of 1599 show, the study of both philosophical and scientific matters was built about his treatises much as the theology course was built about the Questions in St. Thomas's *Summa Theologiae.* Before the *Ratio* was written, it is true, a Jesuit in the Roman College had warned of two dangers in teaching philosophy. One was to allow so much liberty as to endanger faith. The other was to be so rigidly bound to a single author as to make oneself hateful to the students. By the time the *Ratio* of 1586 was written, however, Aristotle's position was undisputed as the ritual for conferring degrees upon Arts' students shows. The presiding officer, according to the *Ratio,* is to receive from an assistant beadle a ring, a cap and a copy of Aristotle. These he will impose upon the candidate saying: "As a sign and pledge of this honor and grade I place this cap upon your head and I give you this volume of Aristotle."[54] Had it been a theologian who was graduating the book would have been a Bible.

Finally, if we adopt the highest possible position as vantage point, it may be possible to trace out the groundwork of basic conviction upon which the Renaissance superstructure of Ciceronianism and Aristotelianism rested. What meaning has that program for generations no longer committed to the very letter of the *Ratio?* Some have maintained that this program of classical literary studies followed by philosophy and science has an absolute value because it is the best recipe for liberal or general education and consequently the best prelude to professional specialization.* Even if one does not go that far one can see that the *Ratio* does suggest that the middle-school student has a particular readiness for language work and for those concrete insights into life which the literature of poetry, fiction and drama afford. No modern secondary school will follow the *Ratio* in deferring mathematics and science to college years just as no Christian secondary school could accept its reduction of formal religious instruction to recital of the catechism during the last half hour of the last day of the week.

Nevertheless, that primary focus upon language and imaginative writing may hold a valuable hint. There is much impressive evidence that young children do learn languages very easily. College admissions officers tell us that skill in use of the mother tongue is the chief key to collegiate academic success. The sixteenth century, convinced as it was of the value of languages in themselves and of their special suitability for secondary schooling, employed Latin and Greek as the means of achieving its linguistic goals. The *Ratio* of 1586 recommended that Greek be

---

* "But they," writes an English Jesuit of the Society's schools, "cling to the notion that the substance of the baptized Hellenic tradition of humanism is permanent; and they are faced with the difficulty, in these days of specialization, of affording time for both the literary formation which humanism entails and for the scientific training without which there cannot be fully effective leadership in a technological age. Those who abandon humanism as an ideal and as the core of education have a flying start in scientific proficiency which cannot be won back: and those who learn in Christian humanism the purpose and value of technology are excluded from directing technology because the technologists have outstripped them." W. Lawson, S.J., "The Jesuit Schools," in George Z. F. Bereday and Joseph A. Lauwerys (editors), *Education and Philosophy: The Year Book of Education 1957* (Yonkers-on-Hudson: World Book Company, 1957), p. 349. It might be noted that many Christian educational theorists would wish explicitly to include both technology and scientific "training" within the compass of Christian humanism itself.

started at the same time as Latin precisely because it would be learned more easily by younger students. A contemporary high school will find, of course, that its own curricular problems are less easily solved. It will feel obliged, for instance, to awaken also the student's interest in mathematics and the natural and social sciences. Even if it does decide to emphasize linguistic and literary studies, it may see little wisdom in identifying these with Latin and Greek. It might well prefer to educate its students to genuine facility in use of their own tongue, to teach them thoroughly at least one other modern language and to introduce them to some outstanding pieces of English and American literature.

Students for the priesthood will always have to study Latin since the papal directives for seminaries require this and it is obviously a necessary professional tool. Jesuit secondary schools, moreover, are reminded by the *Epitome* of Jesuit law to "preserve, so far as possible, the pre-eminence of the classical languages" which are held to be peculiarly apt for the development of intellectual power.[55] But this is not always possible and there are American Jesuit high schools which include a track or stream in which students do not take Latin. There are others which require only two years of Latin and even when the customary four-year Latin course is required it does not monopolize the curriculum.

We need not delay longer on this matter save to note that if Latin does have a place in a modern high school or college it ought not be for purely ritualistic reasons. Writing about the initiation ceremonies which induct youths into male adulthood among the Thonga of East Africa, an anthropologist remarked rather caustically: "Much of this training has the same relation to tribal life as our teaching of Latin has had to our everyday, practical, or even intellectual world; it was done purely for the sake of discipline."[56] Yet such a traditionalistic approach need not be the rule. In *The Classical Heritage* Bolgar has shown that successive ages have always studied the Latin and Greek classics for practical reasons of their own—for useful information, for aesthetic delight, or for personal formation. He suggests that we might today read this literature in its original form precisely for its sociological value, for the light it can throw upon current or perennial social problems through study of the society which created these works and is reflected in them. Whatever the actual value of this recommendation, it appears to point in the right direction. There are, after all, good practical reasons for a balanced dosage of Latin and even Greek in the secondary curriculum designed for students of ability. It may well be true that these studies cultivate the human personality so remarkably as to deserve retention for their aesthetic, disciplinary and sociological potential. Of course, these claims have to be carefully scrutinized. Moreover, if inadequate teaching is choking off the benefits expected there will have to be considerable spading and pruning. But if there are values nourished by these disciplines with special effectiveness, it would be in the best tradition of Ignatian prudence to foster Latin because it seems—useful.

In any case, a Jesuit high school is authentic if it is one in which Jesuits work for their students' growth in knowledge and virtue. Guided by the principles of adaptation and of fidelity to education's basic nature as conveyor of significant aspects of a way of life, the Society has established secondary technical schools and these are no less Jesuit for all that. Indeed, the *Epitome* remarks explicitly that the conducting of non-classical high schools is by no means repugnant to the Jesuit Institute.[57]

A school, nevertheless, is closer to the spirit of the *Ratio,* if it is in that line of literary humanism which reaches back to Periclean Athens. Some students, indeed, believe that when Jesuit education is most characteristically itself, it subscribes to a precise concept of liberal education which distinguishes it even from other Catholic educational traditions. According to this concept, the best liberal education is necessarily founded on literary studies which are followed by science and philosophy. These scientific humanities lead, in turn, to university specialization in the learned professions toward which the whole program is directed. Whatever may be the truth of this view, it is certain that the sixteenth century was most enthusiastic about the first step—the development of *style.* This is an artistry with words which aims at so perfect a union between matter and form as to find, to borrow Pater's terms, for the relative in the world of thought the precise correlative in the world of language. In chapter 6 of the Fourth Part of the *Constitutions,* in fact, St. Ignatius lays it down that the Jesuit scholastics who are being prepared for the ministry, are to work diligently for the acquisition of style: *stilum in compositionibus diligenter exerceant.* This would hardly be a requisite for apostolic work, did not the age itself consider it the hallmark of an educated man.

The *Ratio* of 1591 had this ideal of style in mind when it warmly denounced the mischievous view that it makes no difference, so far as having an acute intelligence goes, whether your speech is cultivated or not. A similar conviction underlies the 1599 *Ratio*'s interest in the exact word, an interest expressed not only in the Rules of the Professor of Rhetoric but even in a directive to the Professor of Hebrew admonishing him to have a special care for words. It is the ideal which Aquaviva believed the Jesuit *collegium* should help all its lay students achieve for themselves so as "to prepare them adequately for the duties of secular life by linguistic studies."[58] It is certainly a relevant ideal today when the power of self-expression is widely esteemed and surely no easier to acquire than it ever was. We are continually encountering scare headlines announcing: Colleges to Fight Decay in English. Or we are told that the director of a space project has to rewrite the reports of his most gifted young men, or that doctoral candidates cannot manage the transition from one paragraph to another. Jouvancy's bleak comment is apparently eternally appropriate: There is nothing more difficult than writing correctly and there is nothing in which there are more ways of going wrong.[59]

If the middle school was to stimulate growth in this power of exact and beautiful expression, the liberal arts course—whose students, remember, were younger than American collegians—was ordered to the initiation of philosophical and scientific thought. In the program of the *Ratio*, the order of the subjects is neither arbitrary nor merely a matter of convenience. *In disciplinis ordo servandus*, said St. Ignatius in chapter 6 of the Fourth Part of the *Constitutions*. The progression which appeared to him both logically and psychologically sound required that tools of expression and analysis be acquired before studying philosophy, science and mathematics and that these latter disciplines themselves precede theology or such professional studies as medicine or law. This precise order of learning may be open to dispute but the notion of a hierarchical principle governing rank and precedence among the subjects taught in school is itself another of those rules now so commonly recognized that its comparative novelty in the sixteenth century is hard to grasp.

Besides prescribing an order of learning, the curriculum of the three faculties of languages, arts and theology implied another principle: that of unity or of general education before specialization. The unity theme is clear enough: first one studied Latin, then the arts, then theology. But at first glance this looks more like specialization than general education. It is not, of course, the frantic specialization of contemporary higher education where the enthusiasm of each faculty member for his own garden patch fosters a luxuriant proliferation of courses and divides the offerings of the English, or chemistry or political science department into dozens of fragments. Still, it seems like a species of specialization—all Cicero, or all Aristotle or all St. Thomas. It is now commonly recognized, however, that a liberal or general education consists not so much in what is taught as in how. "Subject matters," as Peter Drucker observed, "are neither general nor special. There is nothing more specialized for instance than Anglo-Saxon grammar; electronic circuitry, however, is a most general subject integrating a good deal of physics, technology, mathematics, logic, theory of perception and information theory."[60] In much the same fashion, the Jesuit tradition of "one thing at a time" meant not narrowness but preservation of the integrated approach characteristic of general education. The study of the text of Cicero, Livy or Virgil actually brought in sizable doses of art, architecture, history, law and social customs to say nothing of such exotic matters as hieroglyphics and Pythagorean symbols. Around this core of Latinity therefore much else was made to cluster.[61]

Nowadays educators believe that the complex expansion and the dignity of the various disciplines, to say nothing of efficient teaching, require that the major subjects be taught separately by teachers with special competence in the field and not simply as part of the exegesis of Cicero. Nevertheless, the notion of some integrative factor imposing a pattern upon the manifold and facilitating interdisciplinary communication retains its fascination. The search to find it is still going on and in Jesuit institutions philosophy and theology are the leading contenders for this integrative role. The quest may be rather illusory, for it may yet appear that the most satisfactory integration is that which is achieved in the mind of the individual person who has learned something of what the physicist, the anthropologist, the mathematician, the artist, the metaphysician and the theologian each have to teach him about the universe. This subjective integration might be quite as effective as any "integrated curriculum" in reducing the much advertised and rather fictitious division between the "two cultures," scientific and humanistic.

On Teaching

Ut omnes exerceantur .... Non sine praemio[62]

In a meditation upon sin in the *Spiritual Exercises,* St. Ignatius remarks that the trouble with the fallen angels was their unwillingness to help themselves by cooperating with grace. His own ascetical doctrine firmly emphasized the necessity of overcoming indolent passivity and that accent on action became a central pedagogical principle both in the *Constitutions* and in the *Ratio.* The reason is clear in every case: if you will the end, you must will the means. But no growth is possible either in holiness or in secular wisdom without strenuous effort. The goal which is authentic learning is acquired only by the learner's self-activity.

The particular learnings aimed at by the Jesuit course both in Letters and in the higher curricula were enlargements of the personality by genuine entitative additions—growth through the acquisition of new habits or skills which represented a qualitative enrichment of intelligence. Information and formation, as we noted earlier, are not mutually exclusive but are rather points along the continuum of learning and one does not exist without the other. Nevertheless there is a difference between a teaching which aims to survey the detailed history of Rome and one which aims to produce people who can write Ciceronian Latin; between a philosophy course which only expects students to know exactly what Aristotle said and one which expects them also to expound solid reasons for the Aristotelian propositions and defend these against all comers. Since the Jesuit schools intended the second half in each of these alternatives, they may be said to have sought a "humanism of formation" rather than "a humanism of erudition" providing that distinction is not pushed too far. The *Epitome* reflects in the twentieth century this sixteenth-century conviction when it observes: "'In so far as it lies within our power to do so, disciplines should so be selected and taught that the youthful mind is not overwhelmed with a multiplicity of facts and its powers are appropriately developed and fitted for higher studies."[63]

All the concrete Jesuit pedagogy was determined by the character of this preferred learning product. It is the conventional wisdom, both of the common man and the philosopher, that habits are only developed by practice and that practice is most fruitful when the practitioner understands what he's doing. A multitude of small-scale investigations have shown that pupils who are taught how to study or given the rationale of a procedure learn more successfully than those who have not received such instruction. The Jesuit pedagogy was thoroughly committed to both these principles and aimed first at securing understanding and then at developing mastery.

When we page through the sections on education in the *Constitutions* or thorugh the *Ratio,* our first impression is of a welter of regulations for time schedules; for careful gradation of classes; for the selection of authors to be read; for the exact portion of Alvarez's *De Institutione Grammatica* which each grammar section is to cover; for the diversified methods to be employed at various times of the morning and afternoon; for the correction of papers and the assignment of written work; for the precise degree of skill which the small inhabitants of each class will be expected to possess before moving upward. But all these particulars were simply designed to create a firm and reassuring framework of order and clarity within which both teacher and student could securely pursue their objectives.

It was felt that this was the first requirement of any good learning situation—to know just what one sought and how to seek it. St. Ignatius, it will be recalled, was a great believer in method and in a lucid grasp of reasonable and proximate aims. He heartily disapproved of the chaos which obtained in a city like Vienna where the *modus Italicus* was followed and all the students were dumped into one or two classes, logic or humanities, so that the lectures were over the heads of some and too elementary for others. The first Jesuit teachers believed that even little boys could learn a good deal if they were not overwhelmed with too much at one time. The *Ratio* of 1591 warns against multiplication of readings. It maintains that a multitude of books, even though they be useful ones, suffocates talent and impedes mastery of the daily tasks. This conviction was repeated figuratively a century later by Jouvancy who remarked that youthful talents are like narrow-necked vessels. You cannot fill them by splashing everything in at once. You can, if you pour it in carefully drop by drop.[64]

Given this sort of environment of order and care for method, it would be relatively easy to determine precise and limited academic objectives for the individual classes. Once that determination had been made, the teacher set about helping students hit the target. The first requisite was for a general understanding of the materials and aims. This is not identical with mastery of the desired skill but it is indispensable. The characteristic tool employed here was the prelection in which the teacher carefully prepared the students for their own subsequent immanent activity which alone could generate true learning and firm habits. All the versions of the *Ratio* contain detailed descriptions of the prelection. For the *Ratio* was, after all, a handbook for teachers, especially new teachers who needed precise orientation if continuity of the school's tradition were to be preserved.

In the Latin class, for instance, the teacher is advised to begin by planning his procedures carefully beforehand. He will open the lesson by reading aloud the passage under consideration so as to indicate correct pronunciation. Then he will systematically explain its linguistic, literary and perhaps its historical dimensions. This explanation would, presumably, be diversified by drawing out the students' own knowledge through questioning when the issues were those to which they already possessed answers. In literary studies, the prelection would also promote understanding by emphasizing the relation of word to idea, thereby cultivating style and guarding against verbalism. In outlining the prelection devices in rhetoric, the *Ratio* of 1591 insists that the class must understand exactly what Cicero said as well as how he said it.[65]

The *Ratio* of 1586 has a good deal to say about the prelections of the Professor of Philosophy. He has already been warned against dictating his notes. A lively lecture stimulates the auditors, attracts and holds their attention, he has been told, but all this languishes when there is only deadly dictation. For when the teacher dictates the students think of nothing but scribbling it down.[66] The professor should instead begin by reading aloud the text of Aristotle and then briefly explain its connection with what has gone before. Next he will indicate the portion of the present text which is to be memorized and go on to clarify puzzling verbal constructions so that the students will be at ease with the Aristotelian phraseology. When he hits a key text which is much disputed and capable of several interpretations he is to explain it; weigh the more important interpretations carefully and dispose of those which seem less likely. He is advised not to fuss over minor points of dispute, *dubiola,* but neither should he omit them. Finally, he will take up questions raised by the philosophical issue itself and then further points incidental to those main issues.[67] From these examples it is clear that the basic pattern and purpose of the prelection can and ought to be adapted to all teaching and to any subject. It is only too easy, unfortunately, to neglect this work of preparing students for individual study since it is always easier to tell them *what* than to teach them *how.*

After understanding, mastery is to be sought and this means student activity—exercise and more exercise. One of the earliest criticisms made of themselves by Jesuit schoolmasters, before the writing of the *Ratio,* centered upon the comparative neglect of this principle. "Written work," said Ledesma, "is scanty, done coldly and for too short a time and so the students make little progress."[68] In the secondary school pupil activity meant, as we might guess, stress upon Latin composition for the development of style. In the philosophy course it meant not only exact textual study but also a great deal of discussion and disputation or arguing of philosophical problems back and forth. Nothing is more useful than the disputation, said the *Ratio* of 1586, for really getting hold of these issues in philosophy and theology. You see many students, it remarks, very busy reading, writing and binding up their workbooks but quite neglecting these discussions and the result is that their theology is all in their notes rather than in their heads.

You do not get philosophy or theology, it continues, by listening but by discussion for it is then that you discover how shoddy those opinions are which seemed so splendid when you thought them up in the privacy of your room. Only under the press of controversy is a student of ideas forced to extend every nerve, *cogimur omnes ingenii nervos in-*

tendere. When he does so, he plumbs depths of his own thought which he would have never sounded had he remained in shadowy ease, *in otio atque umbra.* Even the little middle school boys were to have some chance at this interchange of ideas which so promotes genuine comprehension. In the *Ratio* of 1599 the Thirty-Second rule for professors of the classes in the lower faculty advises them not to coach their students for every contingency when preparations are on for some public exhibition. They are to leave some room for the boys' own improvisation on the day itself and thereby cultivate not only memory but natural talent.[69] And for all these disputations, St. Ignatius himself had suggested a wise principle as useful for the budding tennis player as for the novice philosopher: If you want to improve take on someone a little better than yourself. "Those who are more advanced should debate with those lower down by taking subjects which these latter are studying."[70]

What is important in all this is, once again, the inner core of the principle rather than any of its historical embodiments: No learning without the learner's own intelligent activity. The authors of the *Ratio* of 1586 admitted that scholastic disputations often became too formal and were consequently sterile but the activity principle was still valid. It was this that produced the *Ratio's* detailed instructions for repetitions—daily weekly, monthly, annually. For these were only further devices for stimulating, guiding and sustaining that student exercise aimed at mastery. So too was the much criticized emphasis on memory. It was believed that mastery implies readiness for use and one cannot use a word or idea which has been forgotten. Again, since acquisition of a habit or skill is the goal, there is no set time for the completion of the language studies. A student moves ahead when he demonstrates control of the materials to be learned and the skill expected at his present class level. Since this will depend to some extent upon his natural endowments, there follows from the chosen learning-objective a concern not only for promotion in terms of mastery but also for individual differences. This found its first expression in the Ignatian text itself: "In the study of humane letters and the languages there cannot be a set period of time for their completion, because of the difference in abilities and learning of those who hear the lectures, and because of other reasons too. These permit no other prescription of time save that which the prudent consideration of the rector or chancellor will arrange for each student."[71]

If there is no mastery without action, so there is no successful action without motivation. The philosophers only repeat what every one discovers for himself when they observe that every agent acts for a purpose, for something conceived of as a personal good, be it only the good of avoiding some pain. The sixteenth-century Jesuit educators consequently gave considerable thought to motivating their students and enticing them along the bumpy road of learning. Indeed, more austere spirits have frowned upon this Jesuit interest in providing tangible rewards beyond the satisfactions (often invisible to students) of knowledge itself. This question of motivation opens out at once upon the moral realm since it treats of values and so we shall defer its discussion until the following chapter. It will be enough to note here that a great deal of care was taken to make learning—*pleasant.* This may scandalize the critics of soft pedagogy and, to tell the truth, the sixteenth-century Jesuit schools would have seemed hard enough by our standards. The fact is, however, that by the measure of their own day they were certainly "progressive." In the Fourth Part of the *Constitutions,* there is a clear recognition of the composite nature of man which finds the spirit so circumscribed by the body's limitations as to require a practical care for sufficient sleep and moderation in mental labors. This humane and Christian spirit is embodied in that central *Ratio* principle: Diversify the classroom activities; variety is good because satiety is bad. *Exercitationes varias . . . pro scholae gradu, modo hanc modo illam, imperet. Nulla enim re magis adolescentium industria quam satietate languescit.*[72]

This principle issues in that multitude of provisions for vacation periods, for games and recreation, for contests and fetes designed to lift the threat of boredom, for "Academies," which kept the more gifted students interested by providing a chance for advanced work, for prizes and rewards of many sorts, for splendidly produced plays and pageants aimed at stimulating the study of literature since, according to the 1591 *Ratio: Friget enim Poesis sine theatro.*[73] Taken all together, these rules demonstrate a prime concern to make the business of education as delectable as it may be.

All these pedagogical principles are, then, closely linked together. The learning product sought is genuine growth which is conceived in terms of abiding habits or skills. Habits are generated not simply by understanding facts or procedures but mastery which makes them one's own and at hand for ready use. Mastery is the product of continual intellectual effort and exercise but fruitful effort of this sort is impossible without adequate motivation and a humane milieu. No part of this chain is particularly original although the strict concatenation had novelty in its day. In any case, it was then and is now hard to put into constant and prudent practice. Nevertheless, as Ribadeneira once said, it is doubtful if any other work gives so much glory to God as the education of youth.[74] That alone sufficiently recommends it.

NOTES: CHAPTER V

1. Document n. 94 in *Mon. Paed., op. cit.,* p. 708.
2. *Ratio* of 1586 in Pachtler, *op. cit.,* II, 26–27.
3. William S. White, "Public and Personal: Old Junior's Progress—From Prep School to Severance Pay," *Harper's Magazine,* 223 (July, 1961), 88.
4. *Constitutions,* IV, 16, n. 1. The phrase quoted here is from the original Spanish version. The context here is concerned particularly with religious practices but as we have shown elsewhere, the early Jesuit schools paid attention also to development of such "little" virtues as courtesy and good manners.
5. For the *concertatio* in the *Ratio* of 1599 see Rule 31 of the Rules Common to Professors of the Lower Classes, Pachtler, *op. cit.,* II, 392: ". . . honesta aemulatio, quae magnum ad studia incitamentum est." Note also the twelfth of the rules for Professors of Rhetoric, *ibid.,* p. 408. The flexible procedures for promotion took care of the needs of the gifted students, needs which contemporary schools and colleges sometimes meet through systems of early college admission or advanced standing upon entry.
6. Jerónimo Nadal, "De Studiis Societatis," *Mon. Paed., op. cit.,* p. 89.
7. *Constitutions,* X, n. 3: "Doctrina exacta et solida et modus eam proponendi populo in contionibus et lectionibus." On this aim of preparing preachers see the long quotation from Nadal in de Dainville, *op. cit.,* p. 15. Nadal reports that Ignatius used to send Jesuits who showed special oratorical promise to exercise their voice and gestures by giving sermons in the Roman ruins before a handful of listeners. In practice, they rarely preached in Latin but the intention seems to have been that they master the vernacular and learn from their Latin studies all Quintilian's rules and Cicero's devices. Thereafter, the whole skill thus built up would prove an effective tool for preaching.
8. *Constitutions,* IV, 6, nn. 8, 10, 12. See *Mon. Paed., op. cit.,* pp. 84–85 for an early *Ordo Studiorum* repeating these directives.
9. Herman, *op. cit.,* p. 249.
10. The *Ratio* of 1586, Pachtler, *op. cit.,* II, 148–49.
11. This paragraph owes a great deal to an unpublished essay of the Reverend Philip H. O'Neill, S.J., of the School of Education, Fordham University.
12. de Dainville, *op. cit.,* p. 131.
13. Herman, *op. cit.,* p. 79. The professor was a certain Father Remondi and his remarks were preserved in a collection of his verses and orations published at Antwerp in 1614.
14. James Bryant Conant, *The Child, the Parent and the State* (Cambridge: Harvard University Press, 1959), p. 1.
15. See, for instance, Myron Lieberman, *The Future of Public Education*

(Chicago: University of Chicago Press, 1960) pp. 15–33 and R. S. Peters, *Authority, Responsibility and Education* (London: George Allen and Unwin, 1959), p. 86.

16. Diego Ledesma, "Annotationes in Ordinem Studiorum Humaniorum Septem Classium, et Trium," *Mon. Paed., op. cit.,* p. 314. The text he had in mind is actually in the Second Book of the Nicomachean Ethics, 1107a and is translated by W. D. Ross: "For among statements about conduct those which are general apply more widely, but those which are particular are more genuine, since conduct has to do with individual cases, and our statements must harmonize with the facts in these cases." See Richard McKeon (ed.), *The Basic Works of Aristotle* (New York: Random House, 1941), p. 959.

17. Diego Ledesma, "De Ratione et Ordine Studiorum Colleggi Romani," *Mon. Paed., op. cit.,* p. 345.

18. James Collins, "The Philosopher's Responsibility," *America,* 102 (November 14, 1959), 189.

19. *Constitutions,* IV, Prooemium. The translation here is that of Ganss, *op. cit.,* p. 283.

20. *Ibid.* Translation in Ganss, *op. cit.,* pp. 281–82.

21. Saint Thomas Aquinas, *Contra impugnantes Dei cultum et religionem,* 11 cited in Thomas Gilby (ed.), *St. Thomas Aquinas: Theological Texts* (New York: Oxford University Press, 1955), p. 33.

22. *Constitutions,* IV, 11, n. 1.

23. *Epitome,* n. 381, 1 and n. 386, 1–2.

24. William H. Kilpatrick's comment was made in the course of a written "debate" with Arthur Bestor, "Progressive Education: A Debate," *The New York Times Magazine,* September 8, 1957, p. 114.

25. *Mon. Paed., op. cit.,* p. 299.

26. These various rules cited from the *Ratio* of 1599 are found in Pachtler, *op. cit.,* II: the Provincial's rules, 234; the Rector's, 268; those of the Prefect of Studies, 276 and those of the Prefect of Lower Studies, 350; the Scripture Professor's rules, 294; the Theology Professor's rules, 300; those of the Professor of Philosophy, 328 and those common to Professors of Lower Classes, 378.

27. John Dewey, *How We Think* (Boston, D. C. Heath and Company, 1910), p. 54. Jacques Maritain remarked in *True Humanism,* trans. M. R. Adamson (London: Geoffrey Bles: The Centenary Press, 1938), p. xi: "There is nothing man desires more than a heroic life: there is nothing less common to man than heroism." For the remark of Lawrence of Arabia which is taken from one of his letters, see Flora Armitage, *The Desert and the Stars: A Biography of Lawrence of Arabia* (New York: Henry Holt and Company, 1955), p. 265. Lawrence's personal philosophy, as Miss Armitage points out here, was a kind of materialism and he had no religious belief.

28. D. W. Brogan, *America in the Modern World* (New Brunswick: Rutgers University Press, 1960), p. 65. For the words of Horace Mann, spoken in a lecture in 1840, see William Kailer Dunn, *What Happened to Religious Education* (Baltimore: Johns Hopkins Press, 1958), pp. 136–37.

29. Suarez, *Tractatus de Religione Societatis Iesu, op. cit.,* V, 6 (p. 298). Speaking of the school's work, Suarez also remarks: "Disciplina enim, et doctrina quodammodo correlativa sunt." *Ibid.,* p. 284.
30. *Constitutions,* IV, 4, n. 2. St. Ignatius is speaking here of Jesuits themselves but a disordered zest for study is not a possibility limited only to religious.
31. *Ratio Studiorum Superiorum Societatis Iesu* (Rome: Apud Curiam Praepositi Generalis, 1954), p. 61.
32. The *Ratio* of 1586 in Pachtler, *op. cit.,* II, 75.
33. *Ibid.,* p. 84.
34. *Ibid.,* p. 134: "Demorari namque in Schola Philosophos totas duas horas et dimidiam, ut modo fit, onerosum est Praeceptori, et molestum auditoribus, quos privato etiam studio consuescere non ab re fuerit, ne tanquam psittaci loqui semper videantur ex praescripto."
35. This apothegm of St. Ignatius's is found in a short list of his "sayings" in a handbook of Jesuit spiritual documents, *Thesaurus Spiritualis Societatis Jesu* (Bruges: Desclée De Brouwer, 1932), p. 448.
36. *Constitutions,* IV, 4, n. 2. Suarez described even the "profane" studies of members of religious orders as "instrumenta virtutis et actionum omnium, quae ad salutem animarum ordinantur." *Op. cit.,* p. 271.
37. de Dainville, *op. cit.,* p. 242.
38. Saint Thomas Aquinas, *Summa Theologica,* IIa IIae, cxlv, i, ad lum. The translation here is that of Thomas Gilby, *St. Thomas Aquinas: Philosophical Texts* (New York: Oxford University Press, 1951), p. 301.
39. *Constitutions,* IV, 5, n. 1. The translation is by Ganss, *op. cit.,* 296–97. The bracketed description of natural philosophy is drawn from a footnote attached to this passage by Father Ganss.
40. This letter was written from Rome, May 21, 1547 and is translated by Young in *Letters of St. Ignatius of Loyola, op. cit.,* pp. 132–37. The words quoted here are found on p. 134.
41. *Ibid.,* pp. 133–34.
42. *Constitutions,* IV, 12, nn. 1 and 3.
43. See Pachtler, *op. cit.,* III, 128. The decree is quoted there in a letter of the sixteenth General of the Society of Jesus, Ignatius Visconti.
44. The *Ratio* of 1586 in Pachtler, *op. cit.,* II, 141. The *Ratio* of 1591 advised the teachers of mathematics to show how the propositions they were demonstrating are useful in the arts and in everyday life since this would attract students. Corcoran, *op. cit.,* p. 222.
45. W. Somerset Maugham, *The Summing Up* (Garden City: Doubleday, 1950), pp. 303–304.
46. Jouvancy, *Ratio Discendi et Docendi, op. cit.,* p. 133. This is the third article of the first chapter of the second part of the treatise.
47. Quoted in Herman, *op. cit.,* p. 226, n. 1.
48. *Constitutions,* IV, 13, n. 2. For the translation see Ganss, *op. cit.,* p. 323.
49. For the document of Pius V see Pachtler, *op. cit.,* I, 1.
50. Herman, *op. cit.,* p. 131.
51. The *Ratio* of 1832 in Pachtler, *op. cit.,* II, 320.
52. Herman, *op. cit.,* 211, 228. In the *Ratio* of 1599 the eighteenth of the

Rules common to Professors of the Lower Classes warns them to observe strictly, *severe*, the practice of speaking Latin; to give demerits to the students who fail to do so and never themselves omit to use Latin: *latine perpetuo Magister loquatur*. Pachtler, *op. cit.*, II, 384. However, the twenty-seventh of these rules explicitly permits use of the vernacular during the prelection and so does the fifth of the Rules for the Professor of the Humanities.

53. For Nadal's phrase see *Mon. Paed., op. cit.*, p. 90. For the phrases prescribing the teaching of Cicero see *ibid.*, pp. 222, 224–225—a few instances among many.

54. For the remark about too narrow an adherence to a single author, see *Mon. Paed., op. cit.*, p. 161 and for the comments from the *Ratio* of 1586, Pachtler, *op. cit.*, II, 113–114.

55. *Epitome*, n. 397.

56. Gladys A. Reichard, "Social Life," in Franz Boas (ed.), *General Anthropology* (New York: D.C. Heath, 1938), p. 476.

57. *Epitome*, n. 397.

58. "Ad saecularia munia usu linguarum sufficienter instructi," Pachtler, *op. cit.*, I, 338. For St. Ignatius's phrase see *Constitutions*, IV, 6, n. 13.

59. Jouvancy, *op. cit.*, p. 36. This is from the fourth article, of the first chapter of the first part of the treatise. It treats of various stylistic defects—of *tumor*, for instance, which is a distended and wordy mode of expression.

60. Peter F. Drucker, *Landmarks of Tomorrow* (New York: Harper and Brothers, 1959), p. 141.

61. For these examples of the material that formed part of the "erudition" in the study of the Latin texts see the *Ratio* of 1586, Pachtler, *op. cit.*, II, 172–173 and the *Ratio* of 1599, Rule 15 of the Rules for the Professors of Rhetoric, *ibid.*, p. 410. One must not make exaggerated claims for this device, however, as though it insured some sort of universal learning acquired while ostensibly studying Latin. The Rule 15 cited above expressly says that this erudition is a diversion for holidays and Rule 5 of the Rules for Professors of Humanities in the *Ratio* of 1599 remarks that the erudition is not to be overdone: *Praelectio eruditionis ornamentis leviter interdum aspersa sit, quantum loci explicatio postulat, ibid.*, p. 420.

62. From Rules 25 and 26 of the Rules Common to Professors of Lower Classes in the *Ratio* of 1599, Pachtler, *op. cit.*, II, 388.

63. *Epitome*, 397, 2. The phrases, "humanism of formation" and "humanism of erudition," are de Dainville's, *op. cit.*, pp. 66, 72. See also the *Epitome*, 345 and 357 b. In these places it is pointed out that in examinations students are not expected simply to parrot opinions but to explain the material under examination and defend it against objections. The ideal of a "humanism of formation" is well expressed in these words of William Cory Johnson, Master of Eton in the late nineteenth century: "At school you are not engaged so much in acquiring knowledge as in making mental efforts under criticism. A certain amount of knowledge you can indeed with average faculties acquire so as to re-

tain; nor need you regret the hours you spent on much that is forgotten, for the shadow of lost knowledge at least protects you from many illusions. But you go to a great school not so much for knowledge as for arts and habits: for the habit of attention, for the art of expression, for the art of assuming at a moment's notice a new intellectual position, for the art of entering quickly into another person's thoughts, for the habit of submitting to censure and refutation, for the art of indicating assent or dissent in graduated terms, for the habit of regarding minute points of accuracy, for the art of working out what is possible in a given time, for taste, for discrimination, for mental courage and mental soberness." Quoted as an epigraph in Samuel Everett, *Growing Up in English Secondary Schools* (Pittsburgh: University of Pittsburgh Press, 1959). In quite a different educational context the same accent is found: "The individual student cannot hope to know the specific kinds of knowledge or particular skills he will need for the different positions he will hold over his working lifetime . . . Therefore, business schools need to concentrate on helping students develop transferable capacities which can be used in many situations and many jobs. Chief attention needs to be placed on fostering qualities of clear analysis, imaginative reasoning, and balanced judgement and on strengthening these qualities through repeated applications to business-type situations. Knowledge of subject matter is essential, but not enough." Frank C. Pierson and others, *The Education of American Businessmen* (New York: McGraw-Hill Book Company, 1959), p. xiii.

64. For the *Ratio* of 1591 see Corcoran, *op. cit.,* p. 209 and for Jouvancy, *op. cit.,* p. 146. For Ignatius's rejection of the *modus Italicus* see Herman, *op. cit.,* pp. 57–77.

65. *Ratio* of 1591 in Corcoran, *op. cit.,* p. 259.

66. *Ratio* of 1586 in Pachtler, *op. cit.,* II, p. 83.

67. *Ibid.,* pp. 130–131.

68. *Mon. Paed., op. cit.,* p. 157. Ledesma seems to be talking here of the work of the Jesuit scholastics but the principle he wished to reinforce applies to any level.

69. For the remarks of the *Ratio* of 1586 see Pachtler, *op. cit.,* II, 103 and for the *Ratio* of 1599, *ibid.,* p. 392.

70. *Constitutions,* IV, 13, n. 3. The translation is from Ganss, *op. cit.,* p. 324.

71. *Ibid.,* IV, 15, n. 1. The translation is from Ganss, *op. cit.,* p. 327.

72. Rule 24 of the Rules common to Professors of the Lower Classes in the *Ratio* of 1599, Pachtler, *op. cit.,* II, p. 388.

73. Corcoran, *op. cit.,* p. 195.

74. Ribadeneira, *op. cit.,* p. 517.

CHAPTER VI

THE EDUCATION OF CHARACTER

Very special care should be taken that those who come to the universities of the Society to acquire letters should learn along with them good and Christian morals.

Constitutions, IV, 16, n. 1[1]

A few years after the publication of the definitive *Ratio* of 1599, Father Francesco Sacchini, the second official historian of the Society, wrote an inspirational tract called *Protrepticon* or Exhortation to the Teachers in the Secondary (Lower) Schools of the Society of Jesus. In the Preface he remarks: "Among us the education of youth is not limited to imparting the rudiments of grammar but extends simultaneously to Christian formation."[2] Then he quotes at once a sentence from St. Ignatius's *Constitutions* to indicate what source he echoes. "The teachers should make it their express purpose, in their lectures when occasion is offered and outside of them, too, to inspire the students to the love and service of God our Lord, and to a love of the virtues by which they please Him."[3] A century later Jouvancy repeated this theme when he said that there are two things which a Christian teacher must teach— piety and letters. The *Epitome,* in turn, adopting the distinction between "instruction" and "education" understood as character formation, lays it down that schoolmasters are to be properly prepared in methods of instruction and in the art of educating.[4] The Jesuit educational tradition in short, has always ratified the sentiment Martin Buber expressed when he said: "Education worthy of the name is essentially education of character."[5]

This emphasis it has been noted, is scarcely unusual. No serious educational theorist was ever content to conceive of education simply in terms of growth in knowledge and intellectual acumen although the work of the teacher would be easier if it were limited by this relatively modest academic aim. "The major difference between Plato's conception of education and our own," wrote Sir Richard Livingstone, "is that his concern was to impart values, ours is to impart knowledge and teach people to think."[6] But most good schools, and certainly all church-related schools, are still struggling for efficacious loyalty to both the moral and the intellectual purposes of education. This naturally condemns them to everlasting discontent for just as this twofold task is too essential to be abandoned so it is also too difficult for any perfect success.

Since a zeal for the development of strong moral character is the single most common feature among philosophies of education from the primitive to the sophisticated and from the Christian to the Soviet, it might be well to clarify a notion protean enough to be at home in such various contexts. The specification of aims and means will show marked differences from one system to another but certain common questions are agitated and certain generic characteristics encountered wherever there is an interest in moral education. The object of such interest is formation of a character both strong and good. The strong character will usually be thought of as one marked by self-motivated perseverance for self-chosen goals and therefore neither wavering, nor driven, nor compulsive. When this psychological description is set within an ethical dimension, character will be denominated not only strong but also good, if its goals, means and motives are all morally valid. It will be the aim of character education to form just such a person.

A teacher who accepts some responsibility for furthering this moral purpose is confronted, to begin with, by the speculative inquiry into the exact nature of goodness. He needs to know the outlines of the ethical ideal he seeks as well as the content of the moral code which transcribes it. This determination of moral principles is not the work of the educational theorist, however, but belongs properly to the moral philosopher who pitches his tent on a plain where disputing theories clash incessantly. Without attempting to describe, much less umpire, their differences, it can still be said that most moralists would agree that the good man is one who chooses the real value over the spurious and the higher over the lower consistently enough to indicate a fundamental allegiance to the good. This itself presupposes that he has an intellectual grasp of what these values are and their proper hierarchical order and that his behavior corresponds to this knowledge. The harmony between the moral ideal and conduct must also be comprehensive since even criminals can be steadfast in one or other virtue whereas educators would agree with the *Meno* that virtue is one and indivisible in the truly good man. This still leaves the precise nature of that goodness largely undefined. An historical overview suggests, however, that most of the great ethical teachers thought of the good man as one in whom the domination of egoism or self-seeking love had been controlled from within by altruism or self-donating love. Even this is very general and requires considerable specification and it is that which the moralists must provide.

But even when he has been furnished with specifications, the classroom teacher still has some thorny practical questions to answer. One such problem is the speculative-practical issue of the relationship between morality and religion and therefore between moral education and religious education. It is certainly not a relation of identity. Morality, in the sense of objective moral virtue, is the conformity of behavior to right principles of conduct. Religion commonly denotes the whole zone of man's relationship to the trans-temporal, to the holy, to the divine—to God.[7] A fully developed or "institutionalized" religion will include a faith or creed, a moral code and a liturgical, sacramental life which serves as a pre-eminent medium for contact with the divine. But since morality and religiousness are not identical there can exist systems of morality and moral education without significant relation to any religion or to religious education. The religious man will consider these systems substantially incomplete but that they exist is proven by the example of such secular ethics as those of Confucius and John Dewey. Conversely, there have been religions which appeared to have little impact upon the ethical theory of their followers. In the *Republic,* for instance, Socrates's devotions contribute nothing of importance to his speculation on the nature of justice.

Most religions, however, have directly influenced the moral life of their adherents and this is pre-eminently true of Christianity. When Christians look about them, in fact, they see that apart from the enlightenment of Faith, many central ethical principles that should govern the lives of all men, whether Christian or not, are simply never known. The Church, however, sets the complete moral code before men and instructs them on the ultimate finality of human existence and the sanctions for sin. It also dynamizes the effort to observe this code and achieve this eternal union with God by providing sacramental nourishment for the life of grace, the life of faith and love.

When the goals of moral education are enunciated within a strictly secular dimension they are generally reduced to respectable commonplaces—ideals of decency, kindliness, responsibility and democratic loyalty which are apt to be hazy if not ambiguous. For his part, therefore, the Christian educator believes that the definition of a good character, as well as the process of educating for it, is essentially linked with religious instruction and the religious life of the student. Alan Paton once expressed this conviction in a very personal fashion when he asked himself whether morality could be taught without the knowledge and practice of faith. "All I know," he replied, "is that for myself, conduct and faith are locked together and that in me a period of faithlessness would inevitably lead to a change of conduct."[8] Certainly any discussion of the Jesuit concept of moral education must necessarily involve some consideration both of the program of instruction in the content of religion and the opportunities provided for practice of the religious life. These are not the only factors in the formation of sound character but they are of prime importance in that process.

Throughout this same process the Christian teacher is guided by one dominant, twofold purpose. He wants his students to achieve a true interiorization of the Christian norms of morality so that their behavior will be controlled from within by their own convictions rather than by social pressures from without. Secondly, the teacher hopes that, throughout their lives, his students, energized by love of God and of the neighbor, will translate these norms into consistent Christian conduct. The practical question raised by so splendid an objective is this: In what sense may it be said that moral virtue can be taught? It is generally agreed that the content of the ethical code can be imparted either by sheer indoctrination or by reflection upon the philosophical and theological reasons for the positions taken. This much may be enough for the moral philosopher but not for the moral educator. An intelligent student can easily bring off a brilliant defense of honesty and remain a liar. The teacher wants to know if people can really be educated to honesty and if so, how. Historically there have been two quite different replies to this question based upon two quite different noetics. The Platonic idealist, for whom the natural object of man's understanding is the intelligible form itself, is inclined to accent the importance in moral training of intellectual vision, that is to say of a profound intellectual grasp of the very nature of moral values. To his way of thinking, a man who has a genuine and appreciative understanding of the essence of honesty cannot lie and if he were to do so, that would only be proof of a defect in his understanding. The Aristotelian realist and empiricist, for whom the natural object of man's understanding is something initially confronted in sensory experience, even though the trans-sensible may subsequently be reached, is inclined to emphasize the importance of practical judgment for developing detailed moral science itself and the importance of practical action for genuine growth in moral virtue.

No doubt both these positions contain valuable suggestions for the educator of character. In the Jesuit program, as we shall see, much depends upon a vital contact with our Lord, the divine Hero, and this is helped by a knowledge of His earthly life and His message. What is looked for here is an intellectual appreciation penetrated by affectivity. This is possible, the Christian believes, only if grace intervenes and transforms the natural resources of mind and heart. Still, the Platonic insight is important for it reminds the teacher that there can be no love without knowledge. On the other hand, the Christian casuist readily grants that moral evaluations must take into account all the pertinent circumstances although he will not agree that the concrete situation is the only determinant of the substance of moral judgments or that pragmatic effectiveness is their sole criterion. Most parents and teachers, moreover, would side with Aristotle and St. Thomas against Plato and deny that virtue can be taught, if that term be taken in the strict sense it has when one speaks of teaching geometry by bringing a student to see for himself that in the Euclidean universe two parallel lines will never meet. When St. Thomas spoke of moral training he did not use *docere* (to teach), the verb he applied to the work of the geometry instructor, but making a significant change he remarked that the child should be accustomed, *assuescere,* to acting virtuously; should be taught, as it were, through practice.[9] This is, indeed, the central conviction of all Christian asceticism: doers of the word, not hearers only.

Educators will most reasonably conclude then, that character formation has two interrelated phases, the instructional moment in which students come to know what the ethical ideal and code are and the moment of practice which develops their personal allegiance to these through living them out in action. The value of cooperation may be taught in the classroom but the virtue itself is developed through generous participation in extracurricular activities. Christian teachers believe, in addition, that grace is strictly necessary for success in this most delicate phase of education. Most of them also think that, naturally speaking, an authentic relationship of reverence and friendship between the teacher and pupil is an invaluable dispositive condition for such success. The Jesuit teacher brings to his work as an educator of character, therefore, both his commitment to the full moral vision of Christianity and some such basic concept of the practical approach as the one indicated here. The business of this present chapter is to review the specifications of that approach which the educational heritage of the Society has emphasized.

This is an even trickier task than summarizing the Jesuit academic tradition. The material is more intangible in this case and the few explicit directives in the *Constitutions* and the *Ratio* are more than ever fragmentary and elliptical—comments, to repeat Lippert's phrase, which do not embody the spirit but only mark certain of its practical applications. Indeed in one or two details, there is a curious division here between the *Spiritual Exercises* and certain features of the *Ratio* program which are rather alien to it. The first Jesuits, it will be remembered, possessed both the *Exercises* and a thorough knowledge of the academic organization codified by the University of Paris. They intended to provide an intellectual training along Parisian lines—languages, philosophy and science, theology—and a moral training inspired by the lessons they had learned themselves through the *Exercises*. The religious and moral pedagogy of these *Exercises* is perennial, for it is rooted in a sure psychological understanding of human nature and a penetration of the Biblical revelation of that nature's history and destiny. The pedagogy of the *Ratio,* however, was sometimes tainted by the ambiguities of the age that produced it. For instance, it thought of religious instruction chiefly in terms of catechetical memory lessons and recommends such dubious devices as preoccupying emphasis on competition for glory. It is necessary to appeal, therefore, to the authentic Jesuit heritage in this matter. That will be found not only in the printed sources but especially in the traditional interpretation of these fonts and in the historic practice which has elaborated the hints preserved in the documents. Our concern is not so much to know how the sixteenth and seventeenth centuries understood or applied the principles of character formation as to discover the radical meaning of the principles themselves.

Such principles will not, to be sure, constitute a full theory of moral education, even when their implications are completely unravelled, any more than the *Ratio's* academic provisions add up to a full theory of intellectual education. The sixteenth century, for one thing, lacked the insight now supplied by psychiatrists and psychologists who have enlarged our understanding of the timetable and mechanics of moral development in childhood and the influence of unconscious forces and motives upon the moral life. They lacked the insight provided by sociologists who have detailed the role of the family and peer-group in the development of character and the part played by the concept of a hero in the formation of a satisfactory self-image. Yet many of these later findings fit so neatly into the theory which the sixteenth century followed, that one might think places had been prepared for them from the beginning.

The Ideal: *Amor et Obsequium:* Love and Service of the Lord

Although moral and religious maturity is not identical with emotional maturity nor with the development of a sound adult personality, it is clearly related to the achievement of these latter aims. The interrelationship here is only a specific instance of the communication between all phases of human life from the biological to the social and spiritual. It is also acknowledged by that basic principle of Christian humanism which holds that Christian personality is not the denial but the transformation of the natural personality. Nowadays the psychological evolution of personality is usually described as a process in which a young person arrives at a clear, firm concept of himself; discovers, so to speak, who he is in terms of his abilities and reserves, his relationships and his vocation. Were he not to achieve this sense of his own identity, his inner life would be one of anxious drifting and his personality as elusive as mercury.[10] The solidification of this definite self-concept, however, requires a grasp of purposes which will serve to integrate or unify the individual and his powers. As one writer put it on the eve of the Golden Anniversary White House Conference on Children and Youth: "The past ten years have taught people, especially the younger ones making their lifetime choices . . . to accept as valuable the idea of permanent commitments, which can liberate more energies and personal resources than the defunct state of remaining uncommitted . . . that serious commitment, voluntary but nonrevocable, is a positive good. . . ."[11]

Now St. Ignatius's contribution to character formation consisted above all in having devised in the *Spiritual Exercises* a wonderfully effective instrument for fostering personal development by fostering the emergence of a satisfactory "self-image" and a "serious commitment, voluntary but nonrevocable."[12] This is not, moreover, a commitment to some ideology or impersonal absolute but to a Person or, more exactly, to the Triune Godhead, to the Father known through his Son Jesus Christ who is encountered in His Church by the grace of the Holy Spirit. Consequently the obligations which commitment imposes are not, for the Christian, coercive or legalistic but a filial homage of service and love.

We do not mean by these *Spiritual Exercises* the text of the terse little manual itself any more than by a Beethoven symphony one means the printed score. It is the *Spiritual Exercises* as actually performed, or a "retreat" as it is called, which constitutes this powerfully educative experience. The students of contemporary Jesuit schools make one of these retreats in abbreviated form for a few days of every academic year. The Jesuit teachers give eight days to their own annual retreat besides following the *Exercises* for a full thirty days twice during their years of training in the Society. Moreover, the practice of "closed retreats" for both students and members of the non-Jesuit faculties is increasingly popular in

American schools and colleges. On these occasions the retreatants go off for a weekend or longer to some retreat house situated in an attractive and secluded country spot and spend the time, under the guidance of a retreat Director, in silent reflection upon the great Christian truths which the *Exercises* have expertly arranged so as to produce a moving and instructive effect. Retreats of this sort are not mentioned in the *Ratio* but they are now a central element of the character formation program of Jesuit schools and are a logical development of the Ignatian tradition. Their influence is not limited to the few days of actual retreat for the attitude and tone they create is communicated to every phase of school life in some degree.

The Ignatian retreat, as we have indicated, does not simply confront the retreatant with an abstract complexus of Christian dogma. Rather it focuses his attention upon the person of Christ, the Lord, and nourishes commitment to Him by evoking, under grace and in a sacramental atmosphere of prayer and quiet, a transforming love for this transcendent figure. All this has clear implications, not merely for religious and moral development but for the formation of stable personality. The encounter with the Lord provides, for one thing, that vision of greatness which Whitehead insisted education must communicate. The love, which is awakened, powerfully sustains allegiance to the Christian world view and to the Christian code. Finally, meditation upon this divine Hero, who for the believer is no mere historical personage but, to use Kierkegaard's phrase, every man's contemporary, marvellously fosters a worthy self-image. For in shaping our concept of the ideal self we hope to become, we usually take some heroic figure as a model and even unbelievers are likely to grant that the Christian Lord is unique among exemplars. Charles Horton Cooley, one of the pioneer American social psychologists, once summed up the moral function of this sort of devotion to noble heroes when he wrote:

> There is, I think, no possibility of being good without living, imaginatively of course, in good company; and those who uphold the moral power of personal example as against that of abstract thought are certainly in the right. A mental crisis, by its very difficulty, is likely to call up the thought of some person we have been used to look to as a guide, and the confronting of the two ideas, that of the person and that of the problem, compels us to answer the question, What would he have thought of it? The guide we appeal to may be a person in the room, or a distant friend, or an author whom we have never seen, or an ideal person of religion.

The strong, good men we have once imagined live in our minds
and fortify there the idea of worthiness. They were free and noble
and make us unhappy to be less.[13]

The Christian spirituality which a retreat serves to heighten aims, one
might say, to help men live in company divinely good.

The *Exercises'* potential for character formation as well as for the
general orientation of Jesuit schools, is not limited, however, to strengthening self-identification and commitment to the Christian interpretation
of life. One who makes the *Exercises* will also have had certain experiences which can teach him how to advance toward a firmly altruistic
personality. To see this, we might recall for a moment the main lines of
the spare and tight dialectic of those *Exercises*. The retreatant is first invited to consider what the divine design of the cosmos requires: that all
its elements reach fruition through man who is to employ them for the
greater glory of God. He is next reminded of the historic fracture of this
design by wide-scale moral evil in the past and of how his own sins have
disrupted, or threaten to disrupt, the order within the microcosm that is
himself. Such failure will be averted and God's purpose fulfilled, if love so
masters the human heart as to preserve fidelity. This sort of energetic
love will be enkindled by contact with the Lord and therefore the retreatant is led to reflect prayerfully upon the great scenes from the Gospel
story. On the other hand, the practice of firm self-control will be required
to bulwark love against the tides of boredom, sensuality, ambition, pride,
hostility and greed so the exercitant also meditates upon the indispensa-
bility of asceticism. Finally, since love is validated in action, the *Exercises*
consistently impel those who are making them to determine how they
will prove their love by service.

These phases of the *Exercises* involve personal rumination rather
than passive attendance at a sermon and consequently they can be un-
usually effective in stimulating progress toward emotional and moral maturity. Reflection upon one's sins and the defects which make sin likely,
often helps a retreatant arrive at some degree of adult objectivity about
himself. The emphasis upon the discipline and abnegation required to
escape a destructive and sterile egoism is clearly valuable, particularly
when the exercitant arrives by himself at agreement with the Ignatian
conviction "that in all that concerns the spiritual life his progress will be
in proportion to his surrender of self-love and of his own will and interest."[14] In similar fashion, the graduated meditations are designed to
deepen men's sense of their central human vocation to love incarnated in
a life of service, to an acceptance of responsibility for the welfare of all

their brethren in humanity. At a critical point in the *Exercises,* this suggestion is encountered: "Those who wish to give greater proof of their love and to distinguish themselves in the service of the eternal King and the Lord of all, will not only offer themselves entirely for the work, but will act against their sensuality and carnal and worldly love and make offerings of greater value."[15] No doubt, this passage is thinking in the first place of those who are likely to make the special choice of life in a Religious Institute. The emphasis upon responsibility and service, however, is not only intended for all Christians but is also the effective solvent of that egocentrism which blights the growth of a mature and ethical personality.

The Moral Significance of the Academic Experience

In the classic dilemmas of educational theory both the extreme positions are in error since the truth is always a synthesis of their respective insights. Thus the sharp antinomy between those who hold that the school's business is "disciplined intellectual training," or the conversion of potential into actual intellectual power, and those who hold that its first concern is for "character building," is to some extent an opposition manufactured by extremists.[16] It can be mitigated, if not eliminated, by recalling that while the formation of character is no doubt the overall aim of education, this requires intellectual maturation. A man who understands nothing about himself nor about the laws governing both the physical and the moral universe will not consistently shape his conduct by those laws. In the Jesuit educational tradition, as in many others, the academic curriculum is thought of as itself having a moral value since the intellectual power and versatility it generates makes possible an adult comprehension of as well as dedication to ethical and religious ideals. This is not to say, of course, either that such intellectual growth is achieved only through formal education or that its sole purpose is to solidify sound character. It might result from self-education through wide reading or from reflective travel or from close association with gifted persons or even from a divine illumination.[17] Normally, however, it is facilitated by formal schooling which is more economical and orderly than informal education. St. Ignatius's appreciation of the moral effect of a civilized intelligence has already been indicated. He esteemed the arts and sciences, as he made clear, because they disposed the mind to understand and use knowledge of things divine.[18]

In addition to this general contribution made by the academic phase of any good education to character formation, a Christian school communicates a message of ethical and religious import simply by teaching a normal curriculum and thereby testifying to its belief in the possibility of synthesizing the religious and the secular dimensions of life. No doubt such harmony is hard to achieve and rarely realized to perfection. In an essay on theory it is enough to point out that, granted the assistance of grace, the ideal is viable, however difficult it may be to incarnate it in practice. If a Christian teacher in a Christian school is a competent scientist and instructor, his students should conclude that the conflict between science and religious commitment is not logically inevitable even if historically rather common. In the first century of the Society's history, Nadal had already laid it down that Jesuit institutions must have capable professors who are not only well versed in their subjects and concerned for their students' moral function but are also men who can impart a religious spirit to the whole school and illuminate it by their good example.[19]

It was expected that in such a school an indirect character education would be quite natural and comments in the early documents suggest that moral formation goes, almost insensibly, hand-in-hand with intellectual growth. Thus Ignatius himself wrote that the students should absorb (*hauriant*) Christian manners along with their letters. The *Ratio* of 1591 spoke of the smallest boys, those in the lowest class, as sucklings imbibing piety along with grammar, whereas the older ones in the Rhetoric division drew these waters of devotion for themselves.[20] None of the versions of the *Ratio* offers a theory explaining how the academic curriculum advances moral virtue but such a theory is possible and rather more subtle than Jouvancy's notion of turning the classic authors into *praecones Christi*. The program of the secondary school, it will be recalled, concentrated upon the literary culture of Greece and Rome. It may seem to us now, reading over the three versions of the *Ratio,* that they interpreted Hellenic humanism quite narrowly and were more concerned with verbal dexterity than with the rich substance of that tradition; more interested in nice Latinity than in the horizons upon which imaginative writing opens windows. But even if this is true, it is irrelevant since we are looking now to the deepest meaning of that curricular theory rather than to its limited historical applications.

It is a theory closely related to that on which Ignatius acted in devising the *Exercises*. Plato formulated it when he observed that the head rules the belly through the heart, that is to say, through generous emotions or magnanimity.[21] H. Boehmer, the Lutheran historian, has nicely pointed up the way in which the *Spiritual Exercises* exploit the resources of the imagination for the spiritual transformation of the retreatant:

> The uniqueness of Loyola's soul-cure, in the last analysis, consists in the stretching or fostering of the imagination, in which exercise he encourages the practitioner most urgently. He starts with the correct observation that one only succeeds in drawing an individual away from his old conceptions and habits and wins him permanently to a new ideal when one understands how to take possession of his imagination. "Visions" were thus conjured up "for him which he could drive away only with difficulty,"—visions which remained longer with him than all the general principles and good instruction one could give him; for good teachings are soon forgotten, but such fabrications of the imagination stick tenaciously in the soul.[22]

The pedagogical principle implied here suggested that, if schooling introduced students to perspectives of beauty and nobility through immersion in great imaginative literature, this would do a good deal to refine and inspirit them. Experiences of this sort, it was thought, are quite within the grasp of persons still too young for metaphysical reflection or advanced scientific work and so the expansion of the aesthetic sensibility was assigned to these early years. Was the aim itself illusory? The mature Augustine upbraided himself for having wept over Dido and perhaps he was right or perhaps Virgil is not food for children. Still, it is also possible that Augustine learned a certain compassion as he mourned that queen who could pity the miserable because she had known misery. In any case, this example, is only emblematic. What counts is the notion that to cultivate the artist in a child, not only through literature but through all the arts, can contribute to making him an integrated and moral person. This surely recommends itself so long as one does not simply equate artistic sensibility with moral virtue.

The curricular ideal which lies beneath the letter of the *Constitutions* and *Ratio* does not make such an equation. It appreciates, to be sure, the ethical potential of great literature but it does not suppose that this is the only value of literary studies nor that the inquiry into life's meaning is limited to reading poetry and drama. Indeed, one of the chief purposes of the philosophic disciplines in the Arts course which follows upon the language curriculum is to help students construct a framework of significance within which their adult lives may satisfactorily unfold. The implications in this for a balanced personality and for conduct are clear enough. Psychiatrists have acquainted us with the disasters that befall men whose lives are devoid of meaning. The philosophical curriculum will not provide such meaning automatically, of course, even though it examines the problems of man, the cosmos, destiny, truth and value, because it bears no immunity from incompetent teaching or the down-pull of an inadequate environment. Yet it must be said again that difficulties and failures do not themselves invalidate an ideal.

The *Constitutions* and the *Ratio* do contain, however, a curricular ambiguity which puzzles the modern reader and has been hinted at before. The total academic experience outlined in these documents not only includes theology but is crowned by it. This discipline was explicitly recognized as the chief means to the end for which Jesuit schools existed in the first place. That purpose was the essentially religious and ethical one of knowing and loving God. In practice, though, only a minority of those enrolled in the secondary school or in the Arts course ever went on to the studies of the Theology Faculty. Moreover, the provision which the secondary school itself made for religious instruction must strike us as scanty and methodologically crude. In two of the five classes constituting the Middle School, that of Humanities (Poetry) and Rhetoric, no time was assigned, at least by the *Ratio,* to formal religion classes. In the three grammar divisions only an hour or half-hour was set aside on the last day of the week in which *memoriter recitatur Catechismus.* Perhaps this was because those classes were often taught by scholastics who had not yet studied theology and were thought capable only of hearing the catechism. Whatever the reason, Jesuit high schools and colleges today would judge these ancient arrangements quite inadequate although by sixteenth-century standards they were both generous and novel. Since the Catholic believes that theological studies contribute preeminently to that framework of significance upon which educated Christians are expected to have some hold, he can hardly approve reserving them to a Faculty of Theology which only seminarians ordinarily reach. Nowadays, the religion department in high schools and the theology department in colleges are integral parts of the program even though the time allotted them is relatively brief. The *Epitome,* n. 382, calls for at least two periods of religion a week in secondary schools but this is obviously a good deal less than Latin or Mathematics or English receive. The strict catechetical method itself is ill thought of by most modern experts on religious instruction although their specialty is still known as catechetics. They advocate instead a variety of new procedures with greater potential for awakening an appreciative understanding of Christian life and dogma than that possessed by repetition of formalized questions and answers.

Because the sixteenth-century Jesuit schoolmasters believed that the academic milieu was itself a shaper of character they took trouble to control that environment so that destructive forces might not weaken its fabric. In the *Constitutions,* for instance, St. Ignatius had advised dismissal of unruly students whom neither counselling nor punishments could reclaim since their retention would do them no good and could serve to mislead others.[23] Still, this decision was not to be made hastily but by the chief administrator, the rector, after he had judged the matter in light of the school's basic aims.

The most controversial regulation for maintaining that controlled Christian environment is, no doubt, the one governing the students' reading program. St. Ignatius had himself directed that no indecent pages from the pagan classics be studied and this is surely reasonable enough. Even the most ardent foes of censorship, as the press likes to call them, do not propose D. H. Lawrence as a high school text. More troublesome, however, were the problems posed by celebrated imaginative works containing passages judged unsuitable for youthful readers and by orthodox theological treatises from writers whose other books were suspect. The first constituted a danger to purity of morals; the second to purity of faith. St. Ignatius's solution to these problems was characteristically forthright. Books in the first category were to be purged of all improprieties and eroticism before being used; books in the second were not to be read at all, for even though they were unobjectionable, their author was dubious and one might acquire a dangerous taste which would lead one from his good to his bad books. Besides, says Ignatius firmly, thinking of all the curious doctrines and the crypto-heretics in the Catholic world of his day, there will generally be some poison in any products of a heart full of poison.[24]

A twentieth-century educator is apt to find this whole business of expurgating the pagan classics a dreary one, although in American schools, major pieces of literature are often edited simply to make them easier for the uncultivated sophomore reader. The device would not have recommended itself at all were it not for the enormous zest for Latin literature in the sixteenth century. It might be thought that Protestant educators were wiser in omitting altogether those items which they could not wholly accept. No doubt, the editors of the *Ratio,* conforming to their general principle of seizing the good where they found it, would have said that these books had positive qualities which it would be too bad to miss when some discreet fumigation would have made them presentable.[25] In any case, the issue itself underscores an instructive conviction of those early Jesuit pedagogues. For although those teachers were less enthusiastic about wide and relatively unrestricted reading than we are, they had perhaps greater respect for the power of books. Since they believed that great books could shape intelligence and hence influence character by reason of the interplay between mind and heart, they also believed that an evil book can corrupt. And unless one assumes that reading and study *can* make a difference, there is little point in educating. The task of the conscientious teacher remains, however, enormously delicate. He surely wants to nurture initiative and a mature, inquiring intelligence. But he also knows that the youthful spirit needs protection against problems and forces which so far exceed its present strength that an encounter with them would shatter rather than develop it. It is certainly hard to work out a practical program and we need not claim that the sixteenth century succeeded perfectly. What can be said is that the principle of making the school a protected milieu in which students can approach life's challenges gradually is sound and it was this principle that underlay the regulation of readings.

Probably it also determined certain other characteristics of the sixteenth-century academic environment whose implications for moral formation make some contemporary Christian consciences uneasy. These were the motivations exploited by those schools as spurs to study—the *quasi calcar pueris admovendum* as the *Ratio* of 1591 once called them.[26] There was then a good deal of hard work laid out for pupils and this in itself was not necessarily antithetical to interest. Indeed, various investigations have shown that modern college students, if not made to work and improve, have no interest in and derive no enjoyment from their classes and study.[27] The little boys whom the *Ratio* bent to Latin and Greek were not old enough, however, or learned enough to savour the intrinsic delights of scholarship. They needed various *incitamenta* or *adjumenta studiorum*. But for the Renaissance man there were two great stimuli to effort, or rather one which possessed a positive and negative face: the love of glory and the fear of dishonor. The Jesuit schoolmasters seem to have uncritically adopted certain methods which exploited this human hunger for honor. There are, said the *Ratio* of 1591 under its rule for teachers of the lowest class, two devices particularly effective for inflaming boys with a zest for study: the hope of honor or praise and the fear of disgrace or punishment. The *Ratio* of 1586 had previously noted this same fact and that of 1599 would ratify the implication by advising teachers that they could accomplish more by the lure of honor and reward and by the dread of ignominy than they could by blows. Jouvancy summed it up quite bluntly when he said that the two mechanisms for ruling a classroom are praise and blame.[28]

The great device recommended by the *Ratio* for canalizing the energies released by this appetite for glory was that of vigorous and incessant competition. It was known as emulation and the aim, as was noted earlier, was to baptize and transform it into *honesta aemulatio, quae magnum ad studia incitamentum est.*[29] Holy emulation is, no doubt, theoretically possible but like just anger it may not be often encountered in a naughty world. The editors of the *Ratio,* however, do not appear to have been at all worried. Classes might be divided into groups of ten with each *decuria* headed by a captain or the whole class might be ranked and commissioned with titles borrowed from Greek and Roman military and civil service. Then all the privates and officers, magistrates and citizens engaged in energetic academic war or *concertatio* with group pitted against group and individual against individual. To the victors went various rewards: first place in the seatings, prizes and emblems of distinction. The *Ratio* of 1586, moreover, recommended that there be also a special bench for those who failed most spectacularly.[30]

Anyone who has ever employed these devices knows that they do wonderfully invigorate youngsters and produce results.* If they can be handled tactfully and with good humor under a wise teacher, it does not seem that they should be morally any more harmful than competitive sports provided at least as much attention is given in the school to fostering the spirit of fraternal cooperation. Indeed, it can be persuasively argued that emulation, when properly controlled, has individual and social values that recommend it as part of any school program. It is of prime importance that people learn how to live cooperatively in community but it is also wise for them to learn their own limitations and to recognize the disparities in abilities among men. Besides, to borrow another of Cooley's formulations:

> The general fact is that the most effective way of utilizing human energy is through an organized rivalry, which by specialization and social control is, at the same time, organized co-operation.

---

* An American Jesuit with considerable experience both in teaching and administration criticized the paragraphs above when he read them in manuscript. The devices of the *concertatio* and *decuriae,* he remarked, are intended to be used only with boys of good character. If that condition is verified, he believes that the devices themselves may well develop such qualities as fortitude, patience, and modesty to say nothing of the spirit of teamplay so much admired by Americans. This may be true and in any case we do not intend here to question the importance of rewards and punishments in actual learning. We are less sure of the value of a one-sided emphasis on rewards that are extrinsic to the satisfactions inherent in learning itself.

An ideal social system, from this point of view, would be one in which the work of individuals in each occupation, the work of occupations in relation to one another, that of class in relation to class and of nation in relation to nation, should be motived by a desire to excel, this desire being controlled and subordinated by allegiance to common social ideals.[31]

In all these cases, nevertheless, one must remember that differences in talent, are not, on the Christian reckoning, supposed to promote pride or despondency and that rivalry really should serve community and co-operation, not weaken them. It can be questioned whether or not the Renaissance passion for glory harmonizes with this latter emphasis. It is curious, in any case, how the *Ratio* on this point inverts the scale of values of the *Spiritual Exercises* which praise goodness, not glory, and urge the Christian to elect humiliations with the humiliated Christ. It is realistic, of course, to exploit for all they are worth the relish for fame and the fear of disgrace but it is a secular kind of realism. The pedagogical device of emulation can be used cautiously. But if it is true, as de Dainville maintains, that *la gloire* is the last word and very soul of the *Ratio Studiorum,* then one must judge the *Ratio* to have been too utilitarian in this matter. The accent, it may be granted, is easily enough explained not only in light of the Renaissance ideology but in terms of the quite practical need of keeping classes of some two hundred exuberant little boys in order, if need be, by Jouvancy's pet machines, praise and blame.

The Liturgical Life of the School Community

A religious sense of the presence of God is directly and powerfully awakened by participation in the liturgical life of worship within the Church. From a brief communal prayer to the most splendid celebration of Solemn Mass, the liturgical moment always constitutes an actually holy situation highly effective for deepening faith in the Divine reality and an effective response to It.[32] Moreover, the Mass also evokes and enlarges the Christians' sense of their own community, of their oneness with each other in the Lord. Even at the level of sociological observation, it can be seen that a sharing in religious ritual unifies the members of a group. They not only act together but their fraternal feeling is strengthened by a spiritual transformation when it is brought into the very sanctuary. This vivid awareness of the Holy God and of the sacred character of the community when once it has been related to Him, contributes profoundly to growth in personal goodness. Consequently, cultivation of the liturgical life is a central element in the plan of Jesuit education for development of moral stature. This does not mean, of course, that the liturgy is thought of chiefly as a means for fostering individual devotion and social unity. Its primary function remains the worship of God and the offering of that homage to which both the person and the community are obliged. The Catholic educator, however, knows that the liturgical action also has these rich moral values and he hopes to cultivate them reverently.

Reverence is, indeed, a primary requisite for without it prayer and ritual may scandalize rather than inspire. St. Ignatius ruled that a short prayer be said before each class but he added that it was to be omitted if it could not be said in a way that would promote edification and devotion. The *Ratio* of 1591, in a similar mood, directs that the littlest boys are never to attend Mass without their teachers also being present to instruct them in reverential attitudes and the *Ratio* of 1599 repeated the idea in the Forty-fifth Rule for the Prefect of Lower Studies.[33]

The heart of the school's liturgical life is the Mass to which the conscientious use of confession is related as a chief means of preparing for fruitful participation in the Eucharistic rite. In the Christian school, in fact, all the activities of the day ought to radiate outward from the Mass for their radical significance is symbolized in the Liturgy. Christian education aims to sanctify all that is worthy in the secular order and it sees this effort mystically prefigured at Mass when the faithful offer themselves and all their human enterprises to the Father along with the supreme oblation of the Son. St. Ignatius himself had directed, therefore, that each day begin with the Mass and had observed that it "would help very much" if all were to attend. He showed great delicacy in this matter, nevertheless. The boys in the secondary school, were, it will be remembered, actually children ranging in age from seven or eight to twelve or fourteen. These could easily be obliged to attend Mass for they would be quite at ease with a paternal direction of their devotion; would expect it and be at loss without it. Older youths, perhaps passing through a phase of hostility to authority, might resent a rule obliging them to attend Mass on a weekday when the Church only prescribed this for Sundays. St. Ignatius was quite likely thinking of these students when he said that those for whom constraint is inadvisable should rather be persuaded gently, *amanter,* to assist at Mass but if they refused they were neither to be compelled nor penalized in any way.[34] This prudent directive was eminently conformed to the Christian spirit which judges a coerced homage no satisfactory homage at all. But the Eucharistic act remains, in every case, the central source of energy in the Christian school whether this is recognized universally or not.

Law and Freedom in the School Community

As we shall say again in the next chapter, the Jesuit school is intended to be a genuine community of teachers and students—a society, partial and incomplete, no doubt, but real. Society requires, however, the embodiment of authority in certain of its members to whom the others are subordinated in order that the social resources of the community may be unified and directed toward the common purpose. This in turn poses the problem of synthesizing authority with individual freedom so that each one may share fully in the social life.[35] Because of the imbalance between the two main segments of an academic community and the natural limitations of extreme youth, one would hardly expect to find the average member of a school participating in authority to the extent of an adult citizen in a small democracy. Nevertheless, the best concept of the school is not that of a prison nor a regiment nor a gang but a rational society in which both law and liberty have their due place. This has clear implications, finally, for the moral development of the members of the school world.

The Jesuit tradition believes that so far as school discipline goes there lies between total permissiveness and coercion a third way when authority is informed by charity and exercised solely for the upbuilding of the community and of each of its members although like every ideal this one may be fitfully understood at times and poorly realized. Basic to it is the conviction that moral excellence can be matured in young people by the pressure of authority which guides them into the pathways of virtue. This pressure has nothing in common with violence, however, and is derived rather from the weight of the teacher's greater wisdom and experience in which the student confidently acquiesces. Exen in the sixteenth century, therefore, when the ancient practice of flogging boys through their studies was still in full vigor, the Jesuit schools dissented from a rule of force. The façades of great French cathedrals testified to the common acceptance of this rule for among the sculptured figures representing the Seven Liberal Arts, Grammar was portrayed as a crone armed with a switch. At Winchester, oldest of the great English "public" schools, there was a vast hall built and first used for classes in the time of Charles II. One of its walls bore a plaque with the intimidating legend: *Aut disce aut discede manet sors tertia caedi*—Learn or leave or, a third possibility, be flogged.[36] In that public school tradition this sentiment is still not entirely extinct.

From the outset, however, the Jesuit concept of discipline departed from the older blend of pessimism and brutality although its sixteenth-century practice may seem to us severe enough. The rod could not be ruled out completely, of course, any more than football and report cards can be eliminated from contemporary high schools. Long before the *Ratio* was written, however, a basic pedagogical principle preserved in the *Monumenta Paedagogica* had been enunciated: *Ubi verba valent, ibi verbera non dare*—If admonition suffices, let chastisement be not imposed.[37] Even if *verbera* did appear called for they were hedged about with restrictions. On no account was a Jesuit himself to administer the penalty. For this purpose a layman called the corrector was hired and his good offices were employed only under supervision and for serious offences, clearly spelled out beforehand. The conviction to be disengaged from this advocacy of humane discipline is that intellectual and moral growth is pre-eminently the product of a student's free cooperation with conscientious, skillful teachers whom he respects and trusts. Contemporary American Jesuit high schools and colleges will define the area of student responsibility and freedom more generously than their seventeenth-century forbears did but the ideal of harmonizing freedom and authority is operative in both cases. A perfect synthesis of these two values is rare and it must, in any event, often be reconstructed since the incidentals of its concrete embodiment change from one period and nation to another. But the conviction that both law and liberty have places in the school community remains a perennial of the Jesuit tradition.

Means of Character Education

In the *Constitutions* and *Ratio* the most precise methods recommended for forming character are not the sort that have much prestige today. There is rather too much trust reposed in brief homilies by the teacher, in sermons and in such other direct means as assigning compositions in praise of virtue or denunciation of vice. In the sixteenth chapter of the Fourth Part of the *Constitutions,* St. Ignatius had himself suggested that one of the students be appointed every week to deliver an exhortation to his classmates. This handy device would serve both to develop the preacher's style and his companions' morals.

In the concept of school life which obtained from the beginning, however, there were two fundamental accents which could be ratified in any age. We have noted already that the oldest wisdom of Christianity has anticipated modern psychological doctrine in holding that character is developed through acceptance of life's challenges and tasks rather than by preachments. The true rationale of any extracurricular program is grounded upon this conviction. In the Jesuit school and college the extra-curriculars designed to promote skill in speaking and writing—dramatics, debates, literary academies and the like—all held positions of honor. The ranking extracurricular activity, however, was an organization called the Sodality. The first of these sodalities or confraternities, was founded in the Roman College more than forty years before the final *Ratio* appeared. It was intended as an association or club aimed chiefly at deepening the religious spirit of its members under the special patronage of the Blessed Virgin Mary. It concerned itself, therefore, not only with their progress in purity of heart, prayer and self-mastery but also directed their energies to various works of the social apostolate since no authentic Christian mysticism can lack this social dimension of active charity. The members of the Sodality were thought of as the school's elite because they were ordinarily outstanding for talent and leadership. When James Joyce was the Prefect of the Sodality at Belvedere, this post was the most distinguished open to a student. Like any human enterprise, the Sodality no doubt often fell short of its noblest aspirations. Wherever it approximated these ideals, however, it formed within the school world a smaller community providing its members with a special opportunity for developing that familiarity with God and that fraternal service of others which are wonderfully effective means for shaping character according "to the mature measure of the fullness of Christ" (Ephesians 4: 13).

In the Jesuit school, however, the chief responsibility for moral as well as for intellectual formation rests finally not upon any procedure or curricular or extra-curricular item but upon the teacher, under God. This school is to be a face-to-face community in which an authentic personal relationship between teachers and students may flourish. Without such a relation of friendship, in fact, much of the unique force of education would be lost. Without it men can communicate information but teaching machines may do this as well or better. The personal relationship with the student is, as the analyses of Buber remind us, the central constituent of the distinctive role of teacher just as any of the distinctive facets that define a self are those which accrue to it through some relationship to another. One man becomes father or son through a relation to his own parent or child and another man is endowed with the character of teacher through his pupil. The *Thou* constitutes the *I*.[38]

No doubt the disparity between the positions of teacher and student makes this relationship somewhat hard to achieve and no doubt it can be poisoned by sentimentality or by any use of it to feed the teacher's own ego and hunger for power. The Christian believes, however, that if the relationship is rooted in supernatural charity, it will be effectively bulwarked against such dangers and able to surmount those disparities. If the members of the academic society are, first of all, in communion with a Divine Person, then their communion with one another will be protected against aberration and their school will be transformed into a Christian community. In such a community, students and masters can stand to each other, as one of the earliest Jesuit educational documents put it, somewhat as sons to fathers.[39]

Within this community, moreover, the teacher will persuasively influence character, for better or for worse, by the example of what he himself is. One way to help others, wrote St. Ignatius to the young Jesuit scholastics studying at Coimbra, "is to be models of virtue yourselves, so as to make them what you are . . . Wherefore, if you would perfect others, be first perfect yourselves." And in the Preamble to the Fourth Part of the *Constitutions* he appears to place personal example ahead of learning or rhetoric as an apostolic means. A comment four centuries later by Max Scheler is to the same point:

> There is nothing in the world that attracts a person toward good so forcibly, so immediately, and so inevitably as the spectacle of a good man doing good . . . Good example, simple and unaffected, is absolutely the best means to make one good.[40]

A variety of specific directives sketch out the range of the teacher's work once it is thought of in this generous fashion. The *Constitutions,* for instance, direct that teachers have not only a special concern for the academic progress of each of their students but that they also look after their moral formation.[41] Yet in fulfilling both their instructional and guidance functions, educators are always to respect the dignity and personality of the pupils. In the classroom, the *Ratio* advises, they should not be hasty nor suspicious nor attribute to the whole group that which is the fault of only one and they should wink, at times, at minor irregularities. They should play no favorites and should avoid all irony, sarcasm and injurious nicknames. The principal is warned, in the forty-eighth of his rules, that he may not himself use the students' work "for writing or anything else," nor allow others to do so.[42]

These negative rules are only a barricade protecting the core of the teacher's vocation as counsellor. To fulfill this properly, teachers need first to know their students and so the *Ratio* of 1591 had recommended that the masters study their pupils at length and reflect upon their aptitudes, their defects and the implications of their classroom behavior. And at least some of the teachers, it remarks, ought to be well acquainted with the students' home background.[43]

In academic matters, students are grouped into rather general categories. In the thirty-eighth of the Rules Common to Professors of Lower Classes, the *Ratio* of 1599 proposes a rough little scale for classifying the pupils through degrees that run from *optimi, boni, mediocri* through *dubii* and *retinendi* to *reiciendi*. But character education requires a nicer and more individual discrimination than this. Here all depends upon the personal equation. That will be variously specified, to be sure, from culture to culture. An American Jesuit high school teacher may smile at Father Odo Pigenat's stuffy insistence in the 1590's that teachers refrain from joining the boys at their games and speak to them always in Latin, never in the vernacular. But about the same time that Father Pigenat was making this rule for the French province, his contemporary, Father Georg Bader, provincial of the Upper German province, wrote a memorandum for the Jesuit prefects of a boarding school at Dillingen and its spirit is quite as fresh today as it was in 1585. The teachers' authority, Father Bader observes, is not proven when students obey their word, or their nod or mere glance. It is rather demonstrated when the boys have an affection for their masters and confidently approach them to discuss their problems without restraint: *ut ament, confidenter accedant ad ipsos et suas difficultates libere proponent.*[44]

Then he touches upon a few attitudes and practices that may promote this easy and friendly relationship. He advises young teachers to be patient with the boys and know how to overlook certain mistakes or put off their correction until the apt psychological moment. They should be much readier with praise than blame and if a reprehension is required it should be made without bitterness. When it seems as though the boys are not maturing fast enough, or in every respect, the teachers shouldn't become fainthearted or desperate. They are not trying, after all, to make monks out of these boys but to assist them in becoming honest, good-living men. The friendly spirit which is nourished by frequent, casual counselling of the students, perhaps in groups of two or three outside class hours, will greatly help this aim along. Even these bits of advice, of course, serve only to apply that underlying concept of the very nature of the school community and of the teacher's role within it. It will be the business of the final chapter to examine more closely certain other characteristics of that community.

NOTES: CHAPTER VI

1. The translation is that of Ganss, *op. cit.,* p. 329.
2. "Non enim apud nos tenerae aetatis disciplina circumscribitur unis

grammaticae rudimentis, sed ad christianam simul institutionem se por-
rigit." Francesco Sacchini, *Protrepticon ad Magistros Scholarum In-
feriorum Societatis Jesu.* Sacchini was born in 1570 and died in 1625.
The *Protrepticon,* which first appeared in 1625, had several editions.
The one used here is that which was included in a *Manuel des jeunes
professeurs* (Paris, 1842). The passage quoted is from the *Prooemium*
and is found in this edition on p. 116.

3. *Constitutions,* IV, 16, n. 4. Translation from Ganss, *op. cit.,* p. 330.

4. "Duo docere debet Christianus Magister, pietatem ac litteras . . ."
   Jouvancy, *op. cit.,* p. 123. "Magistri . . . rite instituti sint . . . in
   methodo docendi et arte educandi," *Epitome,* n. 399.

5. Martin Buber, *Between Man and Man,* trans. Ronald Gregory Smith
   (London: Kegan Paul, 1947), p. 104.

6. Sir Richard Livingstone, *Plato and Modern Education* (Cambridge: At
   the University Press, 1944), p. 32.

7. These definitions can be disputed, of course, as is shown by an interesting contrast between the concepts of religion enunciated in two decisions of the United States Supreme Court. In 1931, Chief Justice
   Hughes in a dissenting opinion in the Macintosh case could write: "The
   essence of religion is belief in a relation to God involving duties superior
   to those arising from any human relation." *U.S. v. Macintosh,* 283 U.S.
   633 (1931). It might be objected that there is some ambiguity here
   since the concept of God is not defined. But in any case, the notion of religion is still much closer to the traditional one than that implied thirty
   years later in the Torcaso case by Justice Black when he spoke of "Those
   religions based on a belief in the existence of God, as against those religions founded on different beliefs." *Torcaso v. Watkins,* 367 U.S. 495
   (1960).

8. Alan Paton, "The Person in Community," in Edmund Fuller (ed.),
   The Christian Idea of Education (New Haven: Yale University Press,
   1957), p. 111.

9. St. Thomas Aquinas, *Commentarium in libros ethicorum,* Lib. 2, lect. 1.

10. For two presentations, popular but not superficial, which approach the
    problem of personality development in youth from quite dissimilar in-
    tellectual backgrounds yet agree in identifying as the central aspect of
    this development the achieving of "self-identification" or the "forma-
    tion of the definite self," see Rudolf Allers, *Character Education in
    Adolescence* (New York: Joseph F. Wagner, 1940) and Edgar Z.
    Friedenberg, *The Vanishing Adolescent* (Boston: Beacon Press, 1959).

11. Nelson N. Foote, "The Old Generation and the New," in Eli Ginzberg
    (ed.), *Problems and Prospects,* vol. 3 of *The Nation's Children* (New
    York: Columbia University Press for the Golden Anniversary White
    House Conference on Children and Youth, 1960), pp. 15–16.

12. For a succinct "psychological analysis of the Spiritual Exercises of St. Ig-
    natius from the point of view of personality dynamics," see the chapter
    by John A. Gasson, S.J., "Religion and Personality Integration," in
    Magda B. Arnold and John A. Gasson, (eds.) *The Human Person: An
    Approach to an Integral Theory of Personality* (New York: The Ronald
    Press Company, 1954), pp. 548–574.

13. Charles Horton Cooley, *Human Nature and the Social Order* (rev. ed.; New York: Charles Scribner's Sons, 1922), p. 386.

14. St. Ignatius of Loyola, *The Spiritual Exercises, op. cit.,* p. 78, n. 189.

15. *Ibid.,* p. 44, n. 97. This is from one of the key meditations or exercises, that on the Kingdom of Christ.

16. The phrases in the text are taken from an exchange, previously referred to, which illustrates well the dilemma under discussion: William H. Kilpatrick and Arthur Bestor, "Progressive Education: A Debate," *The New York Times Magazine,* September 8, 1957, pp. 25, 112–114.

17. In a passage in *The Idea of a University,* Cardinal Newman spoke in this fashion of the way in which forces other than formal schooling can nurture the "habits of gentlemen." Much the same can be said of the acquisition of intellectual maturity through informal educative experiences. See John Henry Cardinal Newman, *The Idea of a University: Defined and Illustrated* (New York: Longmans, Green and Company, 1925), p. xvi.

18. *Constitutions,* IV, 12, n. 3.

19. "Qui praeterea non solum in studiis artium sedulo assidueque tradendis versentur, sed etiam, ac multo magis, qui ad christianam piamque institutionem studiosos provehant, totamque scholam religiose informent et honestis vitae moribus illustrent." This is from a memorandum, "De Ratione Collegiorum Quae Societati Nominis Iesu Eriguntur," which is the first of the documents in *Mon. Paed., op. cit.,* p. 23.

20. See *Constitutions,* IV, 7, 2: "Cureturque . . . ut . . . cum litteris mores etiam christianis dignos hauriant." And the *Ratio* of 1591, Corcoran, *op. cit.,* p. 223: "Ita pueros, qui in Societatis disciplinam traditi sunt, instituendos esse sibi putet, ut e scholis nostris, quas frequentarint, una cum bonis litteris veram etiam animi pietatem imprimis suxisse videantur." To the Rules for Professors of Rhetoric in this edition is prefixed the reminder that care be taken to see that the "Adolescentes . . . una cum bonis litteris veram etiam animi pietatem imprimis hausisse." *Ibid.,* p. 245.

21. Plato, *Republic,* 441 ff. C. S. Lewis calls attention to this Platonic insight in his little book, *The Abolition of Man* (New York: Macmillan, 1947), pp. 15–16.

22. H. Boehmer, *The Jesuits,* trans. P. Z. Strodach (Philadelphia: The Castle Press, 1928), pp. 49–50.

23. *Constitutions,* IV, 16, n. 5.

24. *Ibid.,* IV, 14, A and n. 2. For the *Ratio* of 1599 echoing this directive, see the 34th Rule of the Provincial in Pachtler, *op. cit.,* II, 262. An early document, dating from about 1575 and preserved in the *Mon. Paed., op. cit.,* p. 705, advises teachers gently (*suaviter*) to persuade their students to report on what they are reading so that the teacher may see whether the list includes any objectionable (*prohibiti vel lascivi*) material.

25. For a lengthy discussion of this question see de Dainville, *op. cit.,* pp. 228 ff. The *Constitutions,* IV, 5, E, enunciate the basic principle when, borrowing an ancient image, they say that the good in pagan writers can be used like "the spoils of Egypt."

26. For the phrase from the *Ratio* of 1591 see Corcoran, *op. cit.,* p. 232.
27. See Edward D. Eddy, Jr. assisted by Mary Louise Parkhurst and James S. Yakovakis, *The College Influence on Student Character* (Washington, D.C.: American Council on Education, 1959), pp. 9–39.
28. The *Ratio* of 1591, Corcoran, *op. cit.,* p. 231; that of 1586, Pachtler, *op. cit.,* II, 170 ff; that of 1599, *ibid.,* 396. For Jouvancy, see *op. cit.,* pp. 135–36: "Quamobrem in id unice incumbere Magistri sapientis cura debet, ut his duabus machinis, laude et vituperio, scholam suam regat."
29. The *Ratio* of 1599, Rule 31 of the Rules Common to Professors of Lower Classes, Pachtler, *op. cit.,* II, p. 392.
30. "Designet vicissim in ludo locum quempiam abiectum maxime atque ignobilem. 'Negligentiae scamnum' nominetur. In hoc ignavissimus quisque dejiciatur Qui vero in hoc scamno consederint, frequenter examinentur, pudefiant, obiurgentur, vapulent." *Ratio* of 1586, Pachtler, *op. cit.,* II, p. 171. See also Rules 31 and 35 of the Rules Common to Professors of Lower Classes, *Ratio* of 1599, *ibid.,* pp. 392, 394.
31. Cooley, *op. cit.,* p. 309. The comment on the value of competition for teaching students their limitations has been suggested by a remark in Niblett, *op. cit.,* p. 28.
32. See Rudolf Otto, *The Idea of the Holy,* trans. John W. Harvey (2nd ed.; London, Geoffrey Cumberlege for the Oxford University Press, 1952), p. 60. The original German edition of this book first appeared in 1917.
33. *Constitutions,* IV, 16, n. 4, C. For the comment from the *Ratio* of 1591, see Corcoran, *op. cit.,* p. 220 and for the *Ratio* of 1599 repeating this rule that the smaller boys shall be supervised when in church, see Pachtler, *op. cit.,* II, 370.
34. *Constitutions,* IV, 16, n. 1, A.
35. See Luigi Sturzo, *Inner Laws of Society: A New Sociology,* trans. Barbara Barclay Carter (New York: P. J. Kenedy and Sons, 1944), p. 163.
36. See Ogilvie, *The English Public School, op. cit.,* p. 150 which reproduces an old photograph showing the "Aut Disce" board in the Winchester school room. From the medieval representation of Grammar, see John Evans, *Life in Mediaeval France* (rev. ed.; London: Phaidon Press, 1957), p. 123. The first edition of this book appeared in 1925.
37. This principle of discipline is found in a memorandum given by Nadal to the Jesuit school in Vienna, *Mon. Paed., op. cit.,* p. 821. Another early document prepared for some German schools in 1560–61, recommended that the teacher manifest a paternal spirit toward all his students: "Omnes discipulos scholae affectu paterno prosequetur." Pachtler, *op. cit.,* I, 155. For the office of the *corrector,* who is not to be a member of the Society, see *Constitutions,* IV, 16, n. 5.
38. This theme is developed by Emil Brunner, with acknowledgement of his debt to Martin Buber, in *Man in Revolt: A Christian Anthropology,* trans. Olive Wyon (London: Lutterworth Press, 1939), p. 292.
39. Mon. Paed., *op. cit.,* p. 24 and see the document cited from Pachtler in note 37 above.
40. Max Scheler, *Der Formalismus in der Ethik,* quoted in Franz de Hovre,

Catholicism in Education, trans. Edward B. Jordan (New York: Benziger Brothers, 1934), p. 376. For St. Ignatius's advice to the scholastics at Coimbra, in a letter of May 7, 1547, see Doncoeur, *op. cit.,* p. 91.

41. *Constitutions,* IV, 13, n. 3 and 16, n. 1.

42. See Rules 40 and 47 of the Rules Common to Professor of Lower Classes in the *Ratio* of 1599, Pachtler, *op. cit.,* II, 396, 398 and Rule 48 of the Rules for Prefects of Studies in the Lower school, *ibid.,* p. 370. In the *Ratio* of 1591, the teacher is cautioned against punishing a whole group for the misdemeanors of a single individual. Corcoran, *op. cit.,* p. 243.

43. *Ratio* of 1591, in Corcoran, *op. cit.,* pp. 237, 242. The rating scale is found in the *Ratio* of 1599, Rule 38 of the Rules Common to Professors of Lower Classes, Pachtler, *op. cit.,* II, 394. The ranks of "best," "good" and so on, were to be expeditiously indicated by numbers running from 1 to 6.

44. For Father Pigenat's rulings see *Mon. Paed., op. cit.,* pp. 717 ff. and for the observation of Father Bader, Pachtler, *op. cit.,* I, 411–12. The *Ratio* of 1599 tempers its rather stiff attitude on teacher-pupil relationships with a characteristic pragmatism. Rule 47 of the Rules Common to Professors of Lower Classes recommends that teachers not speak to boys outside of class save briefly and on serious topics. The sixth of these teachers' rules, however, warmly recommends individual "counselling" sessions (*Privatis etiam colloquiis eadem ad pietatem pertinentia inculcabit*) and these would hardly result unless a certain friendly ease marked the relation of the Master to his students. Pachtler, *op. cit.,* II, 398, 380.

CHAPTER VII

THE SOCIAL DIMENSION:
EDUCATION IN AND FOR SOCIETY

Puerilis institutio est renovatio mundi
Juan Bonifacio, S.J.

Pro familia, patria, et Ecclesia viros eminentos praeparabimus
Instructio, Titulus II, art. 7[1]

The corporate personality of a Jesuit school can be studied under two aspects which are different but complementary. In the first place, the school is essentially a society or community of teachers and students united in their common endeavor for a common aim. This union, which is particularly apparent from within, is a moral one but it is analogous to the organic unity of a living being. It is not the artificial unity of a machine or a simple aggregation of straws in a haystack. In addition, the school also has the character of what is nowadays called an organization—an institutional structure whose parts are articulated in an hierarchical pattern and ordered toward specific functions designed for the attainment of a specific goal.[2] This organizational aspect strikes even the outside observer who has no experience of the community's inner life. These two facets of a complex reality stand to one another somewhat as spirit and corporeal structure in man although the comparison is imperfect since a certain degree of organization flows from the very nature of a community.

The foundation documents of Jesuit educational tradition never refer to the Society's schools as themselves communities or societies. They do not need to, for this is what a school naturally is whether everyone recognizes that or not. The group of adults and young people brought together in this academic society have some common interests, share certain values, participate in mutual tasks and spend part of their waking hours in a common setting under the same code of school regulations. All the individuals in this little world are linked, therefore, by a variety of interrelations governed by justice, or respect for the rights of others and charity or friendship. In fact, the authentic moral work of education as distinguished from sheer training, requires a community for its setting, whether that community be the family, the school or the church. For as Emil Brunner observes penetratingly: "Man cannot be man 'by himself'; he can only be man in community. For love can only operate in community, and only in this operation of love is man human. . . True community is the ground and content of Christian 'humanity'; it is fundamentally different from that of individualistic humanism."[3]

The Christian, whose esteem for community has been nourished on such central dogmas as that of the Trinity, which reveals a community of love among Three Persons within the very Godhead, and that of the Mystical Body, which teaches him that the individual is saved through his membership in a divinely founded society, easily appreciates that so central a human enterprise as education requires a societal setting. Any observant person, whatever his beliefs, can also perceive that every education includes the aim of developing man's social potential and that this necessarily requires a social environment even as the development of intellectual power calls for mental tasks and materials. If man is a *zoon politikon,* as Aristotle long ago put it, then society is his natural habitat.

Although the Jesuit school legislation does not spell out this basic principle, it clearly supposes it. The Jesuit schools are, for instance, understood as extensions of the inspiration and action of the Society itself since they are concrete embodiments of its apostolic aim. St. Ignatius would have that Society ruled, however, chiefly by the internal law of charity whose observance the specific regulations are simply designed to expedite.[4] He had, moreover, originally intended that the Jesuit college should enroll together both the lay students or externs and the young Jesuit scholastics making their own studies. In practice, however, this went by the board save in a few places where the Jesuit seminary is one of the corporate colleges of a large Jesuit university. At times the *Constitutions* reflect obliquely this notion of the school as a community which one joins rather than a department store or service station that one patronizes. The seventeenth chapter of the Fourth Part directs that when new students have been in attendance at a *collegium* for a week or so, they are to be invited to enroll and the parts of the *Constitutions* which are concerned with student life are to be read to them. To these they ought to promise observance, although if they are unwilling to do so they may continue on in the school but are to be told that more particular care is taken of those who have matriculated, who have become, so to say, full members of the academic community.[5] The *Epitome,* in similar fashion, indirectly indicates the social character of the school by remarking that its officials should be united by a mutual cooperative endeavor which is guaranteed by their common loyalty to the institution's authority.[6]

This aspect of community is, then, essential but consideration of it cannot be perfectly divorced from consideration of the school as an organization. The roles of men in the academic society are often defined more precisely in terms of the organizational structure. Moreover, although the vitality of a community's spirit is not correlated with its quantitative growth or increased intricacy, still these factors affect organization directly and thereby have repercussions for the inner life of the community.

In the United States today the larger Jesuit universities are organizations of a scope and complexity unimaginable in the sixteenth century. Yet within the memory of men still living many of these institutions were small *collegia* whose six classes covered much the same ground as that now divided between high school and college. The pressure of the surrounding culture brought about a binary fission and evolution of this structure. The three "grammar" classes split off and, with the addition of a fourth year, came to resemble the organization of an American high school. The classes of Humanities, Rhetoric and the year of philosophy, which had been expanded to two, now constituted the ground plan of a liberal arts college. In the twentieth century, particularly after the First World War, the various professional schools and graduate schools matured with astonishing rapidity and the range of the college curriculum was greatly enlarged.

Expansion of this sort means that the organization itself becomes astonishingly more complex. In the Jesuit tradition, the rector of a university has such considerable power that one cannot call the organization he leads a strict bureaucracy since the bureau heads are not entitled by statute to govern. Nevertheless, the organization of a contemporary Jesuit university now often includes various vice-presidents for academic affairs, for business and finance, for student personnel and for public relations or development as well as executive assistants, deans and department chairmen. Although these theoretically function as staff rather than as line, in practice a good deal of policy-making and decisions devolve upon them. In short, a large American Jesuit university or college looks much more like its secular counterpart from the organizational point of view than like any institution sketched in the *Ratio*. This development has some obviously significant effects. For one thing, it necessarily diminishes the atmosphere of a face-to-face community. In an urban university the faculty members of any one college or professional school have all they can do to become acquainted with each other and with the students whom they actually teach. The chief administrative officers are rarely seen by teachers or students and in a large freshman group, two young people from the same high school may not meet for months. The university will have to be a number of communities, if the friendly character of the small school is to be preserved in some part.

An ironic consequence of these realities of growth and complexification is that the *Ratio* of 1599 nowhere seems more primitive than in that precise area for which it was chiefly designed—*de scholarum administratione*.[7] Human nature has not altered substantially during the past four centuries and so the hints for theories of learning and character formation in the early Jesuit documents do not strike the reader as devised for situations radically unlike our own. Many teachers, indeed, might find the procedures suggested quite instructive. The institutional development of modern schools and colleges, however, does mean that a contemporary academic administrator will get little light from the *Ratio Studiorum*. It does not speak of his problems because it does not visualize them. Even the modern high school is subject to the impact of forces unknown to the editors of the *Ratio* while the traditional Faculty of Arts has wonderfully issued in organizations which require highly sophisticated hypotheses of administration. The prescriptions of the *Ratio* stand to these much as sixteenth-century science to that of today. The Jesuit rector is still supposed to be the paternal leader of a community but he is also the chief line official of a vast enterprise. The academic community entrusted to his administration includes, to take but one item, a large number of professionally skilled lay teachers, men and women. In the *Constitutions* and the *Ratio,* it is usually supposed that all teachers will be Jesuits although in the thirteenth chapter of the Fourth Part, St. Ignatius allowed for others when necessary. The *Epitome,* drawn up in the early 1920's, recognized that by now necessity does indeed require augmenting the staffs with non-Jesuit personnel. The full concept of the role of the lay faculty member must, however, go much further than this. It is widely recognized today that the necessity in question is not simply the obvious one created by quantities of students but is imposed by the integral concept of a Catholic university. For such a university must constitute an environment in which the Christian lay scholar can both pursue his vocation and exemplify it for the youth he teaches. "It fills Our soul with consolation and gratitude towards the Divine Goodness," wrote Pius XI, "to see, side by side with Religious men and women engaged in teaching, such a large number of excellent lay teachers . . . All these labor unselfishly with zeal and perseverance in what St. Gregory Nazianzen calls 'the art of arts and the science of sciences,' the direction and formation of youth . . . Let us then pray the Lord of the harvest to send more such workers into the field of Christian education."[8] The rounded theory of the lay teacher's unique role in these Christian schools has not yet been worked out and no attempt to do so can be made here. It is enough to remark that the challenge it poses is an indication of the new dimensions within which contemporary Jesuit school management operates.

In reflecting upon the administrative principles discernible in the foundation documents of the Jesuit educational heritage it will be more than ever necessary, therefore, to distinguish sharply between the elaborate theory called for by one of these modern university complexes and the few basic themes which can actually be discovered in the tradition itself. For there are administrative principles in that tradition, even though they may be scarcely developed, and they do look to the welfare of the school both as a community and as an organization. The ideal of community, for instance, was always cherished, and so the sixteenth century had some relevant comments to make under that heading. Moreover, since there are some organizational problems which are perennial, the primitive tradition had to formulate hypotheses here. It has always been necessary for administrators to overcome both the external pressures and the internal deterioration and conflict which threaten to impede attainment of the organization's purpose.[9] It has always been necessary to maintain the corporate personality of the school and yet allow for benign growth and reasonable change and adaptation. If the system is to be kept working, as well as simultaneously stable and dynamic, the managers will have to provide firm leadership along with opportunity for initiative from below. It has always been necessary to maintain a hierarchical structure of organization and, at the same time, insure what both community and organization require: wise formulation of policy, effective communication of these decisions, mobilization of the community's resources for their implementation and candid appraisal and reconstruction of the original policy. Because the sixteenth-century *collegium* was so much simpler in form than its twentieth-century descendants, its ad-

ministrative techniques can be more easily discerned just as in any relatively unsophisticated community the basic constituents of its distinctive
character stand out more clearly, unobscured by luxuriant growths.

Some of these administrative practices, both of early and contemporary Jesuit educational institutions, will provoke criticism from modern theorists of school management. Control of organization is, for one
thing, highly centralized and the power to make and implement policies
is largely in the hands of the top overseers at the head of the line. On
paper, at least, it would not appear that the actual operators in the organization, the teachers, have much influence upon policy. Yet we can
judge empirically that there is more to the picture than this. For the Jesuit
school over four centuries has shown the vitality that is only preserved
when there is a readiness to reappraise policies, entertain criticism and
then innovate. Without this readiness, the organization would have declined and passed from rigidity to fossilization. In its administrative
practice, then, one may presume a quality which may not have been reduced to a specific rule but which is more important than any single
regulation.

In considering the social dimension of Jesuit education, it will do no
harm to ignore the distinction between community and organization and
simply focus upon that core concept of the school as a community with
attention to the administrative concepts which emerge in this connection.
One might ask first about the principles for organizing the community,
then about the roles of its teachers and students and finally about the
school's method of educating the social powers of youth and preparing
them for a Christian life of social responsibility.

Patterns of Organization

In the management of a Jesuit school all the specific regulations reflect St. Ignatius's own twofold attitude toward law, order and method—
utilization without rigidity. He was firmly convinced of the value of these
factors and their contribution to organization. He especially esteemed
an organization which effectively mobilized the distinctive knowledge
and skills of well educated and dedicated persons. He knew that if a
community's purposes are served by competent, loyal men, then the
power of that collectivity will far exceed the sum of their individual abilities. Each will bring his own special wisdom or professional technique to
bear upon one phase of the cooperative enterprise and will be responsible for its success. Consequently, the organization as a whole will be

uniquely effective, for it will be a corporate person with the versatility of a specialist in every one of its actions and decisions. Although Ignatius was the author of a classic formulation of the ideal of perfect religious obedience, he also believed in genuine delegation of true responsibility adequately equipped with power. Luis Gonzáles, the Jesuit who extracted a few memoirs from the founder, recalled that on a typical occasion Ignatius sent a priest on some mission or other, saying: "I leave to you all freedom to do whatever seems better to you." González also reported that the saint was quite aware of that prime administrative error—the delegation of responsibility without authority—and warned against it. "To do a thing well," he observed, "a man needs power and competence. But in general he is competent who is in charge and who has the affair constantly before his eyes. If you lessen his power, and if the superior himself, although out of touch with the matter, meddles in the business, power is separated from ability with most inconvenient results." The *Ratio* of 1591 reflects this Ignatian spirit when it describes the sort of man the rector of a college should select for the position of dean, or prefect of studies as he was called. He should not look for a harmless or passive person but for one capable of immense and many-sided labors; a man keen, industrious, adroit, tenacious and thoroughly competent for the office. Then the rector should equip this dean with as much real authority as possible so that he may function as a true "prefect" and not as a mere manager or go-between.[10]

These recommendations are rather generalized, but they do represent an application of sound principles of organization. The *Ratio* does not think of the school as an anthill where everyone does the same thing nor as an old-fashioned regiment in which the troops react mechanically but as an organic and heterogeneous structure vitalized by a powerful feeling for harmony and unity. The precise areas of responsibility in it are clearly marked out—for the provincial, the rector, the general prefect of studies, the theology professors, the prefect of lower studies, the secondary school teachers, and the student leaders, *decuriones,* who sometimes functioned as monitors or teachers' assistants. It is this principle of organization which strikes us as contemporary even though we may find its concretizations in the *Ratio* relatively elementary.[11] We may think, however, as we read the various sets of rules, that the conduct of each office has been quite thoroughly predetermined. There is no doubt that the early Jesuit educators were enthusiastic about the value of law for evoking order from confusion. The *Ratio* of 1586 claimed Aristotle and St. Thomas in support of the administrative hypothesis which maintains that whatever can conveniently be regulated, should be. But it added:

"Matters, however, which cannot thus be legislated, such as decisions on individual cases, which are not comprehended by the law, or interpretation of the law itself when this is a bit obscure, should be left to the individual judgment as to a living law."[12]

In this sentiment, the second of the Ignatian attitudes is embodied—that of an intelligent liberty which properly subordinates positive law to the value it is designed to serve. Rules, organizations and method are all desirable, but they are not supreme. They are tools. Laws can, therefore, be dispensed, so long as this involves no sin, in favor of the good to which they were ordered in the first place. In the tenth chapter of the Fourth Part of the *Constitutions,* St. Ignatius remarked that the rector of a college must see that these *Constitutions* are obeyed. He adds immediately that the rector will also dispense from these same rules in individual cases as the welfare of the common good shall require.[13] In similar fashion, the *Ratio* defined, but did not eliminate, the area in which initiative might be exercised and the Jesuit pedagogy was never immobile. In the statutes themselves a good deal was left to the individual teacher. It was he who made many of the concrete decisions and interpretations of the rules. Moreover, the instrumental view of law permitted not only dispensation but innovation. Père de Dainville, reported, from his study of manuscript collections of course outlines in seventeenth-century French Jesuit schools, that these give evidence of constant evolution and adaptation.[14] In an organization with these characteristics one does not feel that sharp conflict between individual and community interests which can rip the social fabric. The individual administrators and teachers of the Jesuit school are to be united by a sincere devotion to the school's goals and to a search for the best means of securing them. They are also to be provided with a milieu and with tasks that will call upon and expand all their resources as free persons. The Jesuits themselves have enrolled in the Society voluntarily and their adhesion to its ultimate purpose is unconditional. This harmony between personal and organizational aims goes a long way toward dissolving that conventional antinomy between individual and collectivity.[15]

Organization does exist, however, and its basic pattern was laid out in the *Constitutions.* At the head of the Society, and hence of all its work, is the General, a chief executive possessing a plenitude of power and responsibility for policies and their execution. The *Constitutions* describe him as having *supremam curam Societatis* and he is, regarding any of the schools, that which recent statutes explicitly call him in relation to the Society's seminaries: The Great Chancellor.[16] Much of this power and responsibility, however, is delegated to a local managerial group, to

the provincials directing the individual provinces and to the rectors
charged with the care of the individual institutions. The rectors are assisted, in turn, by various deans and in the large universities these are
frequently non-Jesuit faculty members. In practice, therefore, a great
deal of educational policy is initiated at the local level and all of it, of
course, is executed there. It is true, nevertheless, that Jesuit schools
and colleges are not managed wholly from within since the repositories of highest authority are elsewhere. Still, the administration is no
more external than it is in a public educational system and the top
board is no more apart than are the trustees of any non-public American college or university. All the Jesuit administrators, moreover, are
from the ranks of the Society; all have had the basic cultural and
spiritual formation provided by the Order; all have had actual classroom
experience. Except for the General, all these principal administrators,
the provincials and rectors, have limited tenure in office and they
are required to listen, at least, to the advice of a panel of consultors.
These qualifications preserve the organization from many of the irritations experienced by schools subject to trustees, who often lack professional educational competence even when they are not actually capricious, or to bureaucrats in municipal and state departments or to political
legislatures in control of school finances.

The objectives of the Jesuit school are also a check upon the organization since they define its essential task. That task is twofold: to
keep the school a genuine Christian community and to keep the teaching function central and satisfactory so that the community may be a
good school. The *Constitutions* made a most significant decision affecting community spirit when they prescribed free tuition for all Jesuit
schools. This principle of gratuity of instruction—"to give freely what
we have freely received"—was in force during the whole of the Society's
first period or until 1773. The schools were then, it will be recalled, almost always secondary institutions offering a very full course from
grammar rudiments up to a capstone year of philosophy together
with some science. In certain cases a Faculty of Theology was joined to
this middle school and then one had a "university." In the first two centuries of the Society's educational work, this meant that instructional facilities were limited to classroom buildings staffed almost entirely by Jesuits. There were no major expenditures required for faculty salaries or
laboratories or large-scale research. The buildings were obtained or
erected through the generosity of individual or corporate donors such
as municipalities. These also supplied the endowment which provided
for maintenance of the plant and the support of the Jesuit faculty. If

there were boarders, these paid only for their own upkeep unless that too was freely supplied in the case of poor students.

Since there were no tuition fees, the atmosphere of the academic community was secured against resemblances to a merchandise mart. Neither the administrator nor the teacher could be regarded as producer of a paid service and the friendship between teacher and student or teacher and parent was not overcast by a contractual relationship. The student body had not the homogeneity of wealth but only that of talent since promising boys were accepted whatever their socioeconomic status. Long before the *Ratio* was written or the lines of the Society's educational apostolate clearly drawn, St. Ignatius had directed in the *Constitutions* that extern students be educated right along with the Jesuit scholastics and that the only conditions of admission be good character and real aptitude. A youth with these endowments gave promise of becoming an apostolic Christian and that "alone is sought in the case of those within and without the Society."[17]

The traces of class consciousness could not wholly be obliterated in the sixteenth century, to be sure, and so the *Ratio* of 1599 suggested that the better seats in the classroom be given to the nobility and that their parents be interviewed by teachers in their own home whereas non-noble parents came to the school themselves. But the set of "Rules Common to the Professors of the Lower Classes" in which this latter observation is found also ends with a warning to the teacher. "He is not to treat anyone meanly. He is to attend earnestly and equally to the academic needs of both his poor and his wealthy students and look after the progress of each of them."[18]

In the world of the nineteenth and twentieth centuries, the restored society had to begin its work afresh and build new schools, sometimes in European cities where public buildings, expropriated years before, still bore the Jesuit monogram over their doorways. It is no longer possible to secure substantial endowments either for the buildings or for the maintenance of small high schools, much less of universities. All American Jesuit schools, therefore, with the exception of Regis High School in New York City, which was founded by a munificent benefaction, now have tuition fees. This does not mean that the ideal of gratuity has been surrendered but only that its practice has necessarily been suspended. Were it not for these fees the schools could not exist. No doubt, the financial sacrifice of the student's parents has its own spiritual value since it is an expression of their religious conviction. Nevertheless, the spirit of the school as a community based solely on Christian charity is somewhat diminished when the school cannot function on a scholarship basis alone. Diminished but not, one hopes, eclipsed. For a second factor building up the academic community ought still to be operative. This factor is constituted by the teachers themselves, the group of Jesuit and non-Jesuit instructors who are committed to the goals of a Christian school. The safeguarding of their central position and the easing of their essential task remains the prime concern of sound administration.

The Teachers . . . *Magistri Sint Insignes*[19]

St. Ignatius did not think that teaching was, under every possible circumstance, the most important work a man could do. In the school itself, however, the Jesuit tradition has always held that the teacher is the single most important educational resource.[20] The teacher thought of, that is, not simply as an instructor but as the stimulating director of all those graduated exercises which evoke the student activity essential to learning, and as the counsellor who discreetly guides the pupil's growth in good character.[21] There is nothing novel about this conviction. Anyone who has given thought to school problems will very likely conclude that the teacher is the key to their solution and that the education improves as the quality of teaching improves. Why would it not? All school reforms have to be realized through the teacher. It is he who is actually on the scene and plunged into the process. The best techniques will shatter ineffectually in the hands of an incompetent or bored teacher, while a good teacher can do a lot even when the other elements are inadequate. He cannot, of course, do everything nor forever. A hard and ungrateful environment will finally defeat the most gifted instructors.

The work of a Christian teacher, however, is even more challenging than that of his secular colleague. His natural credentials as an educator must be the same. The bootless controversy over the relative importance of academic and professional background was sensibly dissolved by Jouvancy when, echoing the *Ratio* tradition, he observed that a good teacher needs to know his subject, know the principles of pedagogy and know all the handy little classroom tricks which lighten the labor of learning and sharpen talent.[22] But the Christian teacher cannot be content simply to teach his subject competently. If the discipline itself is one which, like theology, philosophy, literature or the social sciences, can contribute more or less directly to the maturation of a distinctively Christian outlook, he will want to teach with that purpose also in mind. Of course, if he confuses this with proselytism or thinks that it can be done by moralizing, he will fail to achieve the additional goal and will very likely compromise even his generic instructional aim. No matter what his subject, however, he knows that it should fit harmoniously into the total structure of a Catholic life and education. If, for instance, he is a physicist, he cannot admit an airtight compartmentalization of his science and his faith even though one is certainly not the other. These values ought to be united in the synthesis of the individual's life and the Christian teacher of science exemplifies such a synthesis in his own person. It was this sort of ideal that Father Nadal had in mind when he wrote: "Let the teachers be distinguished for their Christian spirit so that their classes even on secular authors . . . contribute to the education of their students in the charity of Christ."[23]

From the beginning, therefore, from the day when Ignatius sent Peter Canisius, a future Doctor of the Church, as one of the founding faculty of that first Jesuit school in Messina, three facts were recognized by Jesuit school administrators: the crucial importance of maintaining the ideal of good teaching; the difficulties which threaten that ideal; and the program necessary to ward off those threats. Such a program would include careful preparation of teachers, constructive supervision of their work and preservation of their morale. The importance of good teaching hardly needs to be stressed. No one who doubts it could be persuaded by proof anyhow. For his would be a mind like that of La Chalotais, who proposed in 1763 the eviction of the French Jesuits and the creation of a new system of state schools following centrally prescribed textbooks since, he said, "If the books were well drawn up they would dispense with the need for trained masters."[24]

Although the sixteenth-century Jesuits did not have a very detailed theory of education, they did have a substantial theory of life and a set of procedures, advanced for their day, which were designed to facilitate good teaching. Moreover, they had promising candidates for their faculties. From the Athens of Demosthenes to our own time, teachers have often been drawn from the less adventurous members of the lower middle class. If they were people who wanted to get up the ladder and looked upon the profession as the first accessible rung, they didn't stay long in the classroom. Men who did stay were apt to be rather timorous and unimpressive unless they were gifted persons kept in underpaid and poorly esteemed positions by some remarkable sense of dedication. In any religious Institute, however, teaching is neither a stopgap employment nor a refuge and the Institute itself enrolls a wide range of personalities including some who might easily have become successful financiers, explorers or stars of musical comedy had they not elected the vocation of priest, Brother or Sister. Through their history, it is true, the Jesuits, whether in sixteenth-century Europe or nineteenth-century United States, were

sometimes forced to sacrifice academic quality for quantity when necessity appeared to demand it. They lived in a real not an ideal world and
thus it happened that too many colleges were opened in the beginning.
Nadal found the picture discouraging when he visited Germany in the
1560's. Zeal had led his brethren to attempt a shouldering of all the tasks
that were thrust upon them. This may indicate some lack of a cozy prudence but it also suggests that teachers inspired by this sense of apostolic
mission were large-hearted, inventive and courageous. They were hardly
the stuff of which good little civil servants are made.

Nevertheless, their apostolic orientation did not of itself do away
with irritations that readily plague any teacher's life. There were sheer
physical drawbacks, for instance. One of these is hinted at by the frequent
recommendations in the early memoranda, written before the *Ratio*, that
the buildings be kept clean. The sixteenth century had no overpowering
interest in neatness or hygiene but these counted considerably with Ignatius and he passed on that concern. The teaching of boys is always
a strenuous business and the young prefects of the first Jesuit boarding
schools stuck by their charges from morning until night. The work was so
taxing, indeed, that the *Ratio* of 1586 as we saw, reported that teaching in the Grammar classes was often compared to working all day in an
oven, *pistrinum*. The *Ratio* of 1591, when advocating enlistment of selected Jesuits who would devote their lives to the secondary schools, adds
that they should be warned that this vocation is more useful than attractive: *hoc docendae Grammaticae munus magis utile esse quam spe-
ciosum*.[25]

There is perhaps an implication here pointing to a second problem
more delicate than that of material hardship. During the first period
of the Society's history there seems to have been a continual need to defend the status of secondary school teaching against those who took a dim
view of it. Their attitude was not prompted simply by the rivalry en-
demic to any multi-level academic world, although traces of that were
also found. At least one of the documents in which Ledesma had a hand
reported that there was some strife in the Roman College because certain teachers got most of the students' applause or won favor for themselves by conceding privileges. The *Ratio* of 1586 warned the professors
of the higher faculties not to condemn the faculty of Grammar. The
Ratio of 1591 adds that neither must the secondary school teachers make
fun of the Latin used in the philosophical and theological lectures.
The real danger, however, was not in these minor human conflicts but in
a disaffection toward the very notion of teaching in the lower schools.
Some were apparently tempted to regard that work as inferior and un-

desirable and certain unfortunate facts gave this temptation force. It might have been sharpened, for instance, by the rough, and wholly mistaken, comment in the *Ratio* of 1591 that this occupation is suitable for those not so talented.[26]

In the closing pages of the *Constitutions,* St. Ignatius had gravely warned against ambition, "The mother of all evils in any republic or congregation." But the teachers in the lower schools must have felt specially obliged to recall this advice. Their work was naturally fertile in disillusionments, despite its real rewards, for youth is not given to gratitude. It was also physically exhausting. Moreover, it not only gained none of the applause that came to popular preachers but it lacked suitable prestige even among the Jesuits themselves. The authors of the *Ratio* of 1586 felt constrained, therefore, to criticize the tendency to take teachers of the humanities for granted. When there are public gatherings, they wrote, these teachers should not be standing off to one side in the shadows or mixed in with the audience. They should be seated on the platform with the professors of philosophy and theology. Superiors ought, for their part, show equal solicitude for the masters in the lower division and provide them with the same measure of books, clothes and lodging and the same allotment of summer holidays as the members of the higher faculties receive. And when they see one of these middle school teachers laboring strenuously and patiently they ought not immediately pile more work on him.[27] In 1752, the sixteenth General of the Jesuits, Ignatius Visconti felt he had to reaffirm the dignity of work in the *collegium.* He had noticed, he said, that some highly estimable and learned Fathers were deprived of honorable recognition on the grounds that as teachers of rhetoric they occupied an inferior position. Wipe this notion out, said Father Visconti: *Delenda est haec ex nostrorum mentibus opinio.*[28]

The task for the adminstrator, then, was first to establish and then to sustain the morale of all the teachers but particularly of those plagued by these unfortunate irritations. The fundamental solution, of course, was to purify the religious spirit of those oppressed by the chafings of a natural ambition or disinclination for hard work. But it also helped to have all the young Jesuits during their Regency, the period between philosophical and theological studies, get some experience teaching in the middle school. The best rectors for such schools, said the *Ratio* of 1586, are those who have themselves known the burdens its masters bear. Similarly, the best "ministers" (assistants to the rector for the care of an institution's material needs) are those who once taught in a *collegium.* For without this background they are likely to overburden the teaching staff with domestic duties and to show less solicitude for all of them

together than for one coadjutor Brother. The six Fathers who noted these
items also thought that no one should be kept too long in the lower
classes but that the scholastics ought to spend at least three years there
during their regency. Otherwise the faculty would be changing too often;
parents would complain and the teachers would be moving on to other
duties just as they were developing real skill. Young men were thought to
be the best qualified for teaching boys because, "Grammar classes call for
a certain youthful alacrity"—the ability to keep in step with the students,
as it were. Still, if some older men were to volunteer for this work permanently, it would surely be an advantage. "For this long experience
would produce some outstanding teachers and their example would ani-
mate others to fulfill the same office cheerfully, at least for a time, and
would be a model of humility."[29]

The tone here may well strike contemporary Jesuits as curious.
There is no doubt, of course, that university teaching is less taxing physically than high school teaching and that if professors publish or lecture widely they may achieve a modest renown. But ease and reputation are interdicted as motives of Christian action. Besides that, work
in the secondary school provides more of teaching's characteristic intrinsic rewards than higher education does and from an apostolic point
of view it is probably more important, given the crucial significance of
the adolescent years. A middle-aged teacher today might admit rue-
fully that he no longer has the stamina which, as the *Ratio* of 1586
correctly observed, is needed for enthusiastic secondary school teaching. But he would hardly despise such teaching as inferior unless he did
have an itch for fame.

The need to secure status for the vocation to the middle school is
not, therefore, so much of a problem now. The need to prepare good
teachers is perennial, however, and it is instructive to note that the
characteristics of such teachers were stressed in the foundation documents of Jesuit education. It was presumed, to begin with, that the
ideal teacher is intellectually competent and has a thorough mastery
of the material he is to teach. One does not find here the emphasis on
research and publication that one will find in twentieth-century Jesuit
discussions of higher education. But it was always clearly understood
that the good teacher is, first of all, one who controls his subject. Indeed,
Ignatius accepted the management of higher Faculties, or "universities,"
precisely to help prepare men who would "be able to teach with authority what they have learned well." The teachers will be more competent,
suggested the *Ratio* of 1586, in discussing the requisites for a professor
of theology, if they have enough time to prepare their lectures and all

teachers ought to have access to a good library. For without books, the teachers are, as we saw before, unarmed soldiers, *milites inermes*. If there is material which they have not yet mastered, adds the *Ratio* of 1591, they must get it up beforehand rather than go calling for medication after the wound has been inflicted.[30]

Genuine intellectual competence will be better built, of course, upon natural aptitudes and interests and St. Ignatius himself had stressed the importance of taking these into consideration in the preparation of young Jesuits for the Society's work. A man may not be able to excel in every discipline, the founder wrote, but he ought to try to become really adept in one line. Superiors should appraise his talents, his natural inclinations (*propensio animi*), his previous educational background and the benefits likely to accrue from having him specialize in this or that discipline and then assign him to the most appropriate field.[31]

These notions are as valid now as ever. But the scholarly preparation of seventeenth-century teachers also included a thorough immersion in the Renaissance classical humanism at a time when its values had not been widely questioned. It is quite likely that this had a number of good effects. For one thing, it produced men who really believed in the worth of that curriculum. Consequently they might well have presented it more effectively than a twentieth-century teacher who is not so convinced that Hellenism best illuminates contemporary problems or even illuminates them at all. In the second place, those formed by that intensive discipline in language and expression came out with a considerable command over words. Nowadays, studies of communication have helped us to grasp the importance of these verbal skills not just for the transmission of basic meaning but for all those significant attitudes and intangible nuances that a deft speaker conveys obliquely. Any teacher needs some of this power and there is wisdom in the comment of an English writer: "The quality of an education depends most on the quality of the teacher and the quality of the teacher is best indicated by his use of language."[32]

The resources of the good teacher, however, must include more than mastery of his subject and of the power to communicate it. He also needs a certain degree of professional preparation—courses in methods and educational psychology. If teachers lack this professional training, said the *Ratio* of 1591, they will go into their first classroom *rudes ad docendum,* unskilled and forced to learn techniques entirely on the job. So this *Ratio* laid it down that during several summers the future teachers should have education courses for an hour a day from a master teacher who could demonstrate all the best procedures. The ninth of the Rules for the Rector in the *Ratio* of 1599 repeated this regulation but prescribed a somewhat different organization by recommending three hours a week toward the end of the candidate teacher's own arts (philosophy and science) course.[33]

This care for professional preparation is itself only another reflection of an Ignatian attitude. It is also common sense though it has taken several centuries to become everywhere recognized as such. Even today college professors are apt to maintain that all any teacher needs is a good knowledge of his subject. Ignatius, however, did not believe in leaving these important techniques to chance improvisation. In the eighth chapter of the Fourth Part of the *Constitutions*, for instance, he characteristically recommends that scholastics during their studies work up little summaries or outlines for future use in sermons or in the teaching of Christian doctrine to children in a manner psychologically adapted to their mentality. At the time the *Ratio* was being formulated, it was hoped that clearly determined procedures could be devised and all young teachers armed with them. This in turn would diminish the loss accompanying frequent changes in the faculty as the regents departed for their theological studies after three years. For each new regent could pick up where his predecessor had left off and carry on the work in much the same manner. Thus, observed the *Ratio* of 1591, although the teachers change, the method of teaching remains the same.[34]

But this called for a spirit of abnegation in the teacher himself; a willingness to subordinate his own conceptions to a system ready-made in many of its details. And that reminds us that in the ultimate reckoning the most important endowment of the Christian teacher is neither his erudition nor his rhetorical power nor his pedagogical technique but the quality of his spirit. It is expected that the Jesuit has committed himself to teaching out of the purest religious motives; that he is wholly motivated by the charity prescribed in the two great and intertwined commandments: love of God and love of man for the sake of God. To love one's neighbor as oneself is a noble ideal but the Christian imperative goes much further than that. On the night before his redemptive death, the Son of God summoned His followers to His own height: "A new commandment I give you, that you love one another: that as I have loved you, you also love one another" (John 13, 34). Nowhere in the busy pages of the *Ratio* does this note come to the surface and it is scarcely made explicit in the few laconic references to educational purposes in the Fourth Part of the *Constitutions*. There is no need for explicitation. The Jesuit teachers would not be on hand in the first place, if they had not grasped that motivation and were not, howsoever imperfectly, seeking to live by it. Their noviceship, their annual retreats and their hours of prayer had been designed first to educate them under grace to this ideal and then to strengthen their existential adherence to it. For it is this which is to give them their distinctive stamp as Christian teachers.

One further quality is to be added, a natural quality which super-natural charity can mightily enhance: cheerful enthusiasm. This is a motif which reappears time and again. It was a favorite with Ignatius, as we noted earlier. One should live in a religious order, he said, "with spiritual joy . . . with a cheerful heart."[35] The first document in the *Monumenta Paedagogica,* one over which Nadal had worked, describes the ideal teacher as a man who labors "without payment, cheerfully, tirelessly for the love which is in Christ Jesus." The *Ratio* of 1591 directs the provincial to have a most diligent solicitude for preservation of a joyful spirit (*hilaritas*) in the teachers since this is the very bulwark (*praesidium*) of good schools, whereas a melancholy teacher can scarcely fulfill his duties satisfactorily. The theme is repeated in the rules for the rector and touched upon in a practical fashion in the rules for the prefect of the Lower School. This latter administrator is advised not only to exert every effort to keep the teachers working cheerfully but in pursuance of this aim he is to confer with the rector on provision of legitimate vacation periods and recreations for these "will refresh the fatigued and reinvigorate the hard-working." The principle was canonized by the twentieth rule for the rector in the *Ratio* of 1599 which advises him to encourage a cheerful spirit in the faculty and make sure that overwork does not stifle it.[36]

Scholarship, professional skill, eloquence, apostolic dedication, enthusiasm. Certainly the school fortunate enough to possess teachers possessed of these qualifications in some degree is a center of authentic education however meager its material endowments. But even in such a privileged institution the principal or dean is not expected to abdicate his own professional responsibilities for administration and supervision. Thus the Rules for the Prefect of the Lower School, the high school principal, contain a sound outline for supervisory technique. The version of 1591 suggests, for instance, that he confer with the individual teachers at least every fortnight, that he visit classes and note the procedures and whether the teacher's manner is gentlemanly and whether he starts on time. Occasionally, the principal ought to examine the teachers' lesson plans and look over the students' written work. Teachers who are deficient are to be corrected kindly and privately for, as the *Ratio* of 1599 pointed out, the principal must safeguard the teacher's authority and prestige before his pupils. Those masters who cannot improve even after correction are to be removed before they do damage.[37] The *Ratio* of 1599 says relatively less about the principal's supervisory role because it has so much to say about his multitudinous responsibilities for preparing schedules and calendars, enrolling new pupils, attending to promotions, examinations, dismissals (which are to be done very kindly, *perhumaniter*) and looking after curricular and extracurricular affairs. It has all a quite contemporary ring.

There is one contemporary interest of teachers, however, which does not receive much attention in the sixteenth-century documents. This is the twofold concern, on the one hand, for the academic freedom and vigorous research of teachers themselves, particularly in higher education and, on the other, for the development of intellectual curiosity and initiative in students at all levels. Though these values are straightforward, the discussions that have clustered about them have often been complex and there is room here only for the sketchiest of comments. As was noted earlier, in formal schooling these two concerns first came strongly to the fore with the rise of the great nineteenth-century German universities and their motto of *Lehrfreiheit und Lernfreiheit*. It is hardly surprising, therefore, if the impression of this ideal is not found upon secondary schools in 1600. Nowadays, all mature Christian educators appreciate these values but there was little emphasis upon intellectual inquiry and freedom in the *Constitutions* or in the *Ratio*. This seems to have been due not so much to religious convictions as to the temper of the age which, at least so far as secondary education was concerned, put heavy stress upon imitation of Cicero's style and Aristotle's thought and would have both taught by the book of Quintilian.[38]

The *Ratio* of 1591, therefore, in discussing enlargement of the pupils' Latin vocabulary through the keeping of a notebook for choice phrases culled from reading, warns that the small boys must not be allowed to make their own selections lest they mistake some imitation for a real gem.[39] This doesn't prove a great deal, to be sure. A twentieth-century teacher of composition might think that a student's personal enthusiasm for a piece of second-rate writing could do more to awaken his interest in style than dictating his response to better things. But the teacher might be just as apt to interdict firmly the least cliché or gaucherie. At the 1960 annual meeting of the Jesuit Educational Association in Chicago, however, the theme for discussion was: Developing Intellectual Curiosity and Initiative in Our Students. It is a theme that would not have been formulated in precisely these terms by Ledesma or Nadal or by any sixteenth-century schoolmaster. But neither would those Jesuits have disowned it. Nurtured on the spirituality of the *Exer-*

cises, as they were, they would have properly esteemed all well regulated development of human talent and human liberty. Our current appreciation of the school's basic dedication to the maturation of a balanced and informed intelligence able to continue the work of self-education, as well as to make wise practical decisions day by day, is an enlargement rather than a contradiction of the older charter.

Much the same thing is true in the case of the teacher's academic freedom. When we read the directives of the *Ratio,* we are likely to think that it allowed for little freedom of choice in procedures. But closer study shows that there was room for the exercise of responsibility and even for improvisation within a clear framework of determined curricular objectives and materials. One must also exercise the historical sense here and remember that in the sixteenth century the Jesuits were, to a considerable extent, inventing the idea of the secondary school as Europe came to know it. This group of men worked up a program by actual trial in many classrooms and thereby gave to their innovation a form and habitation. The secondary schools comprised most of their educational investment and the inexperienced young teachers who made up a large part of these institutions' staff needed some blueprints. The values of scientific research and academic freedom, central though they are, were no more directly relevant to the ordinary business of those schools than they are to the work of an elementary school teacher today.

At one point, however, a problem is encountered. The only genuine higher education occupying the early Jesuits was in the Faculty of Theology. Now it is true that theology professors in their public lectures on disputed matters were directed to follow the more solid and secure opinion and not to expound views that were useless, antiquated, absurd or clearly false. If this were analogous to expecting a modern biologist to teach Mendelianism, though he might still explain and personally favor Lysenko, it does not appear unreasonable.

It is even better understood, if one recalls the atmosphere of theological controversy which agitated the sixteenth century and the nature of theology itself in the Catholic view. For theology begins with faith in God's word to man, not with facts acquired directly from experience. Its method is therefore authoritarian in the literal sense rather than empirical in the fashion of science or philosophy. It believes its first principles; it does not discover them. The usual formulation of the issue of academic freedom does not, therefore, apply in its case. If a man were not a believer, he would not be a theologian in the first place. If he is a believer, he considers a theological hypothesis to be proven false if it conflicts with the deposit of Faith as that is interpreted by the Church. He would no

more wish to teach it, therefore, than a physicist would wish to expound
as useful a hypothesis which his experimentation had exploded. Moreover, the Jesuit teacher freely accepted the directives which required him
not to teach as his preferred hypothesis, even in disputed questions, one
which appeared less tenable than its alternatives, although not actually
unorthodox. For the seminarians were preparing to become professional
teachers of Christian doctrine and it was felt that they should be
equipped as soundly as possible. The professor might, of course, examine these disputed points in his lectures and debate them with his fellow professors. Ignatius explicitly recommended that the teachers hold
public disputations with one another on moot matters.[40] From the
vigorous coexistence and clash of divergent views considerable clarification could be expected. As for the philosophy professors, whose work at
that time was visualized strictly in its character of a propaedeutic to
theology, they were warned against an addiction to novelties and excessive freethinking (*ingenii nimis liberi*), but they were also advised to
prove their conclusions not by a mass of arguments but by good ones and
to refrain from citing authors whom they had not read.[41]

It has been left, however, for later generations of Jesuit educators to
evolve a fuller understanding of the indispensable freedom which safe-
guards the right of the competent investigator to pursue his professional
researches wherever they lead, so long as this involves no moral devia-
tions, and thereafter to publish or teach his conclusions to audiences
mature enough to receive them. The *Epitome,* in fact, has a neat passage which proposes that a professor be guided in teaching controversial
issues by the threefold norm of charity, truth and consideration of the
best interests of his students. He is then to "give sufficient time to the
various opinions and the principal arguments which support them and
expound them honestly without delaying long upon them" and to advance his own opinion modestly.[42]

A few paragraphs further on, Jesuits are advised by their *Epitome*
that the Society in no way wishes to diminish their freedom in questions
that are still under investigation. Much less, they are told, does it intend
to discourage the employment of learning and the methods of criticism
and all the resources so usefully acquired through the progress of scholarship. Indeed, the members of the Society ought to persuade themselves
that a life devoted to the advancement of learning, although arduous,
contributes enormously to the glory of God and the building up of the
Church.

What is sought for, then, here as in all other matters is a just harmony of freedom and authority. Perhaps a perfect synthesis is impossible

to achieve and in any case the synthesis must be continually reconstituted since the contingent embodiment of its elements is always changing. But the belief that both law and liberty can flourish in the school community remains a perennial of the Jesuit school tradition.

Education for Social Responsibility

Although teachers are the most important of the school's resources, all these resources exist for the sake of the students who are the most important part of the academic community. We have examined some of the basic convictions about the objectives and procedures of intellectual and moral formation which are conserved beneath the letter of the early Jesuit educational documents. Both these phases of education also contribute to the development of a person's social powers. Charmot calls attention, for instance, to a defense of grammar classes which Sacchini made in his *Protrepticon*. Quite like a modern social scientist, that seventeenth-century Jesuit argued that studies in grammar and literature have great social utility because language and communication skills are at the very base of human society.[43] Moreover, character education is always inseparable from a cultivation of the student's potentiality for fruitful participation in community since so much morality is social morality and indeed the basic moral virtue is altruism.

In the school community itself there are constant occasions for developing pupils' awareness of their responsibility to others. Not all the devices used for this purpose by early Jesuit schools recommend themselves to us. Among the older youth, those for instance enrolled in the Theology Faculty, a certain amount of self-government seems to have been envisioned by Ignatius himself.[44] In the secondary school the *decuriones,* or leaders of the subdivisions within the class, sometimes acted as monitors, or teaching assistants as was noted earlier. They corrected papers, heard recitations of members of their band and sometimes, if they were very capable, they explained rudiments to the slower pupils. It often happens, said Jouvancy, that boys learn more easily from their peers in this way than from the teacher.[45]

A less attractive institution was the office of the Censor. He might also be called, said the *Ratio* of 1599, Chief Decurion or Praetor, if the title of Censor is less pleasing, *minus placens*. It is indeed displeasing and some of his duties even more so. He was empowered to act as representative of his fellows in seeking little privileges from the teacher but he was also supposed to keep a sharp eye on the class's behavior and report misdemeanors to the teacher. It was a function that has modern analogues in the scouts whose detailed reports keep corporation and military executives informed about their subordinates' performance. But it was also a function that would be equally repugnant to contemporary American Jesuit teachers and to their students. One wonders, indeed, if it could ever have amounted to much. Yet if this particular use of student leaders is unsavory, still the principle of active student participation in the daily affairs of school life strongly recommends itself.

The social vision of the school cannot be limited, however, to its own little world since that world exists only for the sake of the wider social context. What is called for now, as always, is the education of every Christian student to an ardent sense of responsibility for the welfare of the many communities in which he is destined to play various roles. These communities include the family, the vocational group to which his occupation will join him, the political society at all its levels from the municipal to the international, and the church. At the same time, young people must be provided with some practical experience of this social responsibility during their school days since after all they have been from birth members of at least some communities.

Today the importance of this education of man's social dimension is so widely recognized as to quite monopolize most statements of educational purpose. Philosophies of education in the United States concentrate strongly upon the ideal of the genuinely rational, democratic community and the response which it requires from each citizen not only within strict legal perspectives but in all the ordinary affairs of community living. This ideal is sometimes badly formulated. It may, for instance, be equated with a naive egalitarianism or make an absolute out of majority rule. In itself, however, it is an authentic value, a partial fulfillment of the commandment of fraternal love. The task of organizing the school's resources for the realization of this social goal is clearly as formidable as it is important. We shall not try here even to sketch the principles of such an organization because nowadays a great deal is being expertly said on this topic and besides this present book must have its limits. But at least the central position of this theme of education for social responsibility in the Society of Jesus's concept of school work should be suggested. This can be done succinctly and authoritatively by quoting an exhortation on the point addressed to the Society in 1949 by its twenty-seventh General, John Baptist Janssens:

> It is our aim above all in educating the young men we have accepted in the name of the Church, to instill in their hearts the charity of Christ as it is applied to modern problems in the encyc-

clicals and other papal documents. We should not allow the preju-
dices which they have perhaps learned at home to take deeper root
while they remain with us. There should be no distinction in our
colleges between rich and poor. They should not acquire any spirit
of a special, privileged social class, which I have earlier designated
as a social caste . . . Let them learn to hunger and thirst after justice, the justice which sees to it that all men receive the due reward
of their labors, and that there be a more just distribution of temporal goods, as well as a fuller and more universal sharing of
spiritual goods. They should learn that all men deserve the name
and affection of a brother in Christ; that those who have received
gifts in greater abundance do not have the right of use and abuse,
as the law of pagans proclaimed, but the obligation of using these
gifts for the good of the majority, and indeed of all men, if that is
possible . . . let the young men learn to hate social evils, which far
outweigh those which afflict mere individuals; let them learn, too,
to love the virtues which have a wider scope and tend to the common good; and let them practise these at once within the modest
limits of their own family, school and friends, with the desire to
cultivate them on a broader and fuller scale later on . . . The
Society will certainly achieve a work of no small merit in the eyes
of God, if from her colleges young men, freed of that pagan mentality which adores riches, go forth steeped in that charity which
seeks above all the good of others and is ready to work with the
Church in bettering the temporal and spiritual conditions of the
greatest possible number of human beings.[46]

The spirit informing these words returns us to the point from which
this study of Jesuit educational theory started. A school, for all its intrinsic worth, is not an end in itself. It is an instrument for the attainment of whatever larger purpose men conceive their life to have. The
precise character of that purpose has been widely disputed but so far as
Christians are concerned its nature is clear enough. Life is so to be lived
as to conduct a man to eternal, beatifying union with God through fidelity
in time to His love and service. But this service of love is pre-eminently
a service of others. For the man of faith, indeed, it is a service of Christ,
the Lord in others. Today this vocation to service or social responsibility
imposes upon Christian teachers and students a challenge so awesome as
to discourage comment. But it does surely accent the relevance of that
motive which lead St. Ignatius to the work of education in the first place:
"The teachers should . . . inspire the students to the love and service of
God our Lord, and to a love of the virtues by which they please Him.
They should urge the students to direct all their studies to this end."

NOTES: CHAPTER VII

1. The Spaniard, Juan Bonifacio published in 1576 what was probably the first educational treatise by a Jesuit. His apothegm quoted here, "The education of youth is the renovation of society," is taken from Herman, *op. cit.*, p. 185. The second epigraph for this Chapter VII is drawn from the *Instruction* issued by the Jesuit General in 1948 for the American Jesuit schools and briefly described above at the close of the second chapter.

2. See Talcott Parsons, "Suggestions for a Sociological Approach to the Theory of Organizations—I," *Administrative Science Quarterly*, I (1956–57), 63–64.

3. Emil Brunner, *Man in Revolt, op. cit.*, p. 106.

4. *Constitutions*, Preamble (*Prooemium*), n. 1.

5. *Constitutions*, IV, 17, n. 3, D.

6. *Epitome*, n. 403: "Eluceat in omnibus Collegii Officialibus mutua inter se coniunctio et in unum finem conspiratio, quae maxime per oboedientiae vinculum perficitur."

7. For this phrase see Pachtler, *op. cit.*, II, 30.

8. Pius XI, "Christian Education of Youth," *The Catholic Mind, op. cit.*, p. 87. The reference to the *Epitome* is to n. 398.

9. See Theodore Caplow, "The Criteria of Organizational Success," *Social Forces*, 32 (October, 1953), p. 8 and the booklet by E. D. Duryea, *Management of Learning* (Washington: U.S. Department of Health, Education, and Welfare; Office of Education, 1960), p. 7.

10. The passages from St. Ignatius are taken from Doncoeur, *The Heart of Ignatius, op. cit.*, p. 104. Père Doncoeur extracted the second of these from the *De Vita et Moribus S. Ignatii Loyolae* by Gian Pietro Maffei, S.J. This was one of the earliest biographies of St. Ignatius, appearing in 1585. For the *Ratio* of 1591 on the qualification of a dean see Corcoran, *op. cit.*, p. 199. See also the second of the Rules for the Rector in the *Ratio* of 1599, Pachtler, *op. cit.*, II, 268: ". . . cui omnem tribuet potestatem, quam ad rectam ejus officii administrationem pertinere judicabit."

11. For a discussion of this modern sort of organization, calling for individual exercise of responsible judgment at all levels, see Peter F. Drucker, *Landmarks of Tomorrow* (New York: Harper and Brothers, 1959), pp. 60–110.

12. The *Ratio* of 1586, Pachtler, *op. cit.*, II, 46.

13. *Constitutions*, IV, 10, n. 5, B.

14. de Dainville, *op. cit.*, p. xii–xvi.

15. On the antinomy itself and its resolution in this fashion see Drucker, *op. cit.*, p. 109.

16. *Constitutions*, IV, 11, n. 2. The title, Great Chancellor, is found in the fifth of the statutes in *Statuta Facultatum Theologiae et Philosophiae in Collegii Societatis Iesu Erectarum* (Rome: Gregorian University Press, 1934).

17. *Constitutions,* IV, 3, n. 4, B.
18. It is Rule 29 of the Rules for the Prefect of the Lower Classes in the *Ratio* of 1599 which speaks of the assigning of places, Pachtler, *op. cit.,* II, 364. Rules 46 and 50 of the Rules Common to Professor of Lower Classes contain the other details cited here. See Pachtler, *op. cit.,* II, 396, 398.
19. "The teachers ought to be distinguished." *Mon. Paed., op. cit.,* p. 159. The phrase was that of a certain sixteenth-century Jesuit named Acosta who contributed to the early studies of school organization.
20. In the *Constitutions,* IV, 6, n. 6, F, St. Ignatius observed that Jesuits could be employed in teaching (*in praelegendo*) provided no business of greater importance claimed their time.
21. Just as in the making of the *Spiritual Exercises,* St. Ignatius thought the exercitant's own meditations to be more important than the instructions of the retreat master, so he thought the graduated chain of class exercises more important than the actual explanations or *lectiones* which preceded them. But the guidance of these exercises is a chief part of the teacher's work. See Herman, *op. cit.,* p. 78 and the *Ratio* of 1586 making the same point as it accents the importance of discussions or disputations for the students of philosophy: Pachtler, *op. cit.,* II, 103.
22. Jouvancy, *op. cit.,* p. 7: "Magistri litterarum studiosi eruditio tribus maxime rebus continetur. Primo, cognitione et peritia linguarum. Secundo, Scientiarum quarumdam perceptione, quibus bonarum Artium curriculum quoddam absolvitur. Tertio denique nonnullis ad studendum adminiculis, quibus et levetur labor, et ingenii vis acuatur."
23. Nadal, "De Studiis Societatis," *Mon. Paed., op. cit.,* p. 104: "Sint autem professores ipsi pietatis quoque Christianae egregii cultores, ut lectiones omnes saecularium auctorum, nedum sacros, sua pietate condiant ad aedificationem auditorum in charitate, in Christo."
24. La Chalotais, *op. cit.,* p. 170.
25. For the remark of the *Ratio* of 1586, see Pachtler, *op. cit.,* II, 145 and for that of the *Ratio* of 1591, Corcoran, *op. cit.,* p. 193.
26. For the report from the Roman College, see *Mon. Paed., op. cit.,* p. 163. The warning of the *Ratio* of 1586 is found in Pachtler, *op. cit.,* II, pp. 145–46, and see also Herman, *op. cit.,* pp. 184–85. For the remark in the *Ratio* of 1591 on the qualifications of secondary school teachers ("qui per aetatem et ingenium non magnos in gravioribus studius [sic] processus facturi viderentur") see Corcoran, *op. cit.,* p. 192.
27. The *Ratio* of 1586, Pachtler, *op. cit.,* II, 144–45. St. Ignatius's comment on ambition is found in the *Constitutions,* X, n. 6.
28. This is from a letter of Visconti on the promotion of study of the Humane Letters, Pachtler, *op. cit.,* III, 130.
29. The comments of the *Ratio* of 1586, gathered together in the paragraph to which this note is attached, are found in Pachtler, *op. cit.,* II pp. 148, 152.
30. For St. Ignatius's comment see *Constitutions,* IV, 11, n. 1. The observations of the *Ratio* of 1586 cited here will be found in Pachtler, *op. cit.,* II, 73, 178 and that of the *Ratio* of 1591 in Corcoran, *op. cit.,* p. 207.

31. *Constitutions,* IV, 5, n. 1, C.
32. William Walsh, *The Use of Imagination* (London: Chatto and Windus, 1959), p. 229.
33. See the *Ratio* of 1591, Corcoran, *op. cit.,* p. 193 and that of 1599, Pachtler, *op. cit.,* II, 270.
34. ". . . licet magistri mutentur, docendi tamen rationem manere." *Ratio* of 1591, Corcoran, *op. cit.,* p. 203.
35. *Constitutions,* VI, 1, n. 1.
36. For the document over which Nadal worked, see *Mon. Paed., op. cit.,* p. 23. The directives from the *Ratio* of 1591 are in Corcoran, *op. cit.,* pp. 194, 200, 207. The Rule from the *Ratio* of 1599 is in Pachtler, *op. cit.,* II, 274.
37. See the *Ratio* of 1591, Corcoran, *op. cit.,* pp. 207–208 for the comment on the removal of incompetent teachers.
38. See Herman, *op. cit.,* p. 207.
39. The *Ratio* of 1591, Corcoran, *op. cit.,* p. 229.
40. *Constitutions,* IV, 13, n. 3. The directive to professors of higher studies which tells them not to expound useless, antiquated or absurd views is found in the seventh of the Rules Common to Professors of the Higher Faculties, Pachtler, *op. cit.,* II, 288. In the *Constitutions,* IV, 14, n. 1, professors are advised to base their lectures on books whose doctrine is more solid and safe.
41. It is Rule 16 of the Rules for the Provincial in the *Ratio* of 1599 which says of Philosophy that it ought *Theologiae deserviat* and that its professors ought not be excessively liberal: Pachtler, *op. cit.,* II, 242. For the advice on arguing conclusions see Rules 7 and 8 of those Common to Professors of Higher Faculties, *ibid.,* p. 288.
42. *Epitome,* n. 317, #1. The paragraph beginning "A few paragraphs further on . . ." is a paraphrase of the *Epitome,* n. 322, sections 1 and 2.
43. F. Charmot, S.J., *La pèdagogie des Jésuites: ses principes, son actualité* (Paris Éditions Spes. 1951), p. 50.
44. See Ganss, *op. cit.,* p. 320, n. 4.
45. Jouvancy, *op. cit.,* p. 146.
46. From an English translation, "The Social Apostolate" (Woodstock, Maryland: Woodstock College Press, 1950), pp. 14–16.

APPENDIX

Jesuit Educational Association*
High School Enrollment 1962–1963

	Freshmen	Sophomores	Juniors	Seniors	Specials	Totals 1962–63
Bellarmine College Preparatory, San Jose	266	216	211	179	..	872
Bellarmine High School, Tacoma	125	94	75	78	..	372
Bishop's Latin School, Pittsburgh	52	46	..	..	..	98
Boston College High School, Boston	328	390	323	295	..	1,336
Brebeuf Preparatory, Indianapolis	168	..	..	..	..	168
Brooklyn Preparatory School, Brooklyn	243	240	305	263	..	1,051
Brophy College Preparatory, Phoenix	173	140	130	123	..	566
Campion Jesuit High School, Prairie du Chien ...	181	160	123	127	..	591
Canisius High School, Buffalo	227	240	232	188	1	888
Chaplain Kapaun Memorial High School, Wichita ..	153	193	163	140	3	652
Cheverus High School, Portland, Maine	116	121	97	73	..	407
Colegio San Ignacio, Puerto Rico	59	56	54	45	130	344
Cranwell Preparatory School, Lenox	57	59	53	55	7	231
Creighton Preparatory School, Omaha	296	292	237	184	1	1,010
Fairfield College Preparatory School, Fairfield ..	215	240	219	166	..	840
Fordham Preparatory School, New York	225	223	206	170	..	824
Georgetown Preparatory School, Garrett Park	62	54	56	50	..	222
Gonzaga High School, Washington, D.C.	184	170	182	133	..	669
Gonzaga Preparatory School, Spokane	219	218	192	164	..	793
Jesuit College Preparatory, Houston	104	86	..	..	..	190
Jesuit High School, Dallas	205	165	137	124	..	631
Jesuit High School, El Paso	134	84	83	58	..	359
Jesuit High School, New Orleans	245	243	234	210	108	1,040
Jesuit High School, Portland, Oregon	138	133	132	102	..	505
Jesuit High School, Shreveport	108	93	74	48	48	371
Jesuit High School, Tampa	92	114	95	70	..	371
Loyola Academy, Wilmette	425	397	380	309	..	1,511
Loyola High School, Los Angeles	270	230	226	185	..	911
Loyola High School, Missoula	45	31	26	28	..	130
Loyola High School, Towson	199	205	217	175	..	796
Loyola School, New York	55	52	39	33	..	179
Marquette University High School, Milwaukee	262	253	230	230	..	975
McQuaid Jesuit High School, Rochester	203	210	222	171	..	806
Regis High School, Denver	177	147	138	98	..	560
Regis High School, New York	174	160	140	141	..	615
Rockhurst High School, Kansas City	198	207	152	131	..	688
St. Ignatius High School, Chicago	285	276	276	279	..	1,116
St. Ignatius High School, Cleveland	307	283	280	239	..	1,109
St. Ignatius High School, San Francisco	299	278	273	238	..	1,088
St. Joseph's Preparatory School, Philadelphia	244	220	188	180	..	832
St. Louis University High School, St. Louis	238	212	219	207	..	876
St. Peter's Preparatory School, Jersey City	281	248	262	224	..	1,015
St. Xavier High School, Cincinnati	322	348	309	233	..	1,212
Scranton Preparatory School, Scranton	118	113	94	68	..	393
Seattle Preparatory School, Seattle	159	132	111	109	..	511
University of Detroit High School, Detroit	286	262	265	229	..	1,042
Xavier High School, Concord	149	..	..	..	..	149
Xavier High School, New York	278	244	295	212	..	1,029
Totals 1962–63	9,349	8,578	7,955	6,764	298	32,944

Jesuit Educational Association*

College and University Enrollment, 1962–1963

	Liberal Arts		Commerce		Dentistry	Education Univ. College	Engineering	Graduate	Law		Medicine	Nursing	Pharmacy	Social Work Service	Miscellaneous	Full-Time Totals	Part-Time Totals	Full and Part Totals	Extension Low Tuition	Grand Total	Summer School	
	Day	Night	Day	Night					Day	Night											Graduate	Undergrad.
Boston College	2,199	842	1,556	402		860		1,111	315	111		798		167	424	6,822	1,963	8,785	400	9,185	1,403	1,355
Canisius College	871	496	296	250				660							133	1,384	1,322	2,706	24	2,730	423	583
Creighton University	1,524	78	373	24	176			286	125		297	304	126			2,515	798	3,313		3,313	442	516
Fairfield University	1,343					812										1,360	795	2,155		2,155	412	330
Fordham University	2,212		814	404		2,132		1,895	467	289			315	423		5,727	3,224	8,951	1,103	10,054	1,222	2,100
Georgetown University	1,500		473	84	332			998	461	636	386	261			1,660	5,412	1,379	6,791		6,791	278	2,033
Gonzaga University	966	6	213	9		273	240	65		127		176			213	1,948	340	2,288		2,288	396	488
Holy Cross College	1,811							11							5	1,827		1,827		1,827		
John Carroll University	1,825	1,257	219	134				498								2,210	1,723	3,933		3,933	389	2,440
LeMoyne College	1,393															1,337	56	1,393	125	1,518		556
Loyola College	817	777						379								860	1,113	1,973	46	2,019	331	700
Loyola Univ., Chicago	3,357	2,445	802		379			1,558	111	122	315	400		229	237	5,842	4,113	9,955	1,717	11,672	1,214	4,659
Loyola Univ., Los Angeles	811		209				219	163	156	195					167	1,405	515	1,920	93	2,013	228	329
Loyola Univ., New Orleans	1,026	18	322	452	221			243	112	133			68		123	1,722	996	2,718	436	3,154	125	807
Marquette University	3,069	592	809	637	443		1,594	1,049	180		391	433			968	7,223	2,942	10,165	1,713	11,878	1,500	2,238
Regis College	743	250														716	277	993		993		294
Rockhurst College	664		233	1,218												819	1,296	2,115		2,115		353
St. Joseph's College	1,509	2,984						185								1,723	2,955	4,678	215	4,893	38	1,840
Saint Louis University	2,420	442	674	618	196		984	2,200	111	113	433	494		108	252	6,078	2,967	9,045	79	9,124	2,207	2,102
St. Peter's College	997	178	512	529												1,747	469	2,216	328	2,544		1,173
Seattle University	1,422	63	339	73		555	316	352				188			512	2,862	958	3,820	252	4,072	506	1,033
Spring Hill College	1,220	225														1,059	386	1,445		1,445		620
University of Detroit	2,218	2,115	747	1,259	290		1,365	1,298	100	85					868	5,354	4,991	10,345	3,115	13,460	1,197	3,070
University of San Francisco	682	1,322	309	820		278		117	146	144		214			304	2,159	2,177	4,336	27	4,363	169	2,253
University of Santa Clara	1,051		344	516			256	1,145	88	37						1,746	1,691	3,437		3,437	374	325
University of Scranton	609	234	455	243		237		393							360	1,517	1,014	2,531	113	2,644	461	776
Wheeling College	521															509	12	521		521		52
Xavier University	1,103	409	649	475				1,440							96	1,884	2,288	4,172		4,172	896	897
Totals 1962–1963	39,883	14,733	10,348	8,147	2,037	5,147	4,974	16,046	2,372	1,992	1,822	3,268	509	927	6,322	75,767	42,760	118,527	9,786	128,313	14,211	33,922

* Jesuit Educational Quarterly, Vol. xxv, No. 3 (Jan. 1963)

INDEX

Academic freedom, 204–206, *see also* Freedom
Academies, 153
Activity, principle of, 67, 148, 151–152
Adams, John, 94
Adaptation, principle of, 46, 121, 141, 193
Administration, principles of in Jesuit educational tradition, 188 ff.
Admission policy in *Ratio* of 1591, 65
Aims of education, in mind of early Jesuits, 7; according to Ribadeneira; discussed in first Jesuit documents, 125 ff.; according to Ledesma, 128, 132; in *Ratio Studiorum,* 130; mind of St. Ignatius Loyola on, 130–131; according to *Epitome,* 131; Kilpatrick on, 132; according to Suarez, 134
Alexandria, ancient Christian school at, 19, 49, 136
Alvarez, Emmanuel, S.J., 149
Aquaviva, Claudio, S.J., 32–34, 45, 53
Aristotle, in philosophy course of early Jesuit schools, 68–69, 124, 143, 149, 151; on aims of education, 101–102; cited by Ledesma, 128; noetic theory of, 162; on moral education, 163
Augustine, St., 170
Autobiographical reminiscences of St. Ignatius Loyola, 12, 16

Bacon, Francis, on Jesuit schools, 64
Bader, Georg, S.J., 181
Barcelona, St. Ignatius Loyola studies at, 12
Bellarmine, St. Robert, S.J., 82
Benedict XV, Pope, 54
Bernard, St., on the monk and education, 13
Boehmer, H., 170
Bolgar, R. R., 144
Bonifacio, Juan, S.J., 186
Brethren of Common Life, 38
Brogan, D. W., 100, 133
Brooklyn Preparatory School, New York, 73

Brophy College Preparatory School, Phoenix, Arizona, 73
Brunner, Emil, 187
Buber, Martin, 159, 179

Campion, Blessed Edmund, S.J., 124
Campion Jesuit High School, Prairie du Chien, Wisconsin, 72
Canisius, St. Peter, S.J., 197
Carafa, Gian Pietro, 21, *see also* Paul IV
Censor, office of in early Jesuit schools, 207–208
Censorship, 172–173
Chalotais, Louis Réné de la, 64, 197
Character formation, *see* Moral education
Charmot, François, S.J., 207
Christian education, humanistic ideals of, 77 ff., 90; Pius XI on, 87, 106; some general characteristics of all, 103–110; Pius XII on, 105; role of liturgy in, 175–176
Cicero, as model of Latin style in early Jesuit schools, 38, 68–69, 124, 143, 148, 205
Clement of Alexandria, 19, 49
Clement XIV, Pope, 4
Coimbra, St. Ignatius Loyola to Jesuit scholastics at, 27, 43, 180
Collins, James, 129
Columbia University (King's College), 98
Commission on Higher Studies 1931–1932 (for Jesuit institutions in United States), 55
Conant, James B., 76, 127
Concertatio, 68, 118, 174
Confucius, 161
Constitutions of the Society of Jesus, 8, 16, 28; Fourth Part deals with questions of education, 28, 34, 40–44, 119, 187–188; construction and characteristics of, 42–43; on aims of education, 120, 130–131; on moral education, 133; on curricular questions, 138; on school as community, 187–188